AT SEA LEVEL

AT SEA LEVEL

G W Searle

The Book Guild Ltd
Sussex, England

The Book Guild Ltd
25 High Street,
Lewes, Sussex.

First published 1994.
©G W Searle 1994.

Set in Baskerville.

Typesetting by Formaprint,
Worthing, East Sussex.

Printed in Great Britain by
Antony Rowe Ltd,
Chippenham, Wiltshire.

A catalogue record for this book is
available from the British Library

ISBN 0 86332 897 0

CONTENTS

*Dedicated
to my wife Constance
and my family*

What shall we tell you? Tales, marvellous tales of ships and stars and isles where good men rest.

- James Elroy Flecker,
The Golden Journey to Samarkand

INTRODUCTION

This is a personal account of my wartime experiences from 1939 to 1946 as an Ordinary Seaman at the beginning and a Lieutenant Commander RNVR at the end.

It has been written with the help of notes and records which I was able to keep at that time and memory has been called upon to fill in some of the gaps.

As it is intended to be an account of what I did, what I thought and what I saw, official war records and the works of historians have only been used to describe wider aspects of the war so as to give a background or a reason for my own activities.

I have called the book *At Sea Level* because my service was almost entirely sea-going and for most of that time I served in small ships, very close indeed to the surface of the sea with waves lapping (sometimes pounding) against the wooden hull which formed one side of the bunk where I spent my sleeping hours in harbour and at sea.

1

The Apprentice

I qualified as a Chartered Accountant in 1936, when I was aged 22, and set out to earn my living on audit work for W. B. Keen Co. in the city of London with whom I had served my articles.

It was an old established and, I suppose, an old-fashioned firm. Their senior partner, W. B. Keen himself, had founded the firm having, so the story went, been first in the first examination held by the Institute of Chartered Accountants in England and Wales. He seemed to be of a very great age to us young men. I believe one of his sons or perhaps more than one was killed in the 1914/18 war. There was a memorial stone on the wall of the reception area giving the names of members of the staff who gave their lives in the 1914/18 war; it was a large number for a small firm. W. B. Keen gave a garden party for the staff every summer at his large house in Limpsfield. We played tennis and relaxed in deck chairs to enjoy a fine summer's day with food and drinks served by a large number of maid servants dressed as I thought such servants were dressed only in Edwardian plays. Times were changing in the 1930s but not in the household or the business of W. B. Keen.

Mr and Mrs Keen did entertain us well on those pre-war summer days which kind memory credits with continual sunshine. We enjoyed an excellent lunch and tea and fruit in abundance from the garden. The speciality of the house was gooseberry fool and, all through my five year articles and after, Mrs Keen would address us one by one to ask what we would choose to eat. 'Gooseberry fool, Mr Searle?' she would say every year and I waited expectantly for the time when she would say 'Gooseberry Searle, Mr Fool?'

It was a great relief to have examinations behind me and to have evenings and week-ends free to engage in other things than study. I was paid £250 per annum and as I lived at home rent-free I had enough money to live reasonably well. I enjoyed my sport most — tennis in the summer and badminton in the winter. I became secretary of the Crystal Palace Badminton Club — then one of the largest badminton clubs in the country — and travelled around the London area to play in all the tournaments I could reach by public transport. I was not so well off that I could afford a car.

Behind this period of learning to work and learning to live, I do not think that people of my age had many illusions about the state of Europe. With some friends from the office I had spent a walking holiday in Germany in 1934 and had seen for myself the marching men, the brown shirts, the storm troopers, the bullying of dissidents and the persecution of the Jews. There was fear in the streets and there were state-assisted bullies in the streets.

We spent a drunken evening at an inn in a village near Heidelberg in company with some storm-troopers billeted there. Perhaps we enjoyed the drinking and the singing but we had no illusions about the character of storm-troopers and left with a hope that we might never have to argue with them. In Munich we were warned of the penalties we might suffer if we walked by the guards outside Hitler's headquarters without giving the Nazi salute — so we avoided that street.

At Ulm I became ill with an infection from a broken blister on my heel. I had a high temperature and swollen glands in the groin but I was well and quickly treated by a kindly German doctor. An early lesson of the good and the bad among us all.

In my period of articles with W. B. Keen from 1931 to 1936, nearly all the articled clerks and many of the other young employees belonged to the Territorials. As these five years passed by it was becoming clearer that such service was not just an excuse for drinks on Saturday night or a means of getting an additional week away from the office for summer camp.

War was coming nearer and Germany was becoming stronger. Perhaps I was slow to do my duty because it was not until February 1939 that I joined the reservists. The Army did not attract me neither did the RAF but the Navy always had a glamour for me, so I joined the London Division of the Royal Naval Volunteer Reserve.

No one I knew believed that Chamberlain had achieved "peace in our time" when he returned from Munich in 1938. We believed that it was only a matter of time before war started and so it was, but the delay was probably to our advantage — or that is what we told ourselves.

Having joined the RNVR as an ordinary seaman and being allocated purely by chance to the seamanship branch rather than gunnery or signals, I spent at least one evening a week at *HMS President* or *HMS Chrysanthemum* (moored alongside the Embankment between Blackfriars and Charing Cross bridges). We learned seamanship (out of a book), we tied knots, we learned how to sail (mostly on dry land) and how to row a whaler (on the Thames). We marched up and down the Embankment fixing bayonets, sloping arms and performing other war-like acts.

I should have done my first sea training for two weeks in September 1939 but on 3rd September war was declared on Germany.

It was about two weeks before I was called up. Papers came instructing me to report to *HMS President*. I had a fine new uniform — square sailor collar and bell-bottom trousers — and a new kit-bag with my name and number stencilled on its bottom, LDX 4564.

I well remember arriving at London Bridge station and deciding to be extravagant and take a taxi to the Embankment. There would be time enough to have to carry my kit-bag later on.

On board *HMS President* there was a period of filling in forms — next-of-kin and similar particulars — and then we went back onto the Embankment to take a motorcoach to Chatham Barracks. As we boarded the coach there was a mixture of apprehension and elation. One man said, 'Do you realize we shall get a medal for this?' Despite the excitement and atmosphere of adventure, I well remember my unspoken thought that medals do not come that easily. We might get them but what was the price to be? 'Take what you want,' said the devil, 'take it and pay for it.'

2

Chatham Barracks

Chatham Barracks were approached with awe.

At that time it was a place for gathering reservists together and sending them off in batches to form the crews of ships coming into commission. All the time young men arrived, stayed a few days or a few weeks until they were drafted for a duty for which they were or might possibly become qualified. We new hands did not understand this and wondered why a new and powerful warship was not just waiting impatiently to receive us on board.

We lived uncomfortably. The barrack rooms were sleeping quarters by night and living rooms by day. We ate on tables with so few plates that those who were not first in line had to eat off the unwashed plates of the first or even the second sitting. There was not enough to keep us occupied. At first we were set to sweep up the autumn leaves. Most of us soon understood that a job which could be done in an hour was intended to fill our whole day. One newly-arrived enthusiast was told to sweep a path which, with gusto, he did in half an hour so he reported to the Petty Officer:

'P.O.,' he said, 'I have swept the path. What do I do now?' The P.O. gave him a dirty look and said

'Climb up the bloody trees and shake some more leaves down.'

In the barrack room we slept at night in hammocks and owing to the overcrowding, they were slung very closely together and in long rows covering the length of the barrack room. Throughout the night there was a 'sentry' on duty in the barrack room doing a four-hour shift. We all took a turn at this and I found one of my duties rather unusual. Because in a hammock it was usual to sleep on one's back, snoring became a problem and if unchecked, it disturbed the sleep of those not snoring; so the call was made, 'Sentry! Stop that man snoring!'

Being inexperienced in such matters I asked how this might best be done and was given a lesson in the approved technique which was simply to hold the snorer's nose with thumb and forefinger to prevent the passage of air. This produces a small explosion at the back of the throat and a kind of convulsion in the sleeper but

14

the snoring would stop — for a while.

On Sundays there was an impressive parade and Church service on the very large parade ground. The band played and seamen marched to and fro. Many avoided this by skulking behind buildings and with the very large numbers now in the barracks this could easily be done. At one such parade a defaulter was publicly named and sentenced for being found asleep while supposedly on sentry duty: this certainly had its desired effect as a warning to others. The occasion was so dramatic and awe-inspiring that we almost expected a flogging but he probably only lost his week-end leave.

Week-end leave was greatly prized and there was always a rush on Saturdays for a week-end pass but, as each day men were being detailed to join ships and sent off at short notice, it was not unusual to be stopped at the gate because your name had come up and, instead of a week-end at home, it was a ship one had to join. As we went down to the gate one Saturday, the loudspeakers broadcast 'All RNVR signals ratings report to the Drafting Master-at-Arms', and I regret to say, but understood well enough, that the RNVR signals ratings who were with me cut off their signalman badges and passed undetected through the gate for their week-end.

There was a Gunnery School at Chatham and it was an improvement on sweeping up leaves when I was put on a gunnery course. It was, in retrospect, very primitive and based on procedures of the battle of Jutland. We operated a control mechanism called the Dumaresq (named after Lieut. Dumaresq who introduced it in 1902), and for all its antiquity it was at least a system which might enable guns to project shells towards the enemy with a discipline which could lead to accuracy.

One week-end, when the barracks went quiet with half the inhabitants on week-end leave and the other half with their heads down (i.e. asleep — for war had not yet shaken Britain out of its week-end slothfulness), some six of us — Ordinary Seamen Bonnet, Merz and Foster among them — decided that as our lives might depend on it one day, we had better master the Dumaresq machine. So we applied to use the Gunnery School for a training session which we would organize ourselves. This caused great consternation. The Chief Petty Officer and his assembled Petty Officers had never heard of such an outrageous suggestion. They thought that week-ends were a time of rest and there must be some ulterior motive in our request. But we persuaded them of our honest intentions and spent a week-end in the gunnery control which would have been of great benefit to the country and greatly to the discomfort of our enemies if we had ever had to operate such a gunnery control mechanism. As we never saw such a mechanism in any ships we ever had to man, we neither benefited the country nor discomforted our enemies, but we did at least save ourselves some boredom during the week-end.

It must have been mid-September when I went to Chatham and at least mid-October before I left. One or two week-ends I had as leave and I went by train via London to our home at Horley. The trains ran very well and were reasonably on time; unless the enemy interfered, they ran better during the war than afterwards. My father took me to Purley station at about 5 am on a Monday morning and thus enabled me to get back to Chatham well before 9 am.

At some time perhaps someone will find out that there are some three inches of sand covering the attics of the barracks. When the autumn leaves were all swept up, and because there was a danger of incendiary bombs, we spent much time carrying buckets of sand from a central dump, up endless ladders, and spreading it over the rafters. It was lucky that the buildings were strong. I wondered whether the weight would do more damage than the German fire bombs.

We did fire watch duty at night; we kept watch for enemy aeroplanes in the day, we made tea for the Petty Officers, we marched, we talked and we listened to the rather good Chatham Barracks band. Rumour had it that if you played an instrument well, you might spend the whole war in Chatham Barracks — was that an attraction to become a bandsman?

There was .22 rifle shooting and I was surprised to find that I won first prize which just showed how poor the sailors were at shooting.

Although we were in the part of England closest to the Continent of Europe, we suffered no air raids while I was there. Had we been bombed, the carnage in the crowded barracks would have been terrible and the air raid shelters were for the most part only trenches.

Every day, parties of men left to man ships as they became available or to supplement crews of serving ships or to replace casualties. It was possible to apply (volunteer) for any particular draft if you knew about it and had some reason to be attracted; but for the most part we did not know what was happening and we left things to fate and the drafting office.

There was one rather advertised requirement: a large party to go out to Singapore for service there and in the Far East. At that time in 1939, Singapore and the Pacific were peaceful areas and those who wanted a warm and comfortable life were inclined to volunteer. I wonder whether they were still there when the Japanese captured Singapore?

It was at the end of October when my name came up together with many of my friends from the London Division. We were all innoculated with TAB and as it was the first innoculation for most of us, we felt terrible but had no sympathy. Those who had spent the night before celebrating our departure from Chatham felt worse than terrible and Ord. Seaman John Felix Bonnet collapsed on parade. We were issued with tropical clothing and boarded a train for Glasgow.

For us it was the real departure to war and a seemingly final parting from loved ones which had not been so apparent when we lived at Chatham and often had week-end leave. I recall that one man broke down and cried before he left and no one thought the less of him for that. The parting from his recently married bride was hard for him to accept.

3

HMS Forfar

In the docks at Glagow we joined *HMS Forfar*. This ship was the
Montrose of the Canadian Pacific fleet — a passenger ship which
had previously been engaged on the North Atlantic route. Six six-
inch guns had been mounted on the deck and these were from the
1914/18 war. Not much more had been done to make the peaceful
Montrose into a warlike *Forfar* and as the cabins and the fine wood
panelling had for the most part been retained, it was a floating fire
hazard should anyone land a shell or a bomb on us.

We went down to Greenock and we did sea trials near Ailsa
Craig. With much ceremony and apprehension we fired our guns.
That was appalling! The whole ship shuddered and shook, glass
was shattered and lighting fell down. The raw crew were deafened
and stupefied. We were, therefore, pronounced fit for sea and
service.

The officers were partly RN retired who had been recalled and
partly Merchant Navy (RNR) officers, some of whom were serving
in the *Montrose* before she was 'called up'. We received sailing orders
and set off out through the Clyde boom in early November. The
Captain was on the bridge when we left but after that we did not
see him again. Later in the war I met the First Officer who took
over for the rest of our first voyage. He told me that on passing
the Clyde boom the Captain, who had not been to sea for many
years, had had a nervous breakdown and was put ashore at the
earliest opportunity.

Our first voyage was south through the Irish Sea, round Land's
End and up the Channel to Portsmouth — remember that we had
all been issued with tropical clothing and we all expected to be going
somewhere warmer. I did a spell as crow's nest look-out; it was
very cold and lonely up there.

After a few days in Portsmouth (and I did manage to get home
by train to Horley for a few hours one day, much to the surprise
and delight of my parents who had no idea where I was), we left
again not for the tropics but back to Greenock.

The winter of 1939/40 was spent on the so-called Northern Patrol.

This meant a routine of two to three weeks at sea and two to three days in Greenock. When at sea we patrolled the area Shetlands/Faeroes/Iceland with the purpose of intercepting ships which were either enemy or were supplying the enemy.

In general, it was a highly dangerous and uncomfortable way of spending a winter. It was dangerous because we served in a large and not very agile ship which would have been an ideal target for a submarine — we had no submarine detection devices and no depth charges to drop on them. And with our ancient six-inch guns, some Lewis guns and enough rifles for a boarding party we could not have engaged an enemy surface warship with any chance of survival. We could and did from time to time stop merchant ships from neutral countries and sent over a boarding party to examine their papers and query their cargo and destination. I am not aware we ever found a cargo which was objectionable to our war effort but I disliked lying with engines stopped while our boarding party rowed — yes, rowed! — across to the other ship. For the boarding party used a ship's whaler manned by an officer and about sixteen men: no engines, just long heavy oars and muscular arms. It was here we were grateful for the seamen from Stornoway who formed part of our crew. Rowing heavy boats in rough seas was something they could do very well.

Once we encountered an iceberg and it was decided that we should use it for gunnery practice. That did morale no good at all because we just could not score a hit on it. This lack of success was really not surprising because the training and elevating of the guns was extremely difficult in the cold weather. The lubricating oil seemed to freeze, and if there was spray coming over that added more ice to the open and unprotected gun-sites. In bad weather we had ropes fixed fore and aft to the muzzle end of the gun and a team of men on the end of each rope were prepared to give a heave left or right to help the poor men who were trying to train the guns by the iced-up training handles and frozen mechanism.

One patrol we spent north of Iceland between that island and the permanent ice cap. We did go right up to the pack ice and saw it stretch far and lonely into the northern distance. That was on a fine and clear day but for most of the time north of Iceland we were in a snowstorm with almost nil visibility. We seemed to be doing no good at all in such conditions and the job of the navigating officer must have been more than worrying.

In action stations, my post was in the forward magazine with the job of putting six-inch shells into the hoist for the guns. We were well below the water line and on balance I think I would have preferred a post on deck. But we did not, I am relieved to say, have to fire a shot in anger and only came close to doing so when we encountered another armed merchant cruiser — just like ourselves — on a dark night and discovered her identity, and she ours, before the shooting started.

The crew were almost entirely Reservists, RNR and RNVR. Some Officers and Petty Officers were RN retired who had been recalled. We were the young ones, very raw and inexperienced but most of us did not know how much we did not know and were happy in our ignorance. I think we were a happy ship and the odd assortment of men from so many different backgrounds seemed to provide a mix without any particular problems.

Discipline was good without any pressure. The long days and longer dark nights at sea, often rough and uncomfortable, passed in an orderly routine of watches and sleep, sleep and watches. On Saturday nights sometimes a concert was organized. There was no professional talent that I can remember, but people did their best and I, for one, enjoyed it.

The two or three days we spent off patrol in the Clyde were mainly to replenish stores rather than rest, but each watch did get one night ashore. On those evenings it became the custom for Alec Foster, Roland Merz, John Felix Bonnet and me to take the train from Greenock to Glasgow, have the best meal we could afford, sleep at the Salvation Army Hostel for a shilling and catch the 7 am train back to Greenock.

The narrow roads leading to the embarkation jetties at Greenock (where the liberty boats came and went) were a sad and sometimes a sordid sight as sailors said farewell to their wives or girl friends before leaving for another few weeks at sea. As I passed one embracing couple in the cold darkness of one winter morning, I heard the urgent words of one poor girl,

'It's not a button, dear, it's a hook.'

There is a little story, in the end a sad story, of our evenings in Glasgow. We tried first to go to a rather splendid club but were stopped at the entrance because it was for Officers only so we asked for one of the best restaurants and were directed to Rogano's. Here, too, we found most tables taken by Naval Officers and the appearance of four ratings asking for a table caused the management some surprise and nervousness. However, they gave us a table and as we appeared to behave ourselves they became very friendly and welcomed us each time we had the chance to visit them, which was every two to three weeks throughout the 1939/40 winter. One waiter in particular looked after us well. He was waiting for his call-up and hoped to join us in the Navy. On our last visit in the spring of 1940 when we left *HMS Forfar*, they gave us each a small present and 'our' waiter wished us good luck. That was the happy side.

In the following autumn I had the chance to visit Rogano's once again. They knew me and welcomed me. I asked after our waiter and they told me he had indeed been called up soon after we left. He had joined the Navy as he wanted but his ship had been sunk soon after he joined and he was lost at sea.

On the first of April 1940, I left *HMS Forfar* with a railway warrant for Portsmouth Barracks in order to present myself to a Selection Board for a Commission. It was just before my twenty-sixth birthday and I had spent just on six months in the Royal Navy. Inexperience made us all feel even younger than we were.

I remember little of the discomforts and the undoubted dangers of those early months at sea. I do remember the men and the comradeship, the new experiences and the excitements of the unfamiliar. I remember the ice-capped Faeroes, distant views of Iceland, the ice-packs, the Hebrides and Ailsa Craig. Above all I saw the aurora borealis moving its curtains of colour across the northern sky.

HMS Forfar was sunk in the Western approaches by U99 in December 1940.

Rekyavik

ICELAND

Norwegian Sea

North Atlantic

FAEROES

0   100   200 miles

0   100   200   300 Kms

SHETLANDS

Stornoway

ORKNEY

HEBRIDES

Fort William

Greenock
Glasgow

Methil

Dunoon – Holy Loch

Aberdeen

Troon

Leith

Firth of Forth

North Sea

Holyhead

Hull

Grimsby

Irish Sea

SWEDEN

NORWAY

Kristiansand

Marstrand

Gothenburg

Vorberg

Kattegat

Copenhagen

Baltic Sea

Cuxhaven

Kiel Canal

4

Portsmouth, HMS King Alfred and the Summer of 1940

Portsmouth was nearer the front line. They had air-raids. We awaited our appearance before the Board and meanwhile had no duties.

My good friends Foster, Merz and Bonnet had left *HMS Forfar* with me to attend the same Selection Board. One evening we went to a pub in Havant for a drink and in the bar we met a very charming lady and her daughter. After a round of drinks the mother suggested it might be more comfortable to have the next round at their home which was close by.

The house was indeed a comfortable one. We enjoyed our drink and left with the invitation to return again — which we did and never once did we ask their name. How odd of us! But we so enjoyed our quiet and very respectable evenings in the comfort of a real home, relaxing in cheerful conversation and an hospitable drink, that we asked no questions perhaps thinking that we might cause this window onto peacetime happiness to vanish like a dream.

The Selection Board was duly held, Admiral Kekewich in charge. They had, of course, our history sheets in front of them and I was asked whether one had to come from a wealthy family to become a Chartered Accountant. I had in mind that my father had to pay a premium of £300 (1931) in order that I should be taken on as an Articled Clerk and that my pay as an Articled Clerk was £25 per annum for the first year, rising to £50 p.a. in the fifth. It was on the tip of my tongue to reply that being a Chartered Accountant was 'open to everyone just like the Ritz Hotel' but I thought that might be regarded as flippant, so I gave a more sedate reply. In retrospect I wish I had made the reply I first thought of. I think the Admiral would have preferred it to the colourless one I did give, but in those days we did not really think of Admirals as human.

We were all passed fit and proper persons to attend an Officer's Training Course and before we left Portsmouth we, that is about a dozen of us who were would-be officers, were ordered to attend an inspection by Admiral James who was in command of Portsmouth.

We lined up outside his office and a young Wren came out as a forerunner to the Admiral himself. To our amazement and hilarity the Wren was the younger one (the daughter) of the two ladies we had met in the Havant pub and who had entertained us at their home. While Admiral James solemnly inspected us, this young Wren was making faces at us from behind his back and that nearly ruined our promising careers, since laughing while being inspected by an Admiral is no doubt a crime next door to mutiny. But that is only half the story: when we met the young lady after the parade she disclosed that she was not only on the Admiral's staff; she was also the Admiral's daughter. During our off-duty hours we four Ordinary Seamen had had the honour of being received by the Admiral's wife and daughter, had enjoyed the comfort of his home and the hospitality of his wine cupboard.

I received much kindness from people who realized that Service men and women were often lonely in their hours off-duty and would appreciate a fireside and a cup of tea. I would mention in particular the people of Glasgow where I was often invited home to tea by someone sitting next to me on a tram or bus. The hospitality of Lady James and her daughter stands out in my memory because it was so near to being entertained by the Admiral himself and knowing that, they kept their identity secret. To all those who were so kind to me, I express my gratitude.

We were sent on 19th April 1940 to *HMS King Alfred* at Hove next to Brighton in Sussex. *HMS King Alfred* was the name the Navy gave to a large building they had requisitioned on the sea front. It was recently built and intended as a leisure centre I believe. We slept in dormitories in the large underground car park. The building had classrooms, rest rooms, dining rooms, etc. and outside there were lawns which we used for drill and exercise.

Our particular class was known as Drake Division and consisted of about 45 ratings. Three such divisions were there at any one time; a new one came in each month to take what was a three-month course. From an early morning run to a formal dinner each evening we were worked very hard and I think obtained a good groundwork of the technical side of seamanship and weaponry together with a basic knowledge of an officer's duties and responsibilities. Some of the lessons we learned were acquired from the incidents of everyday life in this Royal Navy establishment run by senior RN Officers who followed closely the traditions in which they themselves had been brought up.

It was routine that the evening dinner was formal and included the Loyal Toast to the King. One evening an Officer Cadet lit a cigarette before the Loyal Toast. Captain Pelly immediately ordered in three Marines with fixed bayonets who arrested the offender and put him in cells for the night. This taught us all a lesson on the etiquette of smoking which would not easily be forgotten. It was perhaps an unfortunate incident because I was told that the particular offender was a Portuguese who had only recently come to Britain to enlist and the rule of not smoking before the Loyal Toast was not something he had previously regarded as an important contribution to the war effort.

While we were under training, the war was being fought on the other side of the Channel. The British Army was forced back and was evacuated from Dunkirk and Calais. Holland and Belgium were over-run and France surrendered.

One night we were called to parade and volunteers were asked for to go to Dunkirk in small boats to help in the evacuation of the Army. Every man volunteered — what else could one expect at an Officers' Training establishment? — so some twenty or thirty were picked at random, but I was not one of them. Foster, who was picked, borrowed my seaman's knife which he lost on Dunkirk beach. It had my name on it so someday perhaps a holiday maker may think I was one of the heroes and one of the casualties of that evacuation.

After Dunkirk we were each issued with a rifle and five rounds of ammunition which we were ordered to keep by us day and night, and, in the event of an invasion, to defend Brighton beach to the best of our ability. The shortage of ammunition was so great that five rounds was the maximum allowance.

In July we 'passed out' as Sub-Lieutenants RNVR. We were asked to nominate which branch of the Service we would like to join. I chose Coastal Forces. That request was noted but further training and experience were to be added before the goal was reached. On 11th July the Drake Division left *King Alfred* and I went back to Horley to spend a short leave with my parents. I was recalled to *King Alfred* on 28th July to join the Eighth M.T.B. Class. This was mainly a navigational course extremely well directed by Instructor Commander Clark RN. What I learned on that course was very valuable to me later in the war. The course lasted only three weeks, then back to Horley for more leave.

That summer of 1940 was a fine one but only two things occupied minds in the South of England. The first was the expected invasion and the second was attack from the air by the German Air Force: the latter, while terrible in itself, being seen as only a preparation for the former. A third possibility much talked about and the subject of wild rumours, was the expected dropping by parachute of German saboteurs and spies as a prelude to landings. Even when off duty we were expected to carry our revolvers or rifles together, of course, with the compulsory gas masks, so that descending enemies could be immediately attacked.

As to my own mind, it was occupied by something quite different. I met, during those summer leaves, a young lady who was spending a holiday in Horley recuperating from a rather serious operation. I asked her to become my wife and later that year on 9th November we were married at the Parish Church in Horley.

Our courtship during my spells of leave that memorable summer took place against the background of air-raids. We had two bicycles and we toured the local lanes enjoying the beautiful summer and each other's company but always keeping watch for aircraft which in a few seconds could turn an ideal summer's day into a tragedy.

I remember sitting with Constance in a field near Balcombe listening at first to the roar of anti-aircraft guns, just like continuous distant thunder, as they opened up against an attack approaching the southeast of London. Then we saw the attack: a terrifying and seemingly invincible cloud of German planes, northeast of us and flying in formation steadily towards London. The next phase followed at once. Small planes like gnats appeared above the German cloud and dived down, through, up again and down again time after time until the enemy formation was broken up. It was the attack of Hurricane and Spitfire pilots on the German formations. We watched hardly believing what we were seeing. As the German formations broke — some shot down, some taking evasive action and some continuing resolutely on to whatever target they elected to bomb, either by design or in desperation — so it became more dangerous for us because planes damaged or driven off course would bomb or fire at anything and they no longer thought of targets in London. Individual dog-fights developed. Planes weaved high and low above us with bursts of machine gun and cannon fire. The sky was a web of vapour trails.

We hid under trees or hedges if the planes came near and once had to shelter in the village school at Balcombe while there was some firing rather too close at hand for us to feel protected by trees and hedges.

To the north of Horley there used to be an attractive restaurant and refreshment place (known in those days as a Road House). It also had an open-air swimming pool which was rather rare at that time. Constance and I used to spend many sunny afternoons beside the swimming pool and so did many others like those, who centuries ago, were described in Shakespeare's Henry V as 'those men in England that do no work today' while others fought and fell at Agincourt.

We were so occupied one day enjoying the sun with many others when there occurred some nearby fighting in the air. Suddenly a plane came over the pool at tree-top height and as it passed over us we saw the German Cross on its Messerschmitt wings. At one moment twenty or more people were lying on the grass sunbathing. A few seconds later all those people had dived into a nearby hedge. By that time, of course, the German plane was a mile away and we all withdrew from the hedge somewhat scratched and feeling very silly.

At the end of August the long, hot and exciting summer in the south of England came to an end. I had spent five months at Portsmouth and Hove with periods of leave at Horley. I had a close view of the evacuation from Dunkirk, the preparations to meet a German invasion by sea and the start of the German air attacks on London. It closely resembled the Napoleonic background of Thomas Hardy's tale of *The Trumpet-Major*, translated into the 20th century.

Now as a very new Sub-Lieutenant RNVR I was ordered back to the Clyde to join another Armed Merchant Cruiser, *HMS Letitia*, which became my home for the months of September and October, 1940.

5

HMS Letitia and a Honeymoon

HMS Letitia was similar to *HMS Forfar*: an ex-passenger ship now fitted with some six-inch guns produced for the 1914/18 war. I suppose these vulnerable and poorly armed ships provided a naval presence and were effective for the interception of merchant ships which might be bringing assistance to the enemy. While I served on her, *HMS Letitia* was engaged on the Northern Patrol between the Shetlands and Iceland and sometimes north of Iceland with the same routine as we endured in *HMS Forfar* — two weeks or so on patrol and two days in the Clyde. One variation of the patrol routine was to escort the *Empress of Australia* and the *Antonia* on a full-speed dash to Iceland and back to carry troops to and from that island. This meant a visit to Reykjavik, but alas no shore leave there.

I had many interesting fellow officers on this ship: John Thom of a well-known Clyde sailing family whom I met again in the Mediterranean; Dick Perrin who spent much of the war afterwards in command of a sea rescue M.L.; Lieut. Richard Hall RNVR, a keen fencer who spent fine days with his foils on the boat deck — often given a hard bout by Reg Anciaume, an RNVR Able Seaman. Skipper Bowles from the trawlers was an experienced grandfather to us young ones.

I left *HMS Letitia* on 5th November, 1940 and was ordered to report to *HMS Osprey* at Portland on 10th November.

On 9th November, 1940 I married Constance Tyrrell at the Parish Church in Horley. To be married on four days' leave meant that much had to be organized in a short time. Special licences from the Bishop and such things. Constance was married from the house of her sister and brother-in-law in Haroldslea Drive and I left from the home of my mother and father on the Balcombe Road in Horley.

After the wedding my father drove us to the Station Hotel at Woking where we spent our wedding night. This place and this hotel was chosen because it was on the main railway line to Weymouth. This is not one of the normal reasons why a spot is

29

chosen for a honeymoon but it did enable us to have a few more hours together. I caught the 11 am train from Woking next morning and my father took a rather sad-eyed Constance back to Kenilworth (later numbered 119) on the Balcombe Road.

I reported to *HMS Osprey*, a shore establishment, at Portland on 10th November 1940. The object of my posting there was to attend a three-week Asdic course to learn how to operate the submarine detection device which was attached to MLs and all other vessels which were or might be engaged in anti-submarine warfare. The principles are now well-known but the equipment was then regarded as secret. Submarine detection was carried out by the emission of a sound wave which if it met with an undersea object was reflected back as an echo. The apparatus measured the length of time between emission of the sound and receipt of the echo and could therefore relay to the operator the range and bearing of the object. Not all reflecting objects were submarines. The same effects could be given by rocks, buoys, shoals of fish and even by the changing density of warm and cold water currents. An experienced operator would be expected to detect the nature of the object which was giving the echo.

The course took place inside the Naval establishment at Portland (*HMS Osprey*) but the members of the course were billeted out in the town of Weymouth. I immediately sent for Constance to join me and so we spent an additional honeymoon in the Trelawney Hotel, Rodwell, Weymouth. There were several other officers at the hotel and some of these were also joined by their wives. With us were Lieut. Peter Loasby RN and RNVR Lieutenants or Sub-Lieutenants Wise, Perrin and Waller. Naval transport took us to and from *HMS Osprey* each day.

At that time air raids were frequent, mostly in the hours of darkness. We often walked into Weymouth for a drink in a pub and had to shelter on the way back from the random bombs and the fall of shrapnel from the anti-aircraft shells bursting overhead. One evening we had just arrived back from the day's training and our transport had left us at the front door. We were all in the hall and waiting to be greeted by our wives who no doubt were in the lounge, when the whistle, turning into the shriek of a bomb sent us all into the recommended survival routine — flat on our faces with hands clasped over the back of our heads. Before we could recover from this recommended but rather undignified position on the floor of the hall, the lounge door opened and the ladies, quite unconcerned about the near miss from a bomb, looked out with amusement and amazement at the carpet of Naval officers on the hall floor.

We suffered some scorn and rude remarks from the ladies but although to us the episode was on the face of it laughable, we really knew that we had been very lucky because the hotel next door had had a direct hit and was completely destroyed. The three weeks at Weymouth were a happy honeymoon with some incidental Asdic training and a spice of danger from the bombing.

The next posting was also for training. This was a course on handling and operating small craft — MLs, MTBs, MASBs, etc. — and was held at Fort William on Loch Linnhe in the west of Scotland. The headquarters, known as *HMS St. Christopher*, was a large hotel now deserted except for the Navy.

Our course consisted of about a dozen young officers. I believe we were the first class there and spent three weeks (1st to 21st December 1940) mainly in practical training in small boats. There were some joint exercises with Army Commando units who were in training nearby. Of course, physical training was included and a highlight of this was a long, very long, run up Ben Nevis — I don't say we ran to the top but it seemed like it at the time.

Being December it had snowed and it snowed again. One of the officers under training was de Mattos whose wife came to stay in Fort William also. He was, I believe, a racing driver or had some such occupation which made him exceptionally good at car handling. He took us over the snow-covered roads to many local towns and even ventured as far as Dalwhinnie in the heart of the Grampians not so far from Aviemore. His car handling on the snow and ice-covered roads was something to be remembered and I have indeed remembered it because he enjoyed skidding into a 180-degree turn without sliding off the road or turning the car over.

One of the instructors was Lieut. Cdr. Chesney RNR, a colourful character with gold earrings who tried to impress on us that he was a mariner of vast experience. We were never quite sure of his credentials, but we proper young officers took a dislike to his theatrical manner. I saw him again in North Africa where he met with disaster and capture.

At the end of the course we were all posted to command a small ship with the exception of de Mattos who was posted as a 1st Lieutenant. He and his wife were very upset about this. I cannot think there was anything to choose between us in our inexperience.

Perhaps they drew our names out of a hat for the ships available. But we did not know and did not think how long the war was going to last and de Mattos need not have worried about his first posting: he still had time to rise to Admiral — perhaps he did.

6

HDML 1007 and A Passage to Egypt

My appointment was to HDML (Harbour Defence Motor Launch) 1007 which was building at Shoreham in Sussex.

Constance and I took a flat in St. Aubyns in Hove and spent January and February there while I 'stood by' the building operation.

At first I was alone. I visited the building yard each day and once a week went to Portsmouth to report. To reach the yard I had to pass through barbed-wire defences manned by Canadian troops. When I first tried to pass through, proudly uniformed as a Sub-Lieutenant RNVR, I was stopped by the Canadian sentry who looked with the greatest suspicion at me and at my Naval pass and said: 'Well, what are you anyway? Home Guard or something?'

Soon I was joined by my First Lieutenant — Sub. Lieutenant Eric Wakeling RNVR — and a crew from Portsmouth. The ratings were all new to the Navy and as keen as mustard. They were led by Leading Seaman G. W. Filmore who was a two-badge long service RN man — in terms of Naval experience, the backbone of the ship's company. I really knew very little of the ship and of naval routine. When the crew arrived, I had to pay for the first few days' food out of my own pocket because I did not know how to get either food or money from any other source.

At our lodgings in Hove, Constance fell badly sick with a form of blood poisoning and had to have a massive blood transfusion. Blood was jealously guarded in those days but my entire crew volunteered and donated a pint each. It was good Naval blood and she recovered quite quickly and it was a proud day when, towards the end of February 1941, ML 1007 was launched by my wife at the Sussex Yacht Works. I bought a barrel of beer and the crew and the Yacht Works' employees enjoyed the great day.

At the end of February we set off for Portsmouth. Handling the ML for the first time was new to us all. I was relieved when we left Shoreham without hitting either side of the harbour entrance. On the way we practised coming alongside a buoy but made a poor show of it. Portsmouth — full of gold braid and Fleet Orders

— was frightening. I was ordered from berth to berth by angry Berthing Officers and did not do any of it very well. I was pleased to be sent on to the Hamble River where there was a Coastal Force base, full of activity and new boats working up.

It was there that I received my next orders and I found them quite shattering. I was bound for duty in the Mediterranean and I was to take ML 1007 to the Clyde where she would be taken as cargo and my crew and I would go by troopship to Suez and thence to Alexandria in Egypt. Some would have welcomed such a posting but I had hoped to be earmarked for duty in the UK and for a young man with a newly-married wife the prospect of a separation of some years made me feel that fortune had treated me unfairly. Why pick on me to go so far away?

Looking back on those days, who knew then what was good and what was bad? In 1939 at Chatham Barracks I had not volunteered to join a naval party going to Singapore although everyone told me it was a nice, quiet and peaceful posting and I would spend the war without hearing a shot fired in anger. Perhaps those who did volunteer for a supposedly peaceful posting did not survive the terrible events to come in the Far East. We were all pawns on the wartime chessboard. What I felt did not matter. You can volunteer to do something but you cannot volunteer not to do something when the Lords of the Admiralty have decided that you should. So the next stop was the Clyde on the way to Egypt.

In company with MLs 1005, 1015 and 1051 we sailed from the Hamble round Land's End to Appledore in North Devon. We berthed alongside the quay. The rise and fall of the tide there is extraordinarily great, and at low tide we found that we were berthed on mud. But as we had no Asdic dome fitted at that time we came to no harm and left next day for Holyhead. We left harbour on a strong ebbtide and one of the MLs — 1015, I think — misjudged its force and collided with a buoy. There was no serious damage but it caused the others some amusement and afterwards the expression 'doing an Appledore' was applied to any misjudgement in our ship handling.

The weather was bad and we arrived tired and salt-coated at a berth near the Holyhead Railway Hotel. I went to the hotel and asked if I could get a bath there — a rather superior young lady at the desk told me it would cost three shillings. I had the bath but it was a large part of a day's pay for a Sub-Lieutenant.

Then across the Irish Sea, past Ailsa Craig to the Clyde where we were ordered to tie up at moorings in Holy Loch. It was now mid-March 1941. The MLs were secured at buoys, the hatches were locked shut and the entire crew departed on leave until a troopship could be found to take us to Egypt.

It was a sad leave overshadowed by the expectation of a long parting ahead of us but for one of my friends (whom I will just call 'Reg' in this story) it must have been more happy than sad for he took the opportunity to get married on the very last day of his leave. Reg and his bride expected to spend their wedding night in a sleeper on the London to Glasgow train but when the (till then) happy couple arrived on the platform they found that their double berth was occupied by an elderly gentleman. He was already in bed for the night and absolutely refused to move or be moved. So two single berths were found for them, one at the front of the train and the other near the guard at the rear.

The great event of a marriage strains a domestic organisation even in peacetime and many a theatrical performance is enlivened by unexpected and unwelcome events in the course of a wedding and the honeymoon which should follow. In wartime the imagination of a novelist is not required to produce the unexpected. From Glasgow, Reg and his bride made their way to Dunoon on the north bank of the Clyde and at the mouth of Holy Loch where our MLs were lying at buoys off the village of Sandbank. We did not have to be ready for sea or for whatever orders might be sent us until the following morning, so when Reg went out that evening by the duty motor-boat to report to his C O he fully expected to be permitted to return ashore for the night. His wife had been left in a teashop to drink endless cups of tea until his return.

Reg's C O was older than most of us. In hushed voices we had speculated that he might be nearly 40 — an unbelievable age to us young ones. He enjoyed his drink too and on being told of Reg's marriage, he got out the gin bottle and insisted on several toasts to the happy couple. In the course of all this, he managed to fall down the hatch and ended up in such poor shape from bruises and gin that Reg could not contemplate leaving him. In any case, during the confusion the last boat for the shore had left, and poor Reg had to spend the second night of his honeymoon applying cold bandages to the head of his skipper.

Constance and I had already travelled up from London by train. I had been out to see that all was well with ML 1007 and had returned to join Constance. On seeking a cup of tea, we found Reg's wife sitting all by herself and when the last boat of the evening came ashore without Reg, we helped her find lodgings for the night as we had already done for ourselves.

Any good novelist would not have continued to part the lovers any longer but wartime stretches suspense beyond the reasonable. The following morning all the MLs were ordered to leave Holy Loch and proceed to Troon on the coast of Ayrshire — some 40 miles south. At Troon we berthed in the harbour and enquiries from the authorities gave us the impression that we might well stay in Troon for a while until shipping and convoys could be gathered together to take us overseas. Reg's honeymoon could now begin! He and I asked our wives to leave Dunoon and join us in Troon and we both found accommodation ashore.

The only duty we had was just to wait and we all spent a relaxed and happy time there — but still under the shadow of an inevitable parting. Some of the crew had more leave and the days passed all too quickly in this unreal time-out from the war.

In May we took our MLs back to the Clyde and they were loaded on *S.S. Belpareil*, a Norwegian ship specially built to carry heavy loads such as locomotives. Now she took aboard some 10 MLs. The officers and crew went on leave again until a troopship became available. Constance and I spent one night in a hotel at Balloch at the foot of Loch Lomond and then took the train south. We had endured that train journey to and from Scotland several times during the winter of 1940/41. It was not a comfortable one and most of our journeys were by night in a crowded stuffy compartment with windows closed and no lights permitted.

At the end of a short leave, Officers and crews of the MLs assembled in a large trainload at Portsmouth and went without stop to the Clyde to board *S.S. Orbita* on 1st June 1941.

Some events stay in one's memory like a photograph, and one of these is my talk to Constance from a telephone callbox in Portsmouth Station. This was a farewell talk before a parting which would probably be for several years.

S.S. Orbita had, we were told, just been transporting Italian prisoners of war. She had only just arrived in the Clyde and the crew had been sent on leave. But a convoy had been assembled, some ships had been waiting for days or weeks for it to sail and the *Orbita*, whether just arrived or not and whether with a full crew or not was ordered to sail with the convoy as soon as all troops — which included our Naval party — were aboard. So we sailed, and as we steamed down the Clyde from Greenock, motorboats were still coming alongside to deliver cooks and other essential crew who had been hurriedly recalled from leave.

S.S. Orbita was filthy. The first few days for all aboard were dedicated to cleaning. The party I was given had the task of cleaning the lavatories which were not only dirty but in most cases blocked.

From the Clyde the convoy went to Freetown on the west coast of Africa and then round the Cape of Good Hope to Durban. The ship was crowded and the conditions were therefore appalling for most of the troops during the long nights in a hot blacked-out ship. I was given the job of duty officer in charge of the lowest deck of all and therefore the hottest, the smelliest and the most dangerous if we had been torpedoed. For myself, I shared a cabin on a deck nearer the waterline and had little to complain of, but when I went round the deck for which I was responsible, I felt I was on a tour of one of the lower reaches of hell. Yet morale was high, I had no real complaints and even had a good many laughs. On one of my early days of duty I stopped and complained angrily that the deck was being made untidy by cigarette ends. Instead of anyone looking shamefaced about it, I thought I heard from the back some stifled laughter which, after a short pause to think what I was doing, made me aware that I had made a fool of myself: smoking was strictly forbidden down there, it was a serious charge I should have brought and here I was, only complaining about litter. Thank God, I reacted without thought and laughed at my mistake; at that they all laughed, too. I believe they considered that I was very understanding and kindhearted. They thought I had deliberately acted that way to give a warning and avoid a punishment. But whatever they thought, I never saw smoking or cigarette ends again.

We found as much work and organized as much play as we could in the daylight hours. The number of look-outs we posted was phenomenal and they were all keen and vigilant — after all, their lives were at risk and few would have survived an attack by a submarine. There were Marines, Air Force, Fleet Air Arm, Army and, of course, our ML party plus a few other Naval personnel. The Marines taught us the rudiments of unarmed combat, we did P.T. and ran races round the deck. Time passed and we saw and suffered no enemy attacks.

The Fleet Air Arm contingent consisted of about sixteen young pilots going out to fly Swordfish in the Eastern Mediterranean. I got to know some of them very well and admired more than I can say their calm and confident courage. I do not believe many of the sixteen survived much more than a year after they arrived in Egypt.

We put into Freetown with the convoy. Only a few of the very senior made a short visit to the shore. It was hot and humid with a misty sun. We enjoyed a day on deck but had warnings about the power of the sun on our northern white bodies. At night there was an impressive thunderstorm over the mountains behind the town, constant lightning and the roar of thunder to remind us that this was Sierra Leone.

To me, our arrival in Durban at the beginning of July, 1941, was dramatic. We had been at sea for a month and the troops had been in a blacked-out ship, sleeping in hot, airless and cramped conditions knowing that one torpedo would give those below decks little chance of escape. Most of these men had only recently left comfortable homes and were new to the discipline of the Forces as well as the hardships of a crowded troopship. What was unforgettable to me was to see their high morale and how they turned out with spirit and pride to march through Durban with uniforms immaculate and with heads held high. I was proud to march with them.

At Durban we changed ships. We had to wait a week for the troopship which would take us north to Suez and during that week we could enjoy a holiday from the war. Together with other Naval Officers I shared a dormitory in an Army barracks. It was basic but comfortable and the winter weather of July was as good as one could expect in an English summer. I remember that I was wakened each morning at 6 am when it was still dark by a black man with a cup of black coffee. All I could see were the whites of two eyes.

The local residents were hospitable beyond belief. We were invited to private houses and cars were always available to take us anywhere we wanted. I paid an interesting visit to the Valley of a Thousand Hills. This was Zulu territory and it surprised me to see the mixture of old and new Zululand exemplified by a huge and handsome Zulu changing the wheel of a car.

I played tennis nearly every day with a young Fleet Air Arm officer whose name was, I believe, Stephenson. We became good friends but I did not see him again after our arrival in the Mediterranean.

On 11th July 1941 we left Durban in the Dutch *Niew Amsterdam*. We had a wonderful send-off from crowds on the quayside and we had the honour of a farewell song from that famous woman who sang *Land of Hope and Glory* to us from the harbour wall — as she did, I was told, on the departure of every troopship.

The voyage from Durban to Port Suez was uneventful. The *Mauretania* was seen also carrying troops but we were not in convoy, we just went as fast as we could and hoped for the best.

Niew Amsterdam was a very big ship. It was crowded and being built for the North Atlantic, it had little deck space and limited ventilation. In the Red Sea it was very, very hot.

We landed on Suez on 27th July 1941 and then went by train to Alexandria. We were well ahead of our MLs which were coming in the heavy freighter *S.S. Belpareil* and so we had another short holiday while we waited their arrival. With some others (Lieutenants Morton and Thomas were two of them, both lost later on when their ML was blown up in the evacuation of Tobruk), I stayed at the Lido House Hotel. This was a small but quite comfortable Pension which, however, had the disadvantage of being opposite a so-called nightclub where music and dancing were to be heard each night and that was a seductive siren call to us lonely sailors. Luckily we did not have enough money to enjoy the delights too often. My main memory of our nights in the Lido House Hotel is listening to South Africans in the nightclub singing South African songs — particularly their favourite concerning the *Old Transvaal* which always reminded me, in its rather yearning homesickness, of the German *Lili Marlene*.

There was a fine sporting club on the outskirts of Alexandria where we could swim and play tennis. The cream of Alexandrian society used it every day. They were mainly of Greek origin, the Italians having left. There were many beautiful young ladies who were attracted by (and very attractive to) the British officers there; but to the dismay of those British officers, it was soon quite clear that a curfew was enforced by the families of these girls — at five in the evening they all left just as if a wand had waved to make them vanish without even leaving a glass slipper behind.

There was sightseeing to be done. The Anfouchi Tombs in Alexandria, the Royal Palace at Ras-el-Tin (if King Farouk was not in residence) and the beaches at Ramleh which were reached by an excellent tramway service. We watched the jugglers and conjurers in the bars (the Gulli-gulli men) and we lived a life of ease for some three weeks.

In the middle of August 1941 our MLs arrived and were unloaded in Suez and we all left Alexandria to take them over.

At Suez we were housed in a down-at-heel hotel until the MLs were ready for us. The cockroaches in the hotel were enormous and numerous and one had to feel brave to fight them out of the washroom and toilets. And the thieves were more agile than any we had met so far. My father had given me a good wristwatch before I left home. I took it off to wash my hands in the hotel and although my back was turned for only a moment, the watch was gone. Later in Port Said, at the great store of Simon Artz facing the harbour, I bought for £5 a Swiss Movado watch which I am wearing as I write these words some 50 years later.

The ship *S.S. Belpareil* was lying off Suez with our MLs onboard. Unloading had begun and because of the local expertise in stealing plus the possibility of sheer carelessness and incompetence, an officer was ordered to be present at all times. I did my tour of duty in the hold of the ship alone amongst some thirty Egyptian stevedores who did not want me there at all. I carried a large service revolver but they had plenty of weapons of their own if they wished to use them. As I stood in the hold one day, a large baulk of timber fell through the hatchway above and would have done my head no good at all had I not just caught sight of it in time. As it was, it caught me a glancing blow on the shoulder and I was lucky to escape without a broken bone or two. Was it accidental?

The huge cranes of the *Belpareil* — a ship which had carried railway engines in peace-time — easily unloaded the MLs and when they were in the water we went aboard to take over, pleased to leave the dirt and cockroaches of the Port Suez hotel.

An unpleasant shock awaited us onboard: each boat had been looted and stripped of everything moveable which was of any value. Sextants, binoculars and the store of liquor which we had stowed away were probably our most serious losses, and were not so easily replaced in a wartime Egypt. The boats had been guarded in Suez so where had the theft taken place? Glasgow, during the voyage, or by the cunning of Egyptian thieves?

Once afloat with engines operational, we set course for Port Said through the Suez Canal on 27th August 1941 — young men in a strange sea excited by the occasion and by the surroundings, passing sailing barges, small feluccas and large ships, watching the native Egyptians irrigating the land and admiring the impressive Memorial to the Defence of the Suez Canal in the earlier war.

Our unimaginative and tradionalist British cook (that is, the seaman detailed to do the cooking) served up Irish stew with dumplings swimming in hot fat as we went through the canal in temperatures of 100 degrees. We did not complain but admired his ability to produce such a meal in the very small overheated galley below decks.

At Port Said were the large and well-equipped workshops of the Suez Canal Company. They were French-managed and staffed by highly-skilled workmen. During the war they did invaluable work for the Allied navies and one of their minor tasks was to make our little fleet of HDMLs operational: tuning up our diesel engines, securing gun mountings, repairing woodwork and generally putting right all the damage, major or minor, suffered in transit from the United Kingdom.

The MLs were painted by the crews and in mid-September 1941 we were dispersed to various parts of the Eastern Mediterranean. On 22nd September 1941, ML 1007 in company with ML 1005 (Lieut. Ken Peacock RNVR) was ordered to escort two freighters — S.S. *Goolistan* and S.S. *Afghanistan* — from Port Said to Alexandria. This was a proud moment: our first operational duty.

Our HDML was 72 feet long, equipped with Asdic and eight depth charges, an ancient (1916 model) 3-pounder gun forward, two .303 Lewis guns and powered by two Gardner diesel engines driving twin propellers giving a maximum speed of about 12 knots. These boats were adequate for what they were called — Harbour Defence — but by their speed and armament were not originally designed to do much more. Nevertheless, in the context of the Eastern Mediterranean where so much had to be done with so little equipment, the HDMLs were given a much wider range of duties and had to do them as well as their design and powers permitted. We were fortunate in having a wonderful spirit in our crews. Backed by a very few experienced long service RN petty officers and Leading Seamen, we had young enthusiasts who had not hesitated to volunteer for the Navy in the earliest days of the war. They were the best of Britain and represented many parts of their country.

They were, to name a few: motor mechanic Woodland who had worked on motor car engines in Somerset before the war; A. B. Bates from Hull, one of the few survivors from *HMS Hood* (who was partially deaf until the Medical Officer in Alexandria discovered cotton wool driven deeply into his ears when the Hood was hit by a shell and exploded in the North Atlantic); A. B. Kent, a very young Lancashire man so enthusiastic that he carried out all his duties at the double whether ordered to or not; telegraphist J. Noone from Liverpool, who would work all hours; the cheerful T. V. Hughes from Rosshire, Scotland; stoker C. E. Ludlow from Essex, always grinning through his grease; J. L. Penfold, A. Hawkins, W. D. Wood, M. J. Ward and so many more in the other MLs whom I regarded as part of the family and whom I remember with affection.

My Cox'n G. W. Filmore, the senior rating, was a long service RN Leading Seaman, later to become Petty Officer. He was steady and reliable in every way and cheerfully put up with my inexperience. The only other officer on board, my No. 1 or First Lieutenant, was Sub. Lieut. Eric Wakeling RNVR. He was enthusiastic and clever. I was lucky to have such a man but perhaps he tried too hard and worried too much. He survived the war and ran a successful business afterwards but became the victim of heart trouble which perhaps was caused by his intense devotion to hard work. Eric Wakeling could be critical and outspoken and I was once told by the Captain of a base in the U.K. before we left that he had been reported to the police for having anti-British sympathies. I knew what had happened — he had made some critical and provocative statements in a pub one evening: he often did that but there was no man more loyal at heart. I told the Captain so and I heard no more about it.

7

The Eastern Mediterranean, ML 355

Alexandria we already knew from the shore; now we experienced it from the sea. It was a great port and a hive of Naval activity with the main Naval Command situated on the point of the harbour called Ras-el-Tin.

After the evacuation of Greece and Crete in April and May 1941, Alexandria was the temporary resting place of ships which had managed to get back to port after the air attacks they had to endure in that disastrous retreat. It is worth remembering the Naval losses the Allies suffered then: 3 battleships damaged, 1 aircraft carrier damaged, 3 cruisers lost and 7 damaged, 8 destroyers lost and 9 damaged. There were only 3 HDMLs involved at that time and two were sunk. Some 2,300 men were lost. This was a major catastrophe for the Royal Navy. It was to be followed by a similar one in the autumn of 1943 but thankfully for our peace of mind, we could not foresee this.

Considering the scale of the losses, all of which were suffered and deeply felt by the local home port and operational headquarters of Alexandria, it was remarkable to me how high the spirit and morale of the Navy had remained. The damaged ships had departed for other dockyards and now only three months later, the harbour looked once more an orderly and major Naval base with battleships, cruisers and destroyers making the newly arrived HMDLs feel quite insignificant.

We did not stay long. With HDML 1005 (Lieut. Ken Peacock RNVR) we were ordered to Haifa to be under the command of Captain Lydekker RN who was the Naval Officer in charge of that port. After an uneventful passage we arrived at Haifa on 30th September, 1941.

There was an oil refinery in Haifa and its products were essential for the Allied Forces in the Eastern Mediterranean. The crude oil for the refinery, however, had to be brought in by sea. It was mainly Iraqi crude oil transported from the Kirkuk oilfield by pipeline to the port of Tripoli in Lebanon. There it was loaded onto a tanker to make the short voyage to Haifa where the crude oil was pumped from the harbour oil jetties to the refinery.

The loading terminal at Tripoli, the voyage by sea and the unloading facilities at Haifa were all vulnerable to attack by submarine or from small raiding parties brought to the eastern Mediterranean by submarine. There had been attacks from the air but the RAF was strong enough to discourage the enemy's long flight from Rhodes or Crete. The sea defences were now strengthened by two HMDLs and we were set to work on a day-on, day-off basis to patrol the waters outside Haifa.

There was a police boat — a rather fast motorboat — with the name of *Sea Wolf* which also carried out duties offshore. Nobody told us about *Sea Wolf* and the first time we met off Haifa on a dark night, we nearly fired at them and perhaps should have done so rather than trust their shouted assurances that they were police and friendly.

Haifa then was a peaceful and pleasant place and Mount Carmel was a great attraction in the fine autumn days. I made friends with the Manager of the Haifa branch of Barclays Bank D.C. & O. and his very charming wife. If I remember correctly, their name was Thompson. They always kept a welcome for the young men from the MLs. Life seemed so stable and peaceful that I opened an account with Barclays as if I expected to be a long term resident.

We got to know Haifa bay very well from our day and night patrols and I always wished I could go ashore to see the crusader town and fortress of Acre on the north side of the bay but I was never able to do so. I admired the graceful Arab dhows which still carried their cargoes up and down the coast. They often gave us some trouble by refusing to keep away from the harbour during the night.

An oil tanker was torpedoed off Beirut one night and we were sent north with orders to find the submarine and pick up survivors from the tanker. We found the tanker still afloat but on fire. There were no signs of boats or men in the water so we considered the burning tanker to be lost and left to carry out a search for the submarine which we continued through the night without success.

On returning to Beirut next morning, I was amazed to find the tanker beached near Beirut harbour with the fires extinguished. Most or all of our crew had stayed aboard and had managed to navigate her to a suitable site for beaching. She was a Norwegian with the name of *Ovula*.

While sitting on board in the harbour one peaceful day we

received a signal from the Admiralty, 'Commence hostilities against Japan forthwith.' Japan and the USA had entered the war. There were no Japanese in sight and I did not take that signal as orders to sail to the Far East so the daily life for us in Haifa remained much as before. We did not fully realize at the time the significance of what had happened on the other side of the world.

This comparatively quiet life was roughly disturbed in the December of 1941 when an urgent signal sent MLs 1005 and 1007 at best speed to Alexandria. On arrival we found alarm and despondency. We had been sent for to help meet an emergency and we had been sent too late: it is just possible that we might have prevented the disaster that had occurred. During the night, while we had been doing our best 12 knots from Haifa, just outside the harbour an Italian submarine launched three explosive devices in the shape of 7-metre torpedoes. Each torpedo was guided by two men sitting astride, one submerged and the other with his eyes just above water. The six men led by Luigi de la Penne (later promoted to Admiral de la Penne in the Italian Navy) penetrated the harbour defences of Alexandria and planted their explosive charges under the hulls of the battleships *Queen Elizabeth* and *Valiant* and an oil tanker where, activated by a timing device, they exploded in the early morning of 19th December.

When we arrived later in the morning, the two battleships still looked formidable but, below the waterline, were seriously damaged and needed major repairs in a dry dock before they could again become operational. The frogmen were taken prisoner, theirs was a one-way ticket, but what a success — six men disabling two battleships and a large tanker!

No one welcomed us in Alexandria. We were made to feel guilty for not having been there before the tragedy and following the precept of locking the stable door after the horse had bolted we were made to work twice as hard in protecting the harbour from further attack. It is interesting to speculate whether the arrival of two HDMLs twenty-four hours earlier in Alexandra would have saved two battleships and whether that would have had any material effect on the course of the war. If we had been on patrol outside the harbour that night, would we have deterred a submarine from off-loading frogmen? Our presence might have done so even if we had not detected the submarine.

Some time later Lieut. E. D. Bennett in HDML 1083 detected a submarine off the coast near the royal palace. Although the

45

submarine escaped, the alarm was given and possibly the landing of spies or subversive elements was prevented not only on that occasion but for the future.

We had little rest that winter and into the early months of 1942. With an occasional day off and even more rarely a night off, each HDML patrolled the approaches to Alexandria whether the weather was good, bad or appalling. To those who may think that the Mediterranean is calm and blue, reference to the Bible will tell them that storms blew up suddenly in those days and I can confirm that they still did so in 1942. The seas are short and steep, there is sand in the air, visibility goes, guns are caked with salt, equipment is thrown about and everyone gets very tired and bad-tempered. I once made myself very unpopular with the Senior Officer of the base by trying to explain that in a storm our small MLs were tossed about like corks: we could not operate Asdic and we could not see anything. All our efforts were directed towards limiting storm damage and staying afloat; as harbour protection we were useless at such times. He made it quite clear to me that we had to be out there whatever the weather and he thought the less of me for suggesting that we might do otherwise.

It would be wrong to infer that we lived a life of endless hardship. On the days off duty the facilities of Alexandria Sporting Club were there to be enjoyed. There was tennis, a swimming pool and excellent catering facilities which even impecunious Sub-Lieutenants could afford once or twice a week. If you wanted sea bathing it was available at Ramleh Beach which could be reached cheaply by tramway.

At the Sporting Club for a small price, we were treated like Lords. We had at least two ball boys on every tennis court and we sat in comfort to have drinks afterwards. The young ladies of the best families in Alexandria (mostly of Greek parentage) were there in the afternoon and would join in tennis and tea. But at 5 pm, just as if a whistle had been blown, they would disappear with their chaperones and be taken home. I remember particularly the sisters Michaelides who were very good tennis players. I remember, too, 'Spike' Spychalla from Poland who had once reached the last sixteen at Wimbledon and was rightly proud of having done so. We had many happy afternoons at the Alexandria Sporting Club with very charming company until curfew time came and the most charming ones went home.

On the shore of the outer harbour, close to the Ras-el-Tin Naval

Headquarters, was the Yacht Club. This was a prestigious social centre where one could meet with great decorum and in much gold-braided company during daylight hours but I do not remember any yachts being used even in the harbour in those days.

Alexandria was well provided with restaurants and bars and the famous Groppi's was there to serve luxurious afternoon teas and to sell confectionery and sticky exotic cakes of splendid appearance and decorative art.

Beween the westernised parts of the city and the harbour was a meaner and rather sordid area such as occurs in most cities which have a significant harbour and a large peace-time sea trade. This could be a dangeorous area to pass through even in a taxi. There were tales of taxis being stopped and the occupants beaten up and robbed. Two Wrens (WRNS) were raped and one murdered when they were stopped one night — that incident led to a reprisal raid on the area by Naval ratings which caused a small riot and added further to the dangers of the passage from the harbour to the city. I usually carried a pistol with me especially if I travelled alone.

Although we faithfully carried out our duties at sea and relaxed with some enjoyment on land, morale among the forces generally began to fall because false elation at the success of an offensive in November 1941 which had carried the advance as far as Benghazi was soon reversed by a retreat in January 1942 and a realization of the strength of the enemy. Now we felt pinned down in the southeast corner of the Mediterranean, threatened by German and Italian forces to the west and to the northwest of us. These forces were being reinforced and a major assault on the Allied forces in Egypt was expected. There was among the troops real doubt about our ability to withstand a strong attack.

In April 1942 I had a welcome change of scenery. B-type Fairmile MLs were being built in Cairo by Thomas Cook & Son. It may be a surprise to read that the organization of Thomas Cook, better known for their travel business, had become builders of minor warships for His Majesty's Government. But it is not so strange because they had for years built Nile River steamers and associated craft for the tourist trade and their excellent Egyptian carpenters were well able to build good wooden-hulled ships in which they installed the Hall Scott high octane petrol engines which were sent to Egypt by sea from the USA.

The first three of the Egyptian-built MLs were shortly to be completed and I was sent to Cairo with Lieut. Rob Young RNVR and Lieut. Peter Bray RNVR to commission them. We lived in Cairo for a few weeks. We saw the final stages of construction; we saw the pyramids and similar sights; we swam and enjoyed our evening drink at the Gazeira Club. Engine trials were carried out on the Nile and on Empire Day 1942 I took over my Fairmile ML from Lieut. Commander C. R. Tribe RN (Retired) who was in charge of the building and commissioning operations in Cairo.

ML 355 was the first — taken over by Lieut. Rob Young. ML 353 came next — which I took over. ML 348 came third with Lieut. Peter Bray in command.

There was, of course, a little ceremony for each one and Commander Tribe was able to provide champagne or something similar to mark the occasion. But he also provided something much more interesting and more lasting, too, for I have it in front of me as I write. This interesting and unusual object is part of a caul and to those who do not know, or have forgotten, what a caul is, perhaps I may explain that a caul is a thin membrane which sometimes covers the head of a child at birth. Its relevance to the occasion is that by superstition it is said that the possession of a caul safeguards a sailor from drowning.

It may be remembered that the fourth paragraph at the start of David Copperfield reads: 'I was born with a caul which was advertised for sale in the newspapers at the low price of fifteen guineas. Whether sea-going people were short of money about that time or were short of faith and preferred cork jackets, I don't know; all I know is that there was but one bidding and that was from an attorney . . . who offered two pounds in cash and the balance in sherry but declined to be guaranteed from drowning on any higher bargain.'

Commander Tribe had lived in Greece as a retired Naval Officer and on being posted to Cairo had been thoughtful enough to provide himself with the caul of a Greek child. He had cut this caul into about eight or more pieces and intended to give one piece to the Commanding Officer of each of the MLs which were to be commissioned by him in Cairo. Accordingly, he attached a piece of the caul to one of his visiting cards and added the words: 'ML 353, may God protect you from the sea.' And this he gave me and I have kept it with me ever since. So far I have not been drowned.

ML 355 departed first. MLs 353 and 348 left together on 24th May 1942. This was not a glorious and spectacular sailing: the only way from Cairo to the Suez Canal is by way of the system of so-called 'sweet water' canals. It would, I suppose, have been possible to go down the Nile but the Nile delta is shallow and treacherous and even if we could have reached the sea that way we then faced a sea trip to Port Said or Alexandria to finish our fitting-out. So we were bound for the workshops at Port Said through the canals.

The sweet water canal was so shallow that we could not use our engines. We had a small Egyptian tug, behind which MLs 353 and 348 were towed.

The sweet water canal was also anything but sweet. Dead animals floated in it and not only small animals: cows and donkeys could be found, but I did not see a camel.

As we were not permitted to use our engines, slowing down and stopping could not easily be accomplished without the two MLs and the tug ending up in an untidy damaged heap. So the MLs had on board some brave local Egyptians who were prepared to dive overboard into the so-called sweet water, swim to the bank, take a line and by hauling backward, slow down and eventually stop the MLs and bring them alongside the canal bank. I feared for the health of these men — that water was filthy.

Slowing down was frequently necessary when we had to pass through places deliberately narrowed and usually stone-faced where there were bridges or facilities for a bridge to be placed across the water. At one spot the ropes were badly handled and the MLs ended up wedged broadside across the entrance of one of these narrow stone-faced bridging points. We were at that time not far from an RAF base and landing field and one Wellington bomber seeing our plight and the pulling and hauling and shouting and swearing which was going on decided to practise dive bombing and low-level attacks on us. This drove all the native labour away in panic and for a time there was chaos and pandemonium to the hilarity of the bomber crews, who came over us so low that we could see from their faces how much they were enjoying the chaos they were creating.

We travelled by day and spent the nights tied up alongside the bank. In the end we reached Ismailia and emerged into Lake Timsah which is about the middle of the Suez Canal. Here we got ourselves organized, started up engines and went north to Port Said.

I have already said how valuable to us were the Port Said workshops of the Suez Canal Company. They maintained the eastern Mediterranean fleet. Now that Malta was a heavily bombed island under constant attack, the only places for any major engineering to be done were at the eastern and western ends of the Mediterranean — Port Said and Gibraltar. At the Port Said workshops we had our armament fitted, engines checked, compasses adjusted and were constrained only by time for the extent of the work which could be done and the finer adjustments we wished to have made.

I can recall only one air raid while we were there. We were berthed alongside *HMS Black Swan* (I think that was her name) and I cannot forget the ear-splitting crack of her 4-inch guns as they engaged the enemy planes. Otherwise one lived in peace at Port Said, bathed at the Plage-des-Enfants, dined at the Officers' Club and shopped at the grand emporium of Simon Artz.

ML 353 was expected to spend perhaps a week or so at Port Said fitting out and working up the crew for sea-going duties. To my great disappointment, however, before the fitting out had been completed Lieut. Mitchelson, RNZNVR arrived from Alexandria with orders to take over command of ML 353 and with orders for me to return to Alexandria to resume command of ML 1007. I was, of course, proud of my new command and hoped I had made the step up from 72-ft. HDMLs to the 112-ft B-type Fairmiles. However, orders had to be obeyed. I wished Mitchelson the best of luck and offered to hand over to him the sailor's good luck charm of the piece of child's caul which had been given me on the commissioning of ML 353. Jim Mitchelson very generously said no to my offer; he said it was a personal gift to me and he thought I should keep it — which I very much wanted to do.

I do hope that in keeping the caul myself I did nothing to impair the fortunes of ML 353. She was sunk three months later on 14th September off Tobruk. Lieut. Mitchelson and the crew were picked up by ML 349 under the command of Lieut. Cdr. Ball, RNVR and brought back to Alexandria under persistent air attacks which caused further casualties.

I returned to Alexandria in June 1942 and took command of ML 1007 once more. I protested to the authorities in Alexandria about my removal from ML 353 and perhaps this did some good, for on 3rd July 1942 I was appointed to command ML 355 but before this could happen there were dramatic events on land which involved both ML 1007 and ML 355.

Tobruk was held but was surrounded after the German advance in the early part of 1942. It was supplied only from the sea and soon after ML 355 was commissioned, Lieut. Rob Young was ordered to take her to Tobruk. She was there when on 20th June 1942 the Germans broke through the defences. By the evening, enemy tanks were in the harbour area.

Ships in the harbour came under fire, many small ships were lost including ML 1069 (Lieuts. Morton and Thomas) which after being hit by a shell suffered an explosion and fire. There were few survivors.

Lieut. Alex Wallace in ML 1048 managed to escape but in an exchange of fire with a tank was wounded by a German tank shell which put a furrow in his cheek as it passed otherwise harmlessly by.

ML 355 stayed almost to the last together with an MTB (Lieut. Solomon RN) who laid a smoke screen in the harbour. Tanks only 300 yards away were being engaged with Oerlikons and Lewis guns.

Many survivors from ships and from Army units were embarked from the jetties (except for a demolition party of a few seamen who continued with their work) and, at 19.50, ML 355 left for Mersah Matruh and was perhaps the last out of the harbour.*

At Mersah Matruh, Rob Young, the CO, became too ill to carry on and his No. 1, Lieut. Ken Hallows RNVR, took the ML to Alexandria. But meanwhile I had not been idle in ML 1007.

When on 21st June, the Germans had captured Tobruk, they pressed on eastwards towards the port of Mersah Matruh and Alemein in the desert behind.

On the evening of 21st June, ML 1007 was ordered to sail urgently westward from Alexandria (as the survivors from Tobruk were hurrying eastward towards us) to help in the evacuation of Mersah Matruh, provided, of course, that we could get there in time.

We approached all alone and with great caution at dawn. Who now held Mersah Matruh? To our horror we saw two craft off the entrance and in the early light we could only see that they carried guns and torpedoes. Were they E-boats? Had the Germans arrived already? Our HDML capable of only 12 knots would look silly against two 30-knot E-boats. We thought we were facing disaster.

But then came flashing lights rather than gunfire from the two ships. They identified themselves as MTBs, perhaps the last of the rearguard escaping from Tobruk or perhaps sent (unknown to us) from Alexandria to help. It was probably the former because having identified themselves they straightway wished us good luck and disappeared east at high speed. They 'got to hell out of it' — to

*See Appendix

51

put it bluntly. Support would have been welcome. We felt very lonely.

Mersah Matruh harbour is small and shallow with a long S-shaped approach through the sand dunes. We went in and found a harrassed Naval Officer doing all he could to evacuate his small staff and his stores in a couple of jeeps. He had no wish for help from us saying, rather surprisingly for an RN officer, that he would rather go by land. He had no idea how close the Germans were but he feared the worst, thought that there were no Allied troops left between himself and the leading German tanks, and told us to get out as soon as possible as he intended to do himself. That was a welcome order. We left the harbour at best speed and had just reached the open sea when we heard machine-gun fire from the direction of the naval buildings in the harbour. Here was a vital decision to be made. We had been ordered 'to get out and fast' but perhaps the leading Germans had caught the resident Naval Officer before he could get his party away.

Could we help him? Could we still evacuate him? Should we even try? Saying, 'Here goes — let's earn a VC,' we turned about and went back through the long narrow harbour approach through the sand dunes — feeling extremely vulnerable. On reaching the harbour again we found that the base staff were using their machine guns to sink buoys and carry out demolitions. We also found the Naval Officer in charge red in the face with anger because we had disobeyed his orders and come back for him. He told us in even more flowery language to 'Get to hell out of it.' Such ingratitude!

Mersah Matruh was evacuated and left to the enemy but it represented his furthest approach along the coast towards Alexandria and was in enemy hands until the Alamein offensive and the advance by the Allies towards the end of 1942.

Many years after the war when I was employed by BP, I met a German employee of the Company who happened to say that he was once an E-boat commander in the Eastern Mediterranean. He had reached that theatre of war via the canals of France and the Italian coast and had been in time to support the big German advance made under the command of General Rommel which took Tobruk and reached Mersah Matruh. He said that he had been the first German boat into Mersah Matruh. I told him that I was the last British boat out of it. Being a solitary HDML, I was glad we were able to get away before the E-boats arrived — but it was a close-run thing. And so, thanks to the escape of ML 355 from

Tobruk and the luck of ML 1007 in getting away from Mersah Matruh, I took command of 355 in Alexandria on 3rd July 1942.

I was lucky to have Ken Hallows as my No. 1. Not only was he an able, cheerful and enthusiastic companion but he had just shown his ability in an engagement with the enemy for which he was mentioned in despatches. He, with the excellent crew, formed an already 'worked up' ship.

The Germans were at Alamein, not too far away. Air raids were more frequent and few ships remained in Alexandria. The summer of 1942 was one of patrols off Alexandria by night and day with an occasional convoy to and from Port Said as a welcome change. The patrols in the B-type Fairmiles took us further to the west than we used to go with our HDMLs. We went as far as the German lines and occasionally, with MTBs, went beyond Mersah Matruh and Sidi Barrani to the Gulf of Solum and the port of Bardia in the hope of catching ships which might be supplying the German forward positions. If there were any such ships we did not find them.

The range of MLs and MTBs was limited by their petrol tanks and by the speed of the ship which naturally consumed more fuel at higher speeds. With a view to increasing the range of the MTBs, someone had the idea of carrying a cargo of petrol on the deck of an ML which would then act as a tanker and refuel MTBs at sea through a pipeline passed between the vessels.

We carried out trials at sea off Alexandria. We did not have the solid Jerry cans which the Germans used for their petrol storage. We only had the then standard and inefficient cans of shiny and very thin metal which were fragile to handle and frequently leaked.

It is horrifying to remember an ML with its own tanks carrying 2,000 gallons of 97 octane aviation spirit loading as many 4 gallon tins (all shiny and sparkling in the sunlight) as there was space available on the upper deck. Then to recall the operation at sea, breaking the seal at the top of each can and on a very unsteady deck pouring the contents by hand into a container at the mouth of a pipeline leading by gravity feed to an MTB close astern. In a seaway much spirit was spilled and the gravity feed was reversed from time to time as the sea lifted the MTB higher than the ML. The cans leaked anyway and the outcome was an ML with petrol running off its decks and the crew wearing petrol-soaked, highly inflammable overalls. I cannot imagine why we did not catch fire and explode. I wonder the enemy aircraft did not see such a brightly shining and inflammable target. If they did see it, they must have thought us quite mad and considered it beyond common humanity to attack those of unsound mind.

Two incidents are worth recalling out of our many patrols off this coast. We were steering due west about five miles from Alexandria and about three miles offshore. It was calm and we were doing about 12 knots. An Asdic watch was normally kept for submarines but for surface activity we relied on sight and sound. So the rule was silence. In this calm, silent, pitch-black night I heard a voice and sent the watch-keeper down to tell the offending rating to keep silent. He came back to say that the look-out thought the sound of the voice came from the water and not from the ship. So I turned 180 degrees and went back dead slow.

We had not gone far when we saw and nearly ran down a man in the water. We hauled him aboard. He was a German pilot from a plane which had been shot down over Alexandria about midday. He had been in the water for twelve hours swimming steadily south where he knew the shore to be. He asked me how far away the shore was when we picked him up and when I said about three miles he smiled and said he did not think he would have reached it. He gave no trouble — he was exhausted. We gave him cocoa and a whisky and handed him over as a prisoner of war when we got back to Alexandria in the morning.

On 21st July 1942, on patrol off Alamein, west of Alexandria, we sighted red flares out to sea. We went off at top speed in that direction and found the crew of a Wellington bomber floating in a rubber dinghy. They had crashed into the sea owing to engine failure on the way to drop flares over enemy shipping north of Crete. The idea of dropping flares was to light up ships as targets for a following wave of bombers.

We took the airmen back to Alexandria when we returned from patrol in the morning, and a few days later the captain of the Wellington, Flying Officer Frame of the Royal New Zealand Air Force, came aboard to thank us. We asked him the question which had been worrying us: if he did not get there to drop his flares, how did the following wave of bombers get on when they arrived to drop their bombs? The answer was disturbing — there were only two other Wellingtons in the raid to carry the bombs. One of these had engine trouble and failed to take off; the other took off, developed engine trouble and turned back. If Flying Officer Frame had not ended up in the sea he would have illuminated the enemy ships off Crete to no purpose. Three aicraft took off and none reached the target.

From time to time we suffered enemy air raids on Alexandria. These were mainly directed at the harbour and were met with considerable anti-aircraft fire from bigger ships. Some bombs did fall on the city and I was in one of the main streets one night when bombs fell rather close. I fell on my face to avoid flying debris but the native population around me just ran. When I returned to the ship I found the marks of bare feet on the back of my white uniform jacket.

Earlier I have mentioned a flamboyant character named Chesney who was an instructor at Fort William. He arrived in Alexandria in command of a large Arab sailing ship where it was fitted with guns hidden under canvas and wooden coverings. It was explained to all who asked and some who did not, that the ship was intended to sail as an innocent trading ship and when an enemy ship was encountered they would surprise and overwhelm it by throwing off the disguise and opening fire. Alexandria had many spies working for the enemy and we all felt that this secret weapon was no secret at all. In due course Chesney sailed with his ship and did not come back. They ran aground near Tobruk, we were told, and were taken prisoners.

There are always some people on the fringe of the disciplined core of the Armed Forces who manage to fight their war almost independently and uncontrollably, often with great bravery and effectiveness but sometimes only with a desire to be seen to be different. Those latter ones make their way rather noisily and less effectively as a result. Chesney's life did not run by normal standards.

In 1926 at the age of 18, Ronald Chesney whose name was then John Donald Merrett, was accused of the murder of his mother in Edinburgh. The verdict of the Scottish Courts was Not Proven on the murder charge but guilty of forging his mother's cheques and he was sentenced to one year's imprisonment. He inherited £50,000 and changed his name to Chesney. In 1954 an inquest in London decided that he had murdered his wife and mother-in-law. Following an international hue and cry his body was found near Cologne with a bullet wound in the head.

In mid-August, ML 355 developed some trouble with valve inserts in the Hall Scott engines and went back to Port Said for repairs. We had a restful time there until early in September. It was during this time that ML 349 (Lieut. Cdr. Ball), ML 352

(Lieut. Worledge, RANVR) and ML 353 (Lieut. Mitchelson RNZNVR) took part in an abortive raid on Tobruk in which MLs 352 and 353 were sunk.

We enjoyed about three weeks rest in Port Said while engine and other repairs were carried out. ML 348 was also in Port Said at this time and the number of Cairo-built MLs was steadily growing through the summer.

By mid-September we were back in Alexandria and renewed our patrols outside Alexandria and into the Arab Gulf which lies to the west.

I have not referred before to units of the French fleet which had throughout this time been lying at buoys in Alexandria harbour. There were two light cruisers and some smaller ships which on the fall of France had escaped from Toulon. While they had not joined Vichy France, neither had they joined the Allied forces to fight the Italians and Germans as some other French units had done. They remained almost as ships of a neutral country in a port which was involved in a war. They kept quiet and took no part in anything going on around them.

At one critical stage however when, in another theatre of war, action was taken to be against the Vichy French it was feared in Alexandria that news of such an Allied action might persuade the French Admiral to leave the harbour with his fleet perhaps to take part in the war against us. On the eve of the action elsewhere against the Vichy French, precautions were taken for a possible conflict should the French ships try to leave Alexandria to join the enemy. Some Allied ships were moved out of the harbour, MLs were placed behind jetties, Army guns (including anti-aircraft guns) were moved into suitable positions, so that with full angle of depression, they could be brought to bear, and finally the MTBs in harbour were so disposed that they could use their torpedoes.

As dawn approached, we in ML 355 sheltered behind our jetty wall and wondered if and when the battle of Alexandria harbour would break out. Just as we sipped out cups of tea in the early grey light, there was the most enormous explosion and, soon after, pieces of rock and stone started falling around us. This is it, we thought! There is now going to be the most awful bloody shambles in this harbour as we fight it out with the French at point-blank range.

But nothing more happened. The harbour was quiet and still. The guns on the French fleet remained in the fore and aft position and the ships showed no sign of moving from their moorings.

It was just by the greatest good fortune that no battle broke out because the cause of the explosion was this: the MTBs would have had to play a major part in any action against the French fleet and they had been deployed round the harbour. In going round his MTB to check the readiness of each torpedo, one MTB officer had pulled a wrong lever or pressed a wrong button and with a woosh — away went his torpedo across the harbour. By great good luck the torpedo missed the French cruisers and exploded with a roar against a jetty behind them. Damage was only caused by flying debris and no one was hurt. But what would have happened if one of the French ships had been hit?

ML355 had at that time two Australian ratings — Baber and Churchill. They were two fine young men and very good swimmers. On coming in from patrol or convoy it was always a matter of pride to be secured to the buoy or tied up alongside a jetty before any other ML in company. If it was a buoy we could win every time because Baber would leap off the bows, swim like a fish to the buoy, catch the rope, secure it and be back on board while other boats were still scratching about with boat-hooks.

We also had among the crew Able Seaman Oliver Ford, an ex-lorry driver. He was a powerful man, a very good friend but dangerous to have around if he was unfriendly. One day Churchill had to go to hospital with a cracked jaw. He said that the cause of this was a fall in the galley and his jaw had made contact with the cooking stove. In a small ship things cannot be hidden for long. All the crew knew that Churchill had called Ford a Pommie bastard or something similar, and they knew that Ford had hit him causing the cracked jaw. If Churchill had wished to complain, then Ford would have been in serious trouble but nothing would shake Churchill's story that the cooker was to blame for his injury. There was no more trouble between Ford and Churchill after that and they were both fine members of the crew on whom I could rely without question.

I don't want to single them out for praise. All the men I had with me in the Mediterranean were in their different ways reliable and devoted to their duty. The troubles they got into were minor compared with the way they behaved when things were difficult. In ML 1007 one of the crew came aboard having had too much to drink and sat in the corner of the mess deck with a pile of plates which he threw at anyone who came near. In the end I thought I would have to intervene and risk personal attack but seeing my

intentions, Able Seaman Bates, the survivor of *HMS Hood*, went in and being a strong lad, knocked out the offender so that all was forgotten in the morning and there was no defaulter to come before the captain. The two Australians, Baber and Churchill, left me around the end of 1942 to take an Officers' Training Course in Australia. I am sure they did well.

On looking back I am surprised how good was the health of all on board. I recall no significant health troubles, although the local food and water in Egypt is known for its ability to cause trouble to European stomachs, and some of the young girls of Port Said and Alexandria were said to be even more dangerous. But we were all young and could throw off quickly the ill-effects of food and drink, and young as we were, we were able to keep clear of the more dangerous of the females by a mixture of celibacy and good sense.

Thoughts of homes and families and dreams of a return were never far away but I think we all accepted that we were on something like a three-year tour of duty and nothing was going to change that unless we were sent home seriously sick or badly wounded. We were kept busy and had a job to do, so we had little time to dwell unhappily on our separation from those at home.

We received mail from home. It came in bundles rather than regularly but was frequent enough to prevent complaints unless we were on the move or in places like Benghazi where the lines of communication were long. Letters were subject to censorship so their subject matter was mainly of personal and family affairs. Only in broad and general terms did we know how the war was going outside our own little area; news from outside came by radio and newspapers (when we could get them) and since the enemy had these too, we all knew that 'the truth, the whole truth and nothing but the truth' was not the cardinal principle of these communications. Later on we did get a confidential Naval news summary to keep us better informed, but even this had to be selective in the information it could disclose.

8

Alamein and Westward

It may appear from reading of my activities in ML 1007 and 355 during 1942 that the war was centred on patrols off Alexandria. My life was centred on such patrols at that time but they must be seen against the background of what was happening on land in Egypt, Cyrenaica and Tripolitania.

The destruction of the Axis forces in North Africa was an essential prelude to any Allied offensive operations against the south of Europe. It was equally necessary to end a constant threat from the enemy across the desert to Egypt and the Suez Canal. To the northwest, the Germans already held Crete and Rhodes enabling them to put Egypt and the Canal under attack from the air.

A British offensive on 18th November 1941 made good headway and Benghazi was captured on 25th December. At that time I was stationed in Haifa but returned to Alexandria just before a counter-attack by Axis forces under General Rommel forced the evacuation of Benghazi in January 1942. A further attack on 26th May 1942 forced the Allied forces back to within 40 miles of Alexandria. A line was finally held at El Alamein which is about half-way between the small harbour of Mersah Matruh and the main Egyptian city and harbour of Alexandria.

While we carried out our Naval duties against the background of the war on land we could observe the change in morale of those on shore. And we did not like what we saw. We arrived in 1941 after the defeats in Greece and Crete when Alexandria was full of damaged ships and the Army was like any Army after a retreat and sea evacuation.

The offensive in November 1941 which took the troops as far as Benghazi raised hopes and morale unduly high. The counter-attack by Rommel early in 1942, the loss of Tobruk and the retreat to Alamein was consequently a really shattering blow. Rommel was being talked of as invincible, and his equipment was said to be better and his troops more numerous than our own.

On the day the Axis forces came nearest to Alexandria and before anyone knew that they had been held at El Alamein, there were disgraceful scenes of panic in the harbour. We had just come in from the night patrol. We had tied up alongside the jetty near the main Naval Stores and I was having a shave when an excited Base officer, white as a sheet and jumping from one leg to the other, called me up on deck.

'Get out,' he said, 'get out of this harbour. German tanks will be at the gates of the dockyard at any moment, they will be at the harbour entrance soon and you won't be able to get away!'

For some reason I did not believe him. I asked him if this was an order and if so where it came from. No, he said, he had no authority to give me orders but he was trying to save me. Well, I had heard no sounds of shooting or battle and as we came into harbour that morning, I saw no activity on land to the west of the city. So, although getting ready to move at short notice, I stayed at my berth and by the evening sanity had returned to the harbour and the base. But I am afraid that the Base officer who tried to panic me into action was perhaps the bravest of the lot for most of them had fled. One I know to have been engaged in loading the furniture from his flat onto a ship bound for Port Said. The Naval stores were left deserted, abandoned and unlocked.

Some of my crew went into the stores and came back with binoculars, sextants and compasses which, if the Germans were really at the gates as they had heard the Base officer tell me they were, was a sensible thing to do.

Next day when the Stores officer and his staff returned, they came round to find out where their valuable stores had gone. We returned what my crew had taken and I was told that those concerned would be put on a charge for stealing. This made me very angry and when I threatened to bear witness that they had deserted their posts and left the stores wide open, I heard no more of the matter. Finally, I was told afterwards by a very senior officer that 'the practice evacuation of the base' had gone very well. I did not tell him what I thought of it because I knew very well that he already knew the facts and perhaps would rather not be reminded of them. It was he who had spent too much of his time saving his furniture during 'the practice.'

This episode I relate only to show that morale had been dropping as the success of the winter of 1941 had been turned to a long retreat during the summer of 1942. At its worst it almost became a panic, and at such times the enemy looks invincible.

After Winston Churchill's visit to Cairo in August 1942, General

Alexander was appointed Commander-in-Chief Middle East and Lieutenant-General Montgomery was appointed to command the Eighth Army. The effect was remarkable. Montgomery had the ability to gain the confidence of the troops very quickly and they began to believe that Rommel could be defeated. But, during the summer we went through the trough of despair and doubt; and whatever we did in our activities at sea, our relaxation at Port Said or our tennis at the Sporting Club, part of us always lived in the atmosphere of events on the land of Egypt and North Africa to the west of us.

The Eighth Army attack at El Alamein was launched on 23rd October 1942.

On the evening of 22nd October, and while there was still enough light for them to be seen from the shore, two merchant ships which had sailed from Port Said passed the entrance to Alexandria and steered due west along the coast.

They were joined by ML 355 and other MLs. When night fell, the merchant ships turned about and went back to Alexandria but the MLs continued for some time towards Mersah Matruh going closer inshore and putting on speed to make maximum engine noise. All this pantomime was intended to make the enemy expect a landing on the coast behind his lines so that part of his forces might be diverted in that direction. We returned in due course to Alexandria to await the outcome of the battle. I have never heard whether we achieved any success in this exercise of deception.

As soon as the Army broke through at Alamein the Navy had a part to play in ferrying supplies of ammunition, petrol, food and other stores along the coast to be unloaded at the nearest port to the Army's advance. ML 355 escorted the first desert convoy and on 9th November we arrived off Mersah Matruh. We were preceded by minesweepers and just before we arrived, the fleet minesweeper *HMS Cromer* hit a mine and sank. Wreckage from the ship was still floating on the surface and other minesweepers were still busily clearing a channel into the small harbour. We anchored for the night in Abu Rasafa Bay to the east of Matruh. To the east of us across the bay we could see several mines floating on the surface.

The night was uneventful and the watchkeepers reported nothing, but when daylight came we found that the mines which were to be seen some way to the east of us when darkness fell now were quite close to the west of us. There was only one explanation: they had drifted through our anchored convoy during the night. Not knowing how long we should have to remain in these waters and heartily disliking the presence of these drifting explosive objects, we set about sinking the mines by rifle fire. While we were doing this we were diverted by loud shouts from the shore where we saw several figures jumping up and down in great distress. On going closer, we discovered that they were a team of mine experts who wanted to capture and dismantle one of the mines we were so busily sinking. I think we left them one to play with, but I had no regrets about sinking the others.

On 10th November we entered Mersah Matruh. There was a large Italian supply ship in the harbour lying half on its side having been bombed by the RAF. It had not been there when we left Matruh earlier in the year.

There was much bustle ashore, shifting stores and so on. Another convoy was being gathered together to go further up the coast with more stores. This convoy consisted of LCMs (small Army landing craft) and some R-boats which were originally German. We were detailed to escort this convoy to Bardia. The LCMs could not go fast and the R-boats could not go slow. None of them had a compass and the night was cloudy and very dark. We nearly went mad trying to keep them together and going in the right direction but we managed to shepherd them through the night and got them all safely to Bardia on the morning of 12th November 1942.

Bardia is a very small inlet which can only generously be called a harbour. It is open to the east and is surrounded on all other sides by high ground. To the west a road zig-zags up the hills and becomes part of the coastal road which leads on westward to Tobruk. The jetties at Bardia had been blown up and the Naval headquarters was established in the small settlement of houses which were on higher ground reached by the zig-zag road. We anchored in this rocky inlet and rolled uncomfortably in the swell which was coming in the open entrance to the east. We were ordered out once when a large supply ship was sighted and we were supposed to guide her in. But her captain ignored us and steered straight in at rather high speed and almost too late he saw what a small harbour it was. So he dropped anchor, went full astern and, turning himself round almost on the proverbial sixpence, he went out again as fast as he had come in. I have no idea where he went to after that — we never saw him again.

The next harbour westward is Tobruk and, after that, Derna.

27th March 1940. HMS Forfar on northern patrol.

Boarding Party leaves to examine merchant ship intercepted south of Iceland.

October 1940. HMS Letitia as convoy escort to the Antonia and Empress of Australia taking troops to Iceland.

Winter 1939/40 HMS Forfar — Cooper, Branch, Wood, Keating, Sykes.

October 1940. Arctic ice floes north of Iceland.

February 1940. HMS Forfar. Timmins, Cooper, Marshall, Savage, Searle, Wood, Metcalf, Foster, Olley.

16th Sept. 1941. HDML 1007 in dock at Port Said.

14th Feb 1942. HDML 1007. Sub. Lieut. Eric Wakeling and Able Seaman A. Hawkins.

25th May 1942. The towing of MLs 348 and 353 from Cairo to Ismailia.

20th June 1942. HDML 1032, Alexandria.

3rd July 1942. Crew of ML 1007, Alexandria. M. J. Ward, J. L. Penfold,
C. F. Ludlow, J. Noone (Tel.), F. Bates, W. J. Woodland (Motor Mechanic).
Front row:- T. V. Hughes, G. W. Filmore (Cox'n), W. D. Wood.

15th July 1942. ML 352 (Lt. G. R. Worledge RANVR) coming alongside,
Alexandria.

8th October 1942. ML 350 (Lt. Cdr. 'Dougie' Russell Senior Officer 43rd ML
Flotilla)

10th November 1942. Italian ship sunk in Mersah Matruh.

9th Nov. 1942. Lt. Ken Hallows — Officer of the Watch — ML 355 in Abu Rasafa Bay.

25th Nov. 1942. Navy House Tobruk.

It was not known whether these harbours were yet clear of the enemy and a pause was considered advisable. We were ordered back to Alexandria.

When we returned to Alexandria, my First Lieutenant — Lieut. Ken Hallows — was posted to the command of an ML (a promotion which he thouroughly deserved) and his place was taken on board ML 355 by Lieut. Crossley. He was known as Butch Crossley and when one saw him, it was obvious that 'Butch' was appropriate. He was very big and very hearty; a great personality and, unlike many ' great personalities,' he was good at his job. Perhaps he enjoyed his drink rather too much and that had to be watched, but drink never interfered with his work. Perhaps many of us drank more than was good for us, but we had a strict rule which was rigidly observed, that officers never drank alcohol at sea. I never saw drinking at sea and perhaps that was used as an excuse for being rather more free with the drink as soon as harbour was reached.

For ratings it was different. Those who wanted it could have their tot of rum every day whether at sea or not — the alternative was 3d per day added to one's pay. Moreover,if you decided to draw your rum ration it had to be drunk on the spot — at least that was the regulation, but in small ships in a rough passage and with half the crew on watch all the time, the rules were not, and perhaps could not, always be strictly carried out. And if the Petty Officer of leading hand did not supervise the issue of the ration properly, rum could be illegally saved up for an occasion when several tots could be taken together, as might happen when celebrating a safe return to harbour.

Of course, this could lead to trouble and even to disaster. I know of one rating who secretly saved up his tots until he had filled a whole bottle of rum. On Christmas Day he sat on the mess deck and drank it all in a very short space of time. He died before anyone could get him to hospital.

After about a week in Alexandria, ML 355 sailed west once more with a very mixed convoy of store ships, water boats, harbour tugs and small landing craft. We arrived off Derna on 23rd November 1942 and followed the minesweeper HMS Calm to the harbour entrance. There we left some of the convoy and returned to Tobruk where we had a short stay on 25th November. Tobruk harbour was a shambles of sunken and half-sunken ships and the jetties and harbour buildings were only heaps of rubble.

Then on to Benghazi with a convoy of LCTs (Landing Craft

Tanks sometimes called A-Lighters) in bad weather and moonless nights. We nearly had an engagement with two of our destroyers and in approaching Benghazi as darkness was falling we could make little sense of the charts of the German minefields which had been given to us. Rather than spend another dark night at sea and trusting to the shallow draft of our convoy and of the MLs, we turned a blind eye on the minefield charts and went straight in. Our luck held, no one was mined and we found a bad berth alongside a half-destroyed jetty in the harbour of Benghazi on 27th November. Benghazi had only recently been bombed by the RAF. One ship was still on fire and there were plenty of sunken ships and jetties half-destroyed by bomb-craters.

They did not want us hanging about in the harbour. We were now quite close to the forward positions of the Army and could go no farther west. We were ordered back for more convoy duty but by that time we were very low on fuel, although we had been running on one engine only (to save fuel) ever since we left Alexandria.

The only supplies brought up by the Army were in those awful shiny, thin-skinned and tinny four-gallon cans. The whole crew, including Crossley and me, worked ourselves exhausted carrying these wretched cans from Army trucks, down the jetty over a plank onto the ML and pouring the contents through a funnel into the fuel tanks. We put in the best part of 2,000 gallons in this way and then set off back eastward.

December 1942 was spent on similar convoy duties to and from Tobruk. Ashore everything was on the move and although everyone was working night and day, morale was sky-high following the rapid advance of the Army.

While in Tobruk, we managed to get a rope round one of our propellers owing to careless handling while we were casting off from one of the very few available berths at a jetty. The coxswain was all ready to go ashore to ask for the service of a diver, but I knew that the few Naval divers in Tobruk were working twenty hours a day in dangerous conditions trying to clear under-water debris from the jetties and the bottom of the harbour. So I told the crew that we had the rope round the propellers through our own carelessness and it was up to us to clear it by our own efforts and not go running to overworked divers for help. We all took turns diving under the stern with a knife and each taking a few quick slashes at the rope before we ran out of breath. Our motor mechanic, a Jew who had originally come from Palestine and had learned his trade in the Mercedes works in Germany, managed to stay longer below water than most by means of a kind of diving helmet which he had very cleverly and quickly constructed from a gas-mask.

After an hour or so we cleared the rope. We were exhausted but I think the crew ended up by being proud of what we had done by our efforts. They certainly learned to be more careful with the ropes.

Just before Christmas, the MLs based in Tobruk seemed to develop an unusual number of defects, all of which they said could only be dealt with in Alexandria. It did not escape the attention of the Senior Naval Officer in Tobruk that 25th December could be better celebrated in Alexandria and so the defect lists were not treated too seriously. It was agreed, however, that two out of the four or five MLs should go back to Alexandria and, because I had been longest in Tobruk, ML 355 and one other ML were sent back and were able to spend the Christmas of 1942 in rather more civilised surroundings than the bombed-out ruins of Tobruk. We also had a rather greater choice of things to eat than they had in the desert. As regards drink, I believe that Tobruk or any desert port did not lack supplies on that day even if they did have to go a little short in the following weeks.

9

Lebanon and Cyprus

The coming of 1943 saw a change of scenery for us. ML 355 and several other MLs were ordered to sail for Beirut in the Lebanon and, at about that time too, I had another change of First Lieutenant when Lt. Norman Stallworthy RNVR took over from Lt. Crossley.

The building of MLs in Cairo had continued so well that despite the loss of MLs 352 and 353 we now had two flotillas of B-type Fairmile MLs: about sixteen MLs in all — the 42nd flotilla under Lt. Cdr. A.H. Ball RNVR and the 43rd under Lt. Cdr. Russell RNVR (known to all as Dougie Russell). These flotillas, however, covered the area from Benghazi in the west to Beirut and Cyprus and on to Turkish waters in the northeast — a coastal distance of over 1,200 miles, which is more than the east and south coasts of Britain from the Orkney Islands through Dover to Lands End. Contact with our flotilla leaders was not only irregular, it was also rare, and ships of each flotilla were more often than not working with the Senior officer of the other flotilla.

We had worked in Alexandria with Dougie Russell who commanded ML 350 and when we went northeast to Lebanon in the early days of 1943, Dougie Russell was the flotilla leader and Senior Coastal Force officer in that area.

The principal reason for our going to the waters in the northeast corner of the Mediterranean was said to be for anti-submarine work in that area. I suppose the success of the Army's advance along the north coast of Africa as far as Tripolitania reduced the need for coastal forces there and released some of the boats for the Cyprus-Beirut area. I wonder, too, whether it was the start of planning for an attack on the Dodecanese and the Aegean Sea which came later in the year.

A word may be appropriate at this stage about the armament of these MLs. Intended primarily for anti-submarine work they all carried an Asdic dome beneath the hull for submarine detection. And on the deck there were twenty depth charges in racks for dropping over the side and on a thrower which could, by an explosive charge, 'fire' two depth charges, one to either side of the boat. Earlier MLs carried a very old (1914/18 war) 3-pounder gun forward, twin Lewis guns (0.303") amidships and a 20mm Oerlikon aft. Later MLs from Cairo were fitted with a Rolls gun forward (in place of the 3-pdr) and later still some had a 40mm Bofors gun fitted in that position. The Rolls gun was a very accurate weapon firing a 2-pdr shell but it was rather slow to re-load. The Bofors gun was a superb weapon.

The armament aft was steadily improved. Another Oerlikon was fitted in place of the Lewis guns. Twin Browning maching guns (0.303") were fitted either side of the bridge. There were other unofficial improvements: guns which were 'acquired' mysteriously — particularly in the desert after the battles had subsided there — and were fitted, quite without authority, whenever a friendly Base Engineer Officer could be persuaded to do so. By such means, ML 355 at its most heavily-armed stage had, in addition to its standard armament, two Italian 20mm Breda fitted aft and, mounted on the deck on either side of the bridge, a Browning 0.5" and an additional Vickers 0.303" machine gun.

I have not mentioned two other offensive weapons which we once had: a Holman projector which fired a grenade — a highly dangerous weapon to all concerned and it was removed from the early MLs which were unlucky enough to have it fitted. And there was a Schermuly rocket mounted on the bridge which fired a coil of thin wire into the air — intended, so I was told, to bring down low flying aircraft by getting them entangled with the wire. I only heard of it being fired twice: once for practice when the wire fell back on the ML causing the greatest confusion until it could be cut away, and once in a gallant attempt to pass a written message from an ML to a destroyer in a heavy sea which made going alongside impossible. In that case the wire became entangled around the destroyer's bridge and mast, causing extreme anger on the destroyer rather than admiration for the enterprise of the ML's captain.

The slowly-increased armament on deck is a reflection and a reaction to the role we were expected to play in the Eastern Mediterranean. Starting as anti-submarine boats it was soon found that other duties became more numerous and that we were at all times liable to attack from the air now that the enemy had airfields in Rhodes and Crete. As time went on we could put up quite a good defence against attacking aircraft.

The weakest point of the ML was the fuel. We ran on 97 octane spirit, a specification then used by some aircraft. We carried some 2000 gallons in large tanks amidships which were covered with a rubbery material which made them self-sealing if penetrated by a bullet but nevertheless vulnerable to an explosive shell. Fire, whether caused by enemy action or by some accident or carelessness of our own, was always our great concern.

As we were likely to operate in shallow waters and in enemy waters too, we were fitted with demolition charges so that the ML could be destroyed rather than captured. These charges were placed under my bunk and, looking back, I wonder why I was not more worried about that. I suppose the thinking was this: if the explosive charges are placed under the Commanding Officer's bunk, he will certainly take the greatest care to control the means whereby the charges were to be fired.

The lack of spares, particularly engine spares, was at times very severe and caused periods of repair to last much longer than expected. This threw greater strain on the boats which were kept operational. I discovered that there was a main stores depot in Palestine somewhere near Tel Aviv, and the idea that I should go there to see what was available was welcomed by the engineer officers in Alexandria and Beirut. I managed to find transport to get there and was amazed at what I found.

This store was an Aladdin's cave and had everything we wanted. But I achieved nothing. The paperwork and authorities required for getting things out of the storehouse were insurmountable. I still do not know whether it was just a matter of red-tape and bureaucracy or whether there was a deliberate policy to keep things there as 'a last resort' against a time of even greater emergency, such as a complete stoppage of all supplies reaching the Eastern Mediterranean from any source. I reported my findings and have no idea whether any improvement to our repair situation resulted from this journey into Wonderland.

For most of January and February we were based in Beirut. ML 350 with Lt. Cdr. Russell in command was the flotilla leader and we carried out anti-submarine sweeps in that area and between the Lebanese coast and Cyprus. We carried out training and exercises, some of which were with our own submarines.

We also used the port of Tripoli to the north of Beirut for it was here that there was the oil pipeline terminal bringing oil from the Kirkuk fields in Iraq. The resident Naval Officer in Tripoli was Commander Courage R.N. who had been given this comparatively quiet post for rest and recuperation after constant and brilliant activities in destroyers, first in the battle of Narvik and afterwards in and around Malta, where *HMS Maori* was sunk under him by attack from the air. Commander Courage was shortly to be posted to Alexandria as Commander Coastal Forces Eastern Mediterranean, where he became an inspiration to all Coastal Forces who served with him, just as he was an inspiration to those in the destroyers which he had commanded before.

There was no enemy action other than submarine reports and consequent searches while we were in the Beirut-Cyprus waters in that January and February. There were, of course, incidents to remember.

We went northwards up the coast and one night anchored in the small port of Latakia: famous in peace-time for its tobacco export trade. Next morning the local priest came aboard to ask a favour: would we please send a party ashore to attend the funeral of an Englishwoman who had just died without any friends after living in his parish of Latakia for many years? We asked her history. She had come to Lebanon and Syria many years ago with a troupe of dancers. She became detached from the troupe and stayed behind earning her living as a prostitute in the local brothel. Now she had died friendless, and seeing our White Ensign the good priest thought we might have been sent by Heaven so that her funeral could be attended by some of her countrymen. I went to the funeral with a small party and found it a moving ceremony. On the way back, the priest showed us the local brothel where she had lived and died. To us at that time it was a sordid sight to see in mid-afternoon a queue of French Senegalese troops waiting outside the door.

A visit or two to Famagusta in Cyprus was an interesting change from routine. It enabled us to go ashore to see the ruins of ancient Salamis which lie just outside the city. We first entered Famagusta on a very dark night after a long, tiring and unsuccessful submarine search in that area. There were four of us and ML 355 was following close astern of Dougie Russell in ML 350. Dougie never went slowly if he could go fast and the entrance to Famagusta harbour follows a longish channel close to the shore, culminating in a narrow entry through ancient fortifications.

I had not been there before and would have liked time to study a chart of the entrance but Dougie having ordered me to follow close astern, just went hell-for-leather into the channel and through the massive stonework of the fortifications. I was convinced that we were all going to end up in a heap on the beach or against the ancient but solid stone walls which I could see flashing past much too close in the darkness. However, trust in Dougie was justified and, although sweating heavily, I anchored safely in the harbour.

I was not so happy on another occasion when having laid a smokescreen in order to test our apparatus, Dougie for some reason caused us to turn and charge back through it in no sort of formation, and MLs 350 and 355 had a very near miss.

Then there was the great excitement when Dougie was faced with a Court Martial. Someone had bought some grapes from a stall in the Beirut market and found that they were wrapped in secret Naval signals relating to the movement of British submarines. Not surprisingly, the Naval Authorities were outraged; enquiries were made in all directions and the copy which was used to wrap the grapes was traced — so it was alleged — to the Senior Officer of the MLs, namely Dougie Russell who, if he was in fact the culprit, should have made sure that it was destroyed after being read — if not before.

We had a Lieut. Gus Roberts in the flotilla who was a very able solicitor in peace-time. He defended Dougie Russell at the Court Martial. I am not sure of the details of his defence because I did not attend, but it seems from what I heard that the history of the offending copy of the signal was so successfuly muddled in the evidence that suspicion of laxity was cast far and wide upon nearly all the base staff and even on the Commander of the base himself. Consequently quite enough doubts were cast on the case for the prosecution to ensure acquittal of Lt. Cdr. Russell and to earn for Lieut. Gus Roberts the undying hatred of all the staff on the base at Beirut.

By March 1943 our tour of duty on the North East station was ended and ML 355 went back to the North African coast.

10

Special Duties

On 7th March we were in Tobruk once again. A certain amount of wreck and jetty clearance had been done but the general picture was still very much of a heavily-bombed and fought-over harbour. The large building on higher ground to the west of the harbour — known to all of us as Navy House because that is where the Naval Officer in Charge maintained his headquarters — was a half-destroyed ruin. The wreck of the Italian cruiser *San Georgio*, her badly damaged upper works just showing above the water, remained near the centre of the harbour, and many other wrecks were still there as memorials to the fighting which was past, and as warnings of fighting which might be renewed.

Then on to Benghazi, another graveyard of ships and a harbour of half-destroyed jetties. Unlike Tobruk, however, the town had not been fought over and the bombing seemed to have been concentrated on the harbour. The large twin-domed Cathedral still stood grandly overlooking the harbour and had suffered only minor damage. The base was in the charge of Lieut. Cdr. J. D. Tooms RNVR. He was a tough and hard-drinking New Zealander who terrified the junior officers, particularly his second in command, Sub-Lieut. Warren. By a happy coincidence, Tooms' brother was a senior officer in the New Zealand Infantry Division in North Africa and at the time we were there the two brothers met in Benghazi.

We spent two or more weeks of March 1943 in Benghazi. There were HDMLs doing harbour patrols (ML 1046 was one of them) and Fairmile MLs awaiting orders. In the spare time we organized rifle shooting and swimming parties for the crew. It was a strangely peaceful few weeks in a front-line harbour. At the end of March we went back to Alexandria and then to Port Said with a convoy. A visit to Port Said was always an opportunity to have a few repairs done in the excellent workshops of the Suez Canal Company.

Soon we were back in Alexandria where Commander Courage was now established as Commander Coastal Forces Eastern Mediterranean and his base there was known as *HMS Mosquito*.

Here I was told that ML 355 was to be detached for Special Duties and before long I was told what, in the immediate future, these duties were to be: I was told to prepare the ship (and myself) for a visit to Crete which for the last two years had been and still was strongly held by the Germans. As with most other occupied countries, we were doing all we could to support the Resistance movement. I felt confident that ML 355 was in good shape for these new duties. We had a very good crew led by Leading Seaman Blyth (later to be Petty Officer Blyth, DCM), who was an excellent Cox'n, tough, uncompromising and absolutely trustworthy and reliable. We had acquired more guns than the other MLs and they were all in good order, but the main problem of getting to the right beach in Crete — and back — was one of navigation and that put a major responsibility right on my own shoulders.

The speed of our MLs was about 16 knots to be comfortable and about 20 knots if one wanted to shake up the engine mountings. From Tobruk to Crete is about 200 miles. From Alexandria it is almost twice as much. So for an ML to get to Crete in reasonable time the North African departure points were Mersah Matruh, Bardia, Derna or Tobruk and then the journey would take about 14 hours to get there (and a similar time one hoped to get back). To arrive about midnight meant a 10 am departure and travelling two-thirds of the way there and back in daylight. Secrecy and good luck were essential if we were to avoid attacks from the air during the daylight hours and not to find that the enemy were on the beach waiting for us.

Our orders were firstly to go to Tobruk by a night passage leaving Alexandria late afternoon on 6th May. After refuelling at Tobruk we were to leave in the morning for a small beach on the south coast of Crete which must have been close to the southern outlet of the Gorge of Samaria and Agia Roumeli.

On the morning of 6th May, before we had left Alexandria, I was awakened from a happy sleep at 6 am with an urgent message to see Commander Courage immediately. I went hurriedly up the jetty wondering what had gone wrong — but nothing had gone wrong. Commander Courage just wanted a word with me to ask if everything was prepared and we were in good order and good heart for the dangerous voyage ahead of us. I assured him that we were all eager to get going, which was absolutely true. It was a great adventure ahead of us with all the attractions of the unusual, the challenge of being the first of Coastal Forces to go back to

Crete since 1941 and the knowledge that some people over there were relying on us. Commander Courage knew all this and he knew that he was responsible for us and our actions. I am sure he wanted to come with us. He wished me the best of luck and did not fuss about details.

Because precise navigation was so important we carried another officer, Lieutenant Matthews RNR, particularly to help us to find the right place at the right time.

The voyage from Alexandria to Tobruk was uneventful. We refuelled and spent the night in Tobruk and set off on the morning of 7th May in good weather to plough our way north to Crete. We had no radar and relied on sun and then star sights to plot our course. About 20 miles off the south coast of Crete and just to the east of our approach lie the two small islands of Gavdos and Gavdopula. We did not know whether they were enemy-occupied or if they had radar on the islands, but we had to go within sight of them and because we passed to the westward in early evening, we would have been clearly visible against the setting sun.

Very soon, and before sunset, we could see the tops of the mountains of Crete ahead of us. With the mountains ahead and the islands to the east, we felt very exposed as long as daylight lasted. We imagined rows of German field glasses and telescopes trained on us and all the resources of the enemy forces being mobilized to make life difficult for us.

It was close to the islands of Gavdos and Gavdopula almost exactly two years before, in May 1941, that the Destroyers *Kelly* and *Kashmir* were sunk by JU87 dive bombers and the cruiser *HMS Fiji* was sunk by bombers a little farther to the west. On 28th May 1941, ML 1030 commanded by Lieut. Cooksey RNVR was sunk by attack from the air 15 miles west of Gavdopula. Two years before the bombers came from airfields 300 miles away in Greece. Now the Germans had airfields not 50 miles away from us in Crete. We felt visible and vulnerable but hopefully not expected.

It was a fine evening and on such occasions in the Mediterranean the horizon at sunset is a firm clear line. This is ideal for obtaining accurate star sights by the use of a sextant. By using several stars now beginning to shine while the horizon remained clear, I carefully worked out and plotted our position on the chart.

From this 'fix' we steered straight for the place where our landing beach ought to be, using our Asdic to give us warning of rocks and in an attempt to estimate our distance from the shore line.

When approaching Crete it is always possible to know that land is near, even on the darkest of nights, because of the smell of the herbs and wild flowers which grow on the hills and whose strong perfume is carried on the air for some miles out to sea.

That perfume may be a romantic welcome to the shores of Crete but it is not an accurate one navigationally and was no guide to our distance from the land. It was a moonless night (a night deliberately chosen as such). We were steering into a dense blackness with the high mountains on shore beginning to tower above us. The echo-sounder still showed plenty of water beneath the keel. The Asdic gave no reading of danger. So we kept right on and hoped our wooden hull would find no surprises which would leave us in trouble on an enemy shore.

Suddenly, right ahead, through the binoculars I saw scores of pinpoints of light. It was rather like looking at a distant Christmas tree decorated with small candles on Christmas Eve. Anything unknown at such a time is worrying, but as we eased off our engines, a brighter light from a torch flashed from the middle of the Christmas tree and appeared to be giving the expected code signal to identify those on shore as the friendly party who expected us. We soon found that the pinpoints of light were about a hundred cigarettes and we found, too, that the party on shore was very large indeed.

It was scarcely a beach ahead of us. There was probably some sand there but it was really a shallow inlet with large rocks visible from the water's edge to the base of the steeply rising land behind. We anchored at 22.20 in about four fathoms but quite close to the rocky shore.

Having been told that we should have a fairly large number of people to embark we had, before leaving Alexandria, practised what we hoped would be the quickest way of getting them on board. We had taken with us two rubber dinghies and we planned to rig up two ropes from the ship to the shore and the people in the dinghies would haul themselves quickly backwards and forwards, thus completing the operation with great speed — so we thought!

Murphy's Law plus unforeseen circumstances were against us.

The main unforeseen circumstance was the number of people on the shore, all of whom seemed determined to get on board as quickly as possible. As soon as the rubber boats grounded on the beach, the crowd rushed them.

The agent on shore who had organized the whole operation from his cave in the hills was Captain Xan Fielding whose exploits on German held Crete became legendary. He had told us via his radio communication with Cairo that he wanted us to evacuate about sixty people. The operation was well-advertised among the local Cretans and besides helping to get the sixty evacuees gathered on the shore, they saw no reason why they should not join in the evacuation and so there were well over a hundred, all determined to get on board. The rubber boats were upturned. The ropes were entangled and jammed in the rocks. Captain Fielding had to use a rifle butt to keep back the unwanted and unruly guests.

Eventually, we took our party on board by paddling the rubber boats backwards and forwards and it all took far too long. We sent ashore some bottles of gin for Captain Fielding and hoped he did not lose too many friends among the Cretans by the force he had to use to maintain some sort of order and prevent us from being overloaded.

We now had on board about fifty-four Australian troops who had been hidden and fed in the mountains by the Cretan villagers ever since the fall of Crete to the Germans in May 1941 — for exactly two years. Two of the Australians had married Cretan girls and they brought them with them — quite rightly, too! The little girls were dressed in traditional black peasant garments and looked thoroughly scared. Even the Australians looked overawed by the surroundings and the events of the night and they slept most of the time with us. One put his arms round the lavatory seat and went to sleep on the floor of the toilet, in ecstasy at the return of such evidence of civilisation and home comforts. We also had on board several Cretans who were said to be on the run from the Germans and with a price on their heads. In all, we had sixty-eight passengers and had to confine most of them below decks in order not to jeopardize stability and to keep them clear of the guns should we run into trouble.

As we steamed away, those who were left on shore seemed to be celebrating for they flashed lights wildly for some time and made the beach and the operation very conspicuous from the sea. I hoped the cliffs would shelter them from possible observers on the land.

We had been about one and a half hours at anchor (far longer than intended) and had kept the engines running for much of the time. When we came to leave and ordered full speed ahead, we sent up for some time showers of sparks like a firework display until the carbon and soot had been blown out of the exhaust tubes.

Luckily the return journey was uneventful despite our too-long stay on the beach. Had it not been for the rugged and isolated mountain region around the Gorge of Samaria, we could have been in real trouble.

We took our passengers to Mersah Matruh where army transport was waiting to take them on to Cairo. I was told that they had a big dinner in Cairo to celebrate their escape and that they drank a toast to ML 355. I wish I had been there. But ML 355 did receive a signal from Commander-in-Chief Levant dated 9th May 1943 saying quite simply 'Well done' and Commander Courage sent me the following letter from *HMS Mosquito* dated 14th May 1943:—

'The following extract from a letter from MO4 is forwarded for our information.

Will you please convey to the Officers and Crew of the ship concerned my gratitude and also my admiration for their seamanship during a difficult and dangerous operation, particularly the efforts of Lieut. G. W. Searle and Sub. Lieut. Steedman. All those rescued were loud in their praise of the way in which the crew of the vessel deprived themselves of sleep, food and tobacco in order that the rescued should be made as comfortable as possible. I congratulate you on your success.'

During the summer of 1943 we were on standby to make more trips to Crete and in between these operations we were engaged on general duties on the North African coast based mainly at Derna.

Derna was a very attractive small port built in Italian style. It lies on a small rather pleasant and green coastal plain at the foot of steep hills which lead to the arid desert stretching away inhospitably to the south. The harbour is small in almost a complete circle of land so that no artificial breakwater is needed. A good jetty on the eastern side was partly obstructed by a wreck. The main distinction of Derna harbour was its smell, probably due to a kind of marsh gas arising from centuries of rotting vegetation and seaweed on the bottom of the harbour. I do not know whether it was good or bad for our health but it did discolour the metal parts of the MLs quite quickly and much work was needed to polish them and keep the inside of the boat looking smart — the metal parts outside were, of course, protected by Naval grey paint.

One RAF air sea rescue boat was based at Derna and usually there was one ML or perhaps two in the harbour. Otherwise it was very quiet. A young Lieutenant RNVR was Naval-Officer-in-Charge and there were usually some Army Nursing Sisters there too, having a break from the Army hospitals in the desert beyond the hills. It was quiet ashore, no sophisticated night life and the very few small cafés were short of almost everything. It is to be remembered with pleasure, however, as a quiet and rather green oasis surrounded by sea on one side and desert on the other. Some had found or acquired legally or illegally some horses, and the sight of seamen on horseback provided entertainment for the spectators.

ML 355 made three more night visits to the south coast of Crete that summer. One was again to the region of the Gorge of Samaria, passing once more the islands of Great and Small Gavdos which always gave me the feeling that our approach was being signalled to the defences on the mainland. The other two visits were further to the east of Crete, one almost due south of Rethimnon and still farther to the east where some of the highest mountains of the island, around Mount Dikti, could easily be distinguished as we approached the shore before night closed in.

My navigation capability was now accepted as reasonably reliable and after the first trip we did not have with us an extra officer to help with the navigational duties. We made all our landfalls on Crete and picked up the recognition signal flashed from the shore without undue difficulty. In each case we used star sights at sunset to give us a reliable fix of our position, and we took similar star sights at dawn, and of the sun later on, to guide us to Tobruk or Mersah Matruh on the way home.

I was rather pleased when on one occasion I constructed a Heath Robinson range finder out of a piece of wood and half a pencil so that I could identify our position by reference to the sharp peak of a mountain (it was either Mount Idi or Mount Dikti) which stood out clearly against the night sky. Our standard nautical range finders could not be used in the darkness, so something which gave me the distance from an outstanding feature on the land had to be constructed before we left harbour, and when the top of my half-pencil was in line with the mountain top I knew exactly where I was.

We were lucky and have to thank the maintenance of secrecy both in Crete and North Africa that we were never attacked by the enemy. I asked one of those whom we evacuated how it was that a hundred Cretans could gather on a beach without the Germans finding out. He said that firstly, the Cretans could be trusted absolutely and secondly, all the beaches were very difficult to reach. All Crete, he said, particularly the Germans, would gleefully be told of our visit next day, but no unfriendly person would hear of the event in time to interfere with it on land.

The fourteen-hour voyage back still gave the enemy a chance to interfere from the air. Such an attack was made on another ML as I shall relate, but not on ML 355.

On one occasion the main purpose was to bring off a British officer who had served his time in the hills of Crete and to land his replacement and an additional wireless set. The officer being relieved came dressed as a Cretan bandit, and not a very attractive one, might be dressed: scarlet handkerchief round his head, red cummerbund, brown breeches, a large dagger at his waist and so on. Not an inconspicuous dress, I thought. They said he had not been a great success as an agent and spy because he loved the quiet life in a cave in the mountains and enjoyed rather too much the Cretan wine.

I think it was on that occasion that we passed a man swimming in the water as we approached the shore. We pulled him aboard and found him to be an RAF officer who had crash-landed or come down by parachute on Crete and had been helped and hidden for some time by the Cretans. He was so impatient to get out of the island that he could not wait for us to take him off the beach in an orderly fashion and had to strip off his clothes and swim out to meet us as soon as he heard our engines.

It was probably a very good thing to strip off clothes and come aboard naked for one of the hardships we had to bear was the cargo of lice and bugs which our passengers left on board when they disembarked in North Africa. The unwelcome parasites got into the woodwork of the ship as well as infesting pillows and blankets, and the only way to make the ship clean again was to have a complete fumigation when we returned to Port Said or Alexandria.

Another trip was made particularly to take off the beach a young lady by the name of Catrina Petrakis. She, a Cretan, had been working in the offices of the German High Command in Crete. I was told that she even worked in the General's office. Information which she obtained in the course of her work was passed on to our agent in the mountains and he passed it on by radio to Cairo. One day she found that her flat had been searched so she ran for it and after hiding in caves for over a month, arrangements were made for ML 355 to get her away. I believe she received a decoration for her work and I also believe she met and married a British Naval Officer in North Africa.

On such trips I did not go below but remained on the bridge

or in the wheelhouse. A short nap in the corner of the wheelhouse was the most I could expect by way of rest. So our lady guest accepted the offer of my empty bunk together with a pillow, sheets and a blanket which were a great improvement on the floor of a cave. Unfortunately, I must ungallantly report that in the caves she, too, had not avoided the attentions of bugs and suchlike pests. For some weeks after that voyage and until the ship could be fumigated, I seemed to do more scratching than sleeping.

Only once did we have some difficulty on the return voyage and that was when we ran into a desert sand and windstorm called a Khamsin. It comes off the shore scorching hot and full of driving sharp sand which is painful to exposed flesh. Visibility goes down to yards. This storm hit us when we were getting quite close to the African shore. We slowed and before long we saw the land — a high, sandy shoreline — only a very short distance off our bows. An instant decision was necessary — as we were too close to the shore for comfort — we must turn to port or turn to starboard: were we to the east or west of the entrance to Tobruk harbour? I chose to turn to port and went ahead slowly, keeping the shoreline just in sight on the starboard side.

Suddenly, in the veil of sand, we nearly collided with another ML. It was the Tobruk-based local patrol ML guarding the approaches to Tobruk harbour. With the aid of a little shouting we found that we had very nearly run straight into the harbour entrance when we first approached. I had turned the wrong way on seeing land and so with a quick about-turn we were back at the harbour entrance and gained the comparative shelter of the waters inside. It was not, however, calm inside: the wind and the sand made it impossible to get alongside and we had to anchor for some hours, waiting to disembark our passengers. Eventually, we found a berth and the Cretan party left in a truck on the way to the comforts of Cairo. That was the occasion when Catrina Petrakis was our passenger — the long delay in port with this young lady on board enabled my ML friends to make several comments about the presence of women on board HM ships in harbour (as well as at sea), pointing out to me the particular Admiralty Fleet Orders which then applied to such a reprehensible state of affairs.

While in Derna, on 17 June 1943, we were involved in a very distressing incident. In the middle of a peaceful afternoon we were ordered to sea to assist two minesweepers. A convoy farther out to sea had been attacked by a submarine and a troopship had been

81

sunk. The minesweepers were part of the convoy and they themselves were on the way to the war in the Pacific. They had picked up survivors from the troopship and were approaching Derna in a heavily overloaded condition.

ML 355 and another ML with me at the time (possibly ML 359) set off immediately and about half a mile out went alongside a motor minesweeper, not very much bigger than ourselves, which was a horrifying sight. Her decks were crowded with the living, the dead and the dying and blood was running across her deck and down her wooden sides. She was overloaded beyond the point of danger and making slow progress through the water. We took off more than we ought to have taken until I called a halt. We had nearly two hundred on board and were in danger of capsizing ourselves but the minesweeper was still in a similarly dangerous state. As we came alongside the jetty we had so much momentum caused by the extra weight that it needed full astern on both engines for an unusually long time before we could berth. Army ambulances collected our cargo of naked or nearly naked men, some of them now only cold and stiff dead bodies. Then back to the minesweeper which was still making very slow progress.

There was not much point in our taking more men from her so we guided her in and she unloaded at least another two hundred.

The skippers of the minesweepers, who were badly shaken and distressed, requested permission to stay overnight in Derna to clean the decks and to recover from their shock. This was refused and they were ordered to sail immediately and to rejoin the convoy as soon as possible. I thought they were very badly treated at the time, but nothing is better for recovering one's nerve than to keep occupied and carry on with one's duties. Now I see it as a good decision, rather like ordering an aviator to fly another aeroplane immediately after he has had a crash.

Shortly after that incident, we did another run to Crete and on that occasion we came back to Derna rather than Tobruk. We were settling down to recover from the loss of sleep during our two-day trip when we had an order to proceed to sea again immediately with the Army Commander for that part of Cyrenaica. There was some sort of apology for such an order so soon after a tiring Cretan mission but the matter was said to be very urgent.

It has been reported that signalling from the shore to the sea had been seen. If the report was reliable, was the signalling to submarines, was it the prelude to a seaborne attack or was it exactly a German copy of what ML 355 was doing in Crete — landing and taking off agents, spies and disruptive elements?

We sailed along the coast that night nearly to Benghazi and back. We saw nothing suspicious but it did give this senior Army Officer an idea of the shoreline and just what might be possible from the sea. Incidentally, we sailed right through a convoy coming in the opposite direction without a challenge or a shot. We were caught up in the centre lane of the convoy and I decided that it was better to remain in silent darkness and let the danger pass rather than flash recognition signals in all directions and hope to be recognized as friendly before someone fired at us.

Coming back to Derna after that patrol, I can distinctly remember that I felt quite exhausted and had the taste of bananas in my mouth although it was months or years since I had seen a banana. After coming alongside I realized I had a fever and soon had a pain every time I took a breath. An Army doctor said something about pneumonia or pleurisy and ordered me to hospital. The nearest hospital was one captured from the Italians at Barce near Benghazi so they put me in an ambulance and we bounced our way over rough roads nearly 200 miles through the coastal mountain range of Gebel el Akhdar. I felt terrible.

At the hospital wonderful work was being done by the Army doctors and the Nursing Sisters. There seemed to be no paperwork, no red tape, they just wheeled you in when you came, did what they could do, and pushed you out again.

The place was alive with mosquitoes and similar insects. We slept under nets and if your arm rested against the net during the night, scores of mosquitoes fed on it while you slept. The nurses had no nets, and moved around day and night ignoring mosquitoes and all other difficulties.

I do not remember the treatment I had but I do remember the large tot of whisky we had every night. Something made me well again fairly quckly and by the middle of July I was sent back by the same bumpy road to Derna — not to my ML but to an Army Rest and Recuperation Camp there. This was a heaven-like break for about two weeks. Besides the rest and good food, I had excellent company among the many others, mostly Army officers, who were recovering from illness or wounds. When we felt well enough we had the use of an Army truck and besides frequent swimming parties, we visited the Greek and Roman ruins at Cyrene which are set in the hills overlooking the sea. It was a very happy time.

For our swimming parties at the many and deserted beaches along the coast, we swam and sunbathed in the nude for the good reason that nobody had swimming trunks. There was nothing unusual in this, but it did have the unfortunate effect that our bottoms became sunburned. Our legs and upperworks had become used to the sun but that part normally covered by a pair of shorts had probably not been exposed to the sunlight since early childhood. The main disadvantage of such a sunburned condition is that sitting down is most uncomfortable. That would not have mattered so much but for a visit to the Camp by General Sir. H. Maitland Wilson who took the chair at a dinner in the Officers' Mess. The dinner lasted at least two hours and my sunburned bottom made me most uncomfortable and might have caused a reprimand for fidgeting.

Discharged from the Rest Camp, I went 'down the road' at Derna to rejoin ML 355. I found that in my absence there had been some activity on the Cretan run and that the news was not all good.

When I went sick, another run for ML 355 was already planned. In my absence it was decided not to send ML 355 with another Commanding Officer. So ML 350 was called upon and, while I was in Barce hospital, set sail for a rendezvous in Crete under the command of Lieut. Cdr. Dougie Russell, senior officer of the 43rd ML Flotilla.

Unfortunately, the weather was bad which caused delay and difficulty in navigation. It was thought too that they had been seen by an enemy aircraft so about half-way there, ML 350 turned back and the mission was postponed. It was, however, quickly re-planned and as I had still not returned to duty, ML 361 commanded by Lieut. R. M. (Bob) Young RCNVR was detailed to carry out the postponed operation. He arrived at the right place in Crete, landed and took off passengers. He left at 0200 which was rather late for near midsummer and at 0655 he was attacked by three Arado 196 aircraft. ML 361 fought off the aircraft in a very gallant action but sustained casualties and damage. An RAF Beaufighter sent out to assist failed to find the ML, but the RAF rescue boat from Derna found her, took off casualties and escorted ML 361 back to Derna.

As a result of this attack we had the luxury of a Beaufighter to cover us for the daylight part of our return trip on later missions to Crete. We did, however, object to these aicraft using us as a target to practise low-flying attacks — perhaps our nerves were not as good as they should have been.

Our last Cretan voyage was on the night of 7th/8th September when once more we landed some Army personnel, arms and wireless sets and we took off other Army people plus about twenty Cretans who were being evacuated either for their own safety or for training prior to their return to help the Resistance on the island.

This last mission was carried out against a quickly changing background of events in the Mediterranean war. On 8th September 1943, Italy surrendered to the Allied Forces. Our opposition on sea and land in this part of the world had up to now been German and Italian. Now it was to be solely German but in the meantime to the north of us we had islands which were either Italian occupied or occupied by both German and Italian forces. There were clearly opportunities to be taken by both sides and there was going to be confusion and fighting as each side tried to make the best of a new situation.

The completion of our operation and our return to Tobruk on the morning of 8th September marked the end of my time of seagoing service on the North African coast which had lasted for over two years from July 1941 to September 1943 and extended from the borders of Tripolitania in the west to the borders of Turkey in the northeast. The rest of my Mediterranean service was to be in and around the Aegean.

To end this chapter of North African service in MLs 1007 and 355 one incident remains to be told and that was when I went to sea on another ML and came nearest to losing my life.

It happened in the winter of 1942/43 although I do not have a record of the date. I had been engaged on normal convoy and coastal patrol duties based on Alexandria. HDML 1048 had been having an extensive refit, and her officers and crew had been living ashore for about a month. The great day came when they were once more ready for sea and were ordered out on a normal night patrol off Alexandria harbour. However, seagoing in an ML and particularly a patrol at slow speed in a rough sea is a tough assignment; one is constantly bouncing up and down and rolling from side to side which is hard on the legs and the stomach. It is particularly bad after a spell on shore — one gets soft and out of practice.

So those in command of us decided that another officer should go out with ML 1048 to assist them in this first patrol after their long rest. I had just come into the harbour and what could be more suitable than to send me straight out again?

The CO of ML 1048 was Lieut. Alex Wallace from Glasgow, an old friend of mine who had come out to the Mediterranean with me. He was the man whose ML had exchanged fire with a German tank at Tobruk and had the furrow of a tank shell across his cheek as a reminder of that action. We went out as darkness fell: it was a black night with a rather disturbed sea. After a few turns along the inshore coastline we decided, as was quite common practice, to tie up at a buoy at the seaward end of the long approach channel to the Alexandria harbour. A line was put on the buoy and a hydrophone watch was set to listen by means of our Asdic for sounds which might indicate ships or submarines. Alex Wallace and I sat in his cabin talking until about 10 pm, leaving his No. 1 on watch. It was getting rougher when suddenly the line to the buoy snapped as a heavy sea hit us. By the time we were on deck the seas looked high indeed, and were quickly getting higher with the wind and spray howling from the North West.

The Biblical stories of a storm springing up are no exaggeration. These storms can come almost as suddenly as a flash of lightning and the shallow sea can be whipped up almost as quickly.

We set the engines at slow ahead and steamed slowly into the wind. The small 72-foot ML started to climb up and charge down the sides of seas which, in the pitch-blackness and constant salt spray, only showed their broken crests as they towered above us, rushing down on us and breaking over us. It would be suicide to turn: for one thing, we could not stand such a sea on our beam and even if we did turn safely we would then be driven towards a shore with no lights and with no hope of finding the narrow channel through rocks and shallows into the safety of Alexandria harbour.

The next problem was the crew. There was no doubt that they were out of training and an exceptionally rough return to ML duty was the worst thing that could have happened. Within an hour Alex Wallace, the cox'n, the motor mechanic and myself were the only men on board who were capable of any reasonable action. The rest were seasick to the point of unconsciousness and throughout the long night the three of us took turns on the bridge and at the wheel while the excellent motor mechanic sat by his engines.

The long night was spent climbing up frightening waves. The telegraphist was unconscious and I tried to get the set to work without success: but what did we have to report other than that we were off station, steering North West and had no idea when they might see us again?

As daylight came it gave us some relief to see a little of what was going on but we knew we must seize an opportunity to turn. The sea, although still very high, had moderated a little. We turned. Now the waves lifted our stern high and the danger was to keep from broaching-to as we were carried forward almost out of control. A hard time for the man on the wheel.

Where were we? We had steamed dead slow into a gale for over eight hours. Had we made any distance, had we stood still or had we even been carried backwards by wind and sea? Spray and flying sand was all we could see. Visibility was almost nil, we were covered by sand-filled salt spray driving into our tired eyes.

We steered slightly south of a reverse course and kept as sharp a watch as our tired smarting and salt-caked eyes permitted. Most of the crew were still incapable of intelligent action.

Suddenly, quite close, we saw the shore off the starboard bow. Alex Wallace gave an order to take us to port as the land was no more than a few hundred yards away with huge breakers churning up the shallows, and waves behind us carrying us fast into danger.

I went into the wheelhouse to look at the chart and had just leaned over the chart table when there was a shout of 'Rocks Ahead!' and the cox'n on the wheel said 'Oh, my God.' I looked past him out of the wheelhouse window and there right ahead, quite close and just showing in the trough of a wave, was a jagged line of rocks. There was nothing to do. I waited for the crunch — but I had forgotten the sea.

There was a huge wave behind us, it lifted us up, the rocks disappeared beneath us as the trough of the waves became a peak we were carried right over. Dead silence. We went on. No more rocks. We had been carried over one reef which we saw and if there was another one which we did not see we were carried over that, too.

But it fixed our position for the chart showed that off the headland which lies at the westerly point of the large bay which covers the entrance to Alexandria harbour, is a shallow reef extending out to sea from the headland. Working on that we set a course for the entrance of the channel into the harbour. We found it and in a windswept, squally and sand-covered afternoon we crept back into Alexandria. There we were greeted with some disbelief. They thought we were lost — as we very nearly were. All we did lose was our Asdic dome left on the reef which, as the loss of the dome confirmed, was within a few feet of ripping the bottom out of the boat.

11

The Aegean

Plans for the seizure of small islands in the Aegean as bases for raiding operations against enemy lines of communication had been under consideration for some time. As the Allied success in North Africa continued, these plans were enlarged during 1943 and a major assault was contemplated with Rhodes and Scarpanto as the principal objectives.

The invasion of Sicily and Italy took priority however and this limited the available resources from the Eastern Mediterranean. General Sir H. Maitland Wilson reported 'during the nine months from May 1943 no less than seven plans were produced for the capture of Rhodes, Crete and other islands in the Dodecanese and the Aegean.' This is an interesting sidelight on the importance of our visits to the beaches of Crete in order to land and take off Army Officers who were working with the Cretan Resistance.

'On four occasions,' General Maitland Wilson reports, 'a force was assembled and partially prepared to undertake the capture of Rhodes.' A force was ready to sail on 1st September 1943 but the transports then received orders to proceed to India. When on 8th September the Italian armistice was announced, the force which could have immediately landed on Rhodes had been dispersed.

The priority given to the Italian front on one side and the Indian front on the other, left the Eastern Mediterranean command starved of resources and unable to take best advantage of the Italian capitulation.

The Germans were always in strength on Crete and the capitulation of Italians there gave them little concern. Scarpanto (Karpathos) was at once reinforced by the Germans and its occupation consolidated. In Rhodes, however, the Italians outnumbered the Germans by six to one and this appeared the best chance for the Allied forces to gain a foothold in the Aegean with, most importantly, airfields. All depended, however, on the attitude of the Italians and this depended on the speed with which the Germans on the one hand and the Allies on the other could act and show their strength.

Major the Lord Jellicoe and another officer parachuted into Rhodes to establish contact with the Italian Governor and to ask for his co-operation in the landing of Allied forces. All depended on timing and it was clear to the Governor that German forces were in the island of Rhodes and in the city of Rhodes while Allied forces were not. It appears that the British 234th Infantry Brigade which was assigned to these operations could not be ready to sail to Rhodes until 18th September. On 11th September the Italian Governor, with Germans on his doorstep, indicated that he did not wish to have further dealings with the British. The Germans took over Rhodes.

At the time of these momentous happenings, when the nature of our operations was evolving rather than being decided, ML 355 was ordered from Tobruk to Alexandria on 10th September.

It is not surprising that there was considerable confusion. The priorities of troops and equipment, of ships and airplanes had been given to other areas of war. The Commander of the forces in the Eastern Mediterranean had not been able to use the capitulation of the Italians to any great stretegic advantage. The hope of persuading the Italians in Rhodes to join forces with the Allies against the Germans had not been realized. Rhodes with its airfields, port and large Italian garrison, the key to a major Aegean operation, remained a strong enemy fortress.

There were still Italian garrisons and no German forces in Cos, Leros and Samos. They were thought to be well-equipped and prepared to join forces with the Allies. With the limited forces available and with no time to lose, it was decided to send small detachments of troops to Cos, Leros and Samos to help the Italian garrisons deny those islands to the Germans. It could only be a hastily flung together team which could be sent at such short notice.

This background has been given because otherwise the operations now described would seem inexplicable to a reader unacquainted with the circumstances. So far the operations I took part in along the North African Coast are easy to understand in the context of the to-and-fro of the land battles which took place from Egypt to Tunis. North Africa was a major theatre of war with large armies and air power involved on both sides. We helped to protect the seaward flank and to maintain seaborne supplies. Now in the Aegean we became engaged in operations individually small, designed to pin down enemy troops, harrass his communications

GREECE

Pireas
Athens •

Mediterranean Sea

| 0 | 25 | 50 | 75 miles |
| 0 | 50 | 100 | Kms |

R•

Gorge of
Samaria →

Aegean Sea

KHIOS

Izmir

TURKEY

SAMOS

IKARIA

Kusadasi

PATMOS

LEROS

KALIMNOS

Bodrum

Marmaris

Kapi Cove

AMORGOS

Pencik

COS

Krio

NAXOS

STAMPALIA

NISSIROS

SIMI

TILOS

CALCHI

RHODES

CASTELORISO

SCARPANTO
(KARPATHOS)

Heraklion

CRETE

Mount Ida

Mount Dikti

Kasos Straits

and establish bases for larger operations later on. It was going to become an operation similar to that of the Resistance fighters in the occupied countries, and in future we would have to work very much with those Resistance fighters who could be both Greek and Italian.

The eight MLs of the 42nd Flotilla (whose senior officer was Lieut. Cdr. Ball in ML 349) had, before the capitulation of Italy, been assigned to the proposed invasion force for Rhodes. As related, the main ships and most of the troops for this invasion had been withdrawn and sent to India or Italy. The 42nd ML Flotilla was left in the Eastern Mediterranean and was assigned to operations on a much reduced scale now urgently planned for the landing of troops on Cos, Leros, Samos and other Italian-held islands. ML 355, which had been on Special Duties during the summer, was recalled to Alexandria to join the 42nd Flotilla in the forthcoming Aegean operations.

Cyprus was to be the main departure point for small craft, and from there the route to the Aegean was expected to be by way of the island of Casteloriso, which lies close to the Turkish coast about two hundred miles west of the nearest point in Cyprus and about one hundred miles east of Rhodes. From Casteloriso the route would be through the channel (about 10 miles across) between Rhodes and the Turkish coast, past Simi, on to Cos and then the whole Aegean lay ahead.

Casteloriso, however, was held by the Italians and their attitude to events was not known. Immediately after it was certain that Rhodes had been taken over by German forces, ML 349 and ML 357 (Lieut. R. L. Jones RNVR) left Cyprus for Casteloriso on 11th September 1943. They carried a number of troops of the Long Range Desert Group who after distinguished service in the North African desert had been training for sea-going and island warfare.

The two MLs arrived off Casteloriso in the early morning and were fired upon by the Italian garrison. Following their orders that no hostile acts were now to be committed against the Italians, the MLs passively submitted to this uncomfortable but not too heavy fire. Meanwhile, two Army officers disembarked in a small boat and having paddled close to the harbour they persuaded the local commander that they were allies rather than enemies, whereupon everyone was invited into the harbour and greeted cordially. A small show was put on: the Union flag and the White Ensign were hoisted, a Guard of Honour was supplied by the MLs and everyone drank everyone's health — probably in gin also supplied by the MLs.

In this way the first of the Dodecanese was taken over by forces of the Allies and at a total cost of one slightly wounded — the First Lieutenant of ML 357 (Sub-Lieut. Moore RANVR) who had his hair parted and a strip of skin removed from the top of his head by a bullet during the preliminary fire which greeted the MLs. Alas, Casteloriso was to see many sad days before the Aegean story ended.

In Casteloriso there were several small craft which had sailed from Rhodes to escape from the German take-over. These small boats, tugs and lighters were at once sent back in convoy to Beirut and Haifa escorted by ML 357.

Back in ML 355: on returning to Alexandria on 10th September, Commander Courage sent for me and told me that he wished me to take stores and a base maintenance party to Casteloriso: he apologised for giving me such a dull job after our previous Cretan assignments. Little did he (or I) know that dullness was not going to be the main trouble!

We loaded up with all kinds of spare parts, with wireless sets and batteries and with people who knew how they worked and how to fit them into MLs and MTBs. C-in-C sent aboard a complete W/T station for Casteloriso, and other unidentified people kept putting things on board until we had little space anywhere to put a foot on the deck.

Lieut. Cdr. Tooms RNVR, who had been in command of the Coastal Force base in Benghazi, was under orders to take command of the new Casteloriso base. We awaited his arrival in Alexandria so that we could take him to Casteloriso with all the assorted stores we had for his new command.

By the evening of 11th September we were told that Lieut. Cdr. Tooms had gone by air from Benghazi to Cairo and it looked as if he would find his own way from there. No one knew how but Tooms was a determined and resourceful man. So at 16.00 on 12th September, we sailed from Alexandria directly to Paphos in Cyprus — some 300 miles — and we took with us: Sub-Lieut. Goodworth RNVR and eight men of the ML base staff, one leading telegraphist and three telegraphists for the Casteloriso W/T station and one Special Services Sergeant telegraphist and his equipment. Off Paphos we encountered ML 354 and a French sloop and saw ML 358 (Lieut. Michelson RNZNVR) entering harbour. We followed and secured at Paphos at 11.20 on 13th September.

Paphos is in the southwest of the island of Cyprus. Behind the ancient castle which stands by the tiny harbour and above the white lighthouse on the point can be seen the mountains rising to the imposing heights of Mount Troodos (Mount Olympus) which lie towards the centre of the island.

The harbour was indeed very small with a narrow entrance through a dangerous reef. There was a wooden jetty with water deep enough for small craft and sailing schooners to go alongside but around the sea wall which encloses the harbour and where the Customs House was placed, the water shallowed to only a few feet.

There were not many buildings round the harbour. The nearest town was about a mile away and looked down on the sea from higher ground. Apart from RAF planes which were approaching and leaving a nearby airfield, it was wonderfully peaceful: the inhabitants quietly went about their business of unloading schooners or cultivating the land in the pleasant warmth of a fine September day. Nevertheless, a close inspection of the small harbour revealed unusual visitors and unusual activity. With sterns secured to the jetty were ML 358, the famous *Hedgehog* (of which I shall say more later) under the command of Lieut. Brian Coleman RNVR, an Italian MTB (known to the Italians as a MAS boat), and an Italian fast motor boat with red crosses painted on it, which presumably had been used for hospital work.

The two Italian boats had only arrived the previous evening: the torpedo boat with her own Italian crew and the other manned by the Army and RAF. Both had come from Rhodes via Casteloriso and it was at Casteloriso that the RAF had taken over the Red Cross motor boat.

The Italian officer and his crew of the MAS boat sat on their small deck looking lost and downhearted. They had fled from the Germans in Rhodes and were now berthed alongside the British who, presumably, were now their friends or at least did not seem belligerent. In fact they found that no one was taking much notice of them at all and so they sat gloomily on board, unmolested and still fully armed. I invited the Italian officer on board for a drink. That cheered him up a little more and he said, 'Now I have to work with the British Navy, I shall have to learn to drink gin.' He drank rather a lot of it.

The *Hedgehog* was a small coasting vessel; she was of steel plate construction, about 60 tons displacement with a noisy engine which pushed her along at 5 knots if all went well, and she had a stout mast to take a spread of canvas if the wind was favourable. She had earned fame in the evacuation of Allied troops from Crete on and after the fall of that island. There is a story to be told by those who know more about it than I, of the 5-knot voyages which saved so many British, Australian and New Zealand troops and contributed to the work of the Resistance forces in the island of Crete. Now Lieut. Coleman was taking her to the Dodecanese to add further chapters to her story and, as it came to pass, to end her days of loyal service in the waters of the Aegean.

I doubt if any HM ships had visited Paphos before, which is strange, for it was here — so legend says — that Aphrodite arose from the waves, and British sailors are not usually so ungallant as to ignore an event like that. There was no Naval Officer ashore or Naval headquarters at Paphos and the nearest Naval authority was N.O.I.C. Cypriot Ports, who flew his flag at Famagusta on the other side of the island. It was just possible to communicate with him by telephone if one had sufficient patience. A knowledge of Greek and Turkish would also have been helpful in dealing with all the strange voices which were encountered in such a telephonic Odyssey.

Captain MacDonald R.N. was N.O.I.C. Cypriot Ports, and when I spoke with him on the telephone he seemed to be in a state of bewilderment. He appeared to have been given no operational orders nor any details of what was going on farther west and towards Rhodes and the Dodecanese, yet before his amazed eyes he found a crowd of light craft passing his island and stopping if they felt like it in the almost-unknown and unprepared port of Paphos, and ringing him to ask if and when they should sail west into what he believed to be enemy territory. He must have had a good Naval cook (cooks are the source of all Naval Inteligence) and he must have had a lively sense of enterprise and initiative because from a slow start he quickly became very interested. He was keen to know who and what was in Paphos harbour, and when I gave him details, he and his office were deeply grateful. He must have regarded me as a reliable friend because I had to ring him up twice a day to report what was in the harbour, to tell him what they were doing there, and whether they expected to sail east, west or even south. And in reverse, his office used to ring me to ask their own questions regarding the 'goings on' in Paphos harbour.

All this will probably sound unbelievable or at least exaggereated but it is a realistic picture of the confusion surrounding a hastily-thrown-together expedition trying to make the best of a situation when all the best-laid plans had been frustrated. The Middle East Command, having had their plans torpedoed and their strength removed just at a time when there was a wonderful chance to take advantage of the Italian capitulation and a temporary weakness in the German camp, might well have thrown up their hands, sulked and done nothing. Instead, they threw forward all they could and hoped that some advantage might be gained. It is unfair now to complain that the organisation was not as good as it might have been. At the time, those on the spot found the situation rather worrying — but it had its excitement and even amusement.

For example, the telephone conversations. There was a service line installed for us but it was defective and it was impossible to hear and to be understood at the other end. So the normal civilian telephone service had to be used, which was a very dangerous thing to do when security of information was necessary. In an attempt to overcome this we tried to speak in the form of riddles which the intended receiver of the call would be more likely to understand than an ill-disposed eavesdropper. Here is the sort of conversation which ensued and on which I relied for my orders:

'Do you know that ship whose Commanding Officer's name begins with R which recently sailed from a port with biblical connections?''

'Yes, I think so, if it is the one whose stoker I put in cells the last time he was here.'

'I don't know about that, Sir, but I will check. If we are talking of the same ship, she came here two days ago and he wants to sail to the place I came from.'

'I can't remember where you came from but I'll look it up. When does he want to go?'

'Tomorrow, at a similar time to that of the man who sailed yesterday whose name reminded you of a musical instrument.'

'All right, tell him to go and I will send off the necessary signals.'

All that was not a bad substitute for *The Times'* crossword puzzle.

Both the Army and the RAF had camps nearby and they were very good to the orphans of the Navy. They provided us with food, water and fuel and lent us transport to go into the town to buy local fruit and wine.

Because there was too little jetty space to tie up alongside, the MLs and other ships were anchored by the bows and secured by the stern to the jetty. Access was by way of a plank from the jetty to the stern.

At first, fuelling ship was slow and the cause of much bruising and swearing. Fuel came in 40 gallon drums delivered to the head of the wooden jetty by an RAF truck. The drums were then trundled down the jetty, manoeuvred over planks onto the ML, and the contents poured through a funnel into the ML's tanks. Then some genius with higher education pointed out that oil and motor spirits are lighter than water and after that revelation the crew flung the drums straight into the harbour from the RAF truck which brought them and swam with them to the MLs where they were hoisted aboard with the dinghy davit. This meant a swim of about a hundred yards and the operation took nearly all day but the weather was warm and they liked swimming (at least they did when the job started) and a fairly good time was had by all.

My main responsibility was to find the missing Lieut. Cdr. Tooms. I had his base staff and his stores but I did not see how he was going to get to Casteloriso unless ML 355 or another boat from Paphos took him there. I spent much of the time on the telephone trying to find out if he could or might have arrived in Casteloriso by air or any other means.

A minor trouble, rather like a persistent mosquito, was an RAF Officer who continually button-holed me trying to pesuade me to unload all my stores and take on board drums of 100-octane aviation spirit instead. Someone had ordered him to get the stuff to Casteloriso but had given him no means of doing it — that was left to his initiative. His arguments were persistent, unscrupulous and tiring.

The Commanding Officer of the Italian torpedo boat was also continually on the prowl up and down the jetty trying to explain something to us in all languages but English. Eventually we understood that his crew had no food, no drink and no money. We saved them from starving or dying of thirst and we invited their captain on board for another drink. He was getting on well with gin.

September 14th was a tiring day. In the evening, alarm was caused by the coast guards who reported many ships approaching the shore from the west. As the west had up to now been nothing but enemy territory, the approach of these ships caused some running to and fro by the Cypriots and the Army. However, Jim Michelson and I climbed to the top of the castle and identified a very strangely assorted convoy as the evacuated craft from Rhodes and Casteloriso being led back to Famagusta or Beirut or Haifa by ML 357.

Then the Italian was sent orders to sail for Haifa and he left as darkness fell. It seemed very odd to see him priming his torpedoes and loading his guns before leaving — was he really on our side now?

We were just settling down to the quiet of the evening when our deck watch came clattering down to tell me that there was a light to seaward flashing S.O.S. I let go everything and went out of harbour towards the light. There was our Italian friend in his torpedo boat. He had gone out of the harbour right into the shoal of rocks which lies to the east of the harbour entrance. When we reached him he had managed to re-float himself and, getting one propeller to turn, he followed us back into harbour. The poor man was almost in tears at the damage he had done.

Some of us walked to the town later in the evening and decided to pay a visit to a small cinema which was showing a rather ancient film. We paid our money and went inside and as soon as we entered the back of what was really a village hall with a screen hung on the wall at one end, the show was stopped, the lights were put on and everybody stood up. We were embarrassed to find that it was our arrival in our best Naval uniforms which had caused this. We were shown to front seats, the audience sat down again and the performance was resumed. This was a great honour for us but it did mean that we had to stay to the end and could not slip quietly out if we were too tired to appreciate the film.

Next day, ML 351 (Lieut. Ken Hallows) arrived with orders to proceed to Casteloriso and at 14.20 on 15th September we left with ML 351 escorting four RAF rescue launches. We carried the base staff for Casteloriso and a full cargo above and below decks of equipment, petrol and oil. We left Sub-Lieut. Goodworth with an ML base staff at Paphos.

It had been a short but very busy two days. Besides the needs of ML 355, I had had to act as Senior Naval Officer present, arranging berthing and fuelling, feeding Italians, getting the telephone installed and in working order and trying to maintain contact with the Naval Headquarters in Famagusta.

At daybreak on 16th September, we arrived off Casteloriso. One could not take anything for granted and we had no reliable information as to the state of affairs in the island. Who was manning the gun we could see at the harbour entrance? We could only find out by looking to see, and were relieved when we identified the troops as British (at least they had British uniforms on) although the gun was probably Italian. So, feeling reasonably happy we went into the almost circular harbour, taking soundings as we did so. We dropped anchor and secured our stern to the jetty near enough to jump ashore.

We were watched by a crowd of the inhabitants. The men and women kept to their houses and looked from the windows but the children crowded round and were soon begging for food and cigarettes. They looked starved and their sunken cheeks and eyes which seemed to have known no childhood told a pitiful story of the suffering of war and were a strange contrast to the background of a beautiful island. Some people may dispute that an almost treeless island can be beautiful, but I saw it as such, and a worthy introduction to the Dodecanese. It lies in a Turkish bay. Turkey lies to the north and the east and the channel between the island and the mainland is not more than a mile wide at its narrowest part. Where the channel is wider it is dotted with the tips of large rocks and with small islands so that swimming to Turkey would not be difficult.

Like most of the south coast of Turkey, the mainland here is mountainous with the mountains rising high and steeply from the sea. Although generally rocky, they appear green and pleasant but are mostly too steep for cultivation. There is snow on the heights in winter and tracks wind over passes between peaks which travellers must use to move between the villages which lie in those places where there is enough of a level site to support some agriculture.

Near or in those coastal towns or villages there are usually the ruins of a castle and signs of other settlements in earlier centuries. Whether these ancient remains or ruins are Greek or Roman or from earlier settlers, they witness centuries of coastal traffic and because there are in some cases remains to be seen with no present habitation, this rugged but pleasant coastline must once have been more prosperous and more populated than it was in 1943.

The island of Casteloriso is exactly like the coast to which it clings. It rises to a peak of some 1,000 feet high in the centre and consists of about four square miles. There is scarcely any flat land and the town is built in terraces like a vineyard around the almost-circular and very deep harbour. When I walked up the hill and looked down on the town with houses clustering so closely around the ships at anchor, I found the scene extremely beautiful. Every house seemed to be a different shape and a different colour. Although there appeared to be no plan, each house was placed just where it should be placed so as to compose the picture. There was a church and behind the church I could see a minaret. Beyond the narrow entrance, the still blue water of the sound was dotted with tiny green islands before it joined the open sea. It reminded me of a stage back-cloth as the scene spread out before me in the soft September sunshine.

Casteloriso first became involved in the war when this island, which was held by an Italian garrison supported by naval and air forces from Rhodes, was the target of the first Mediterranean combined operation of the war. That was in February 1941 and although a considerable British naval force was employed and a landing was made, the island was not held and the operation was a failure. Admiral Cunningham reported: 'The taking and abandonment of Casteloriso was a rotten business and reflected little credit on anyone . . .'

Now it was to be involved again. The peace I saw that September evening lasted not much longer and some months later when I saw Casteloriso once more, the harbour and those pretty little houses were mostly blackened heaps of bricks and stones and burned timber.

This, my first visit to Casteloriso, was short. As soon as we had put a line onto the shore, the so-far-missing Lieut. Cdr. Tooms came aboard and wondered why we had been waiting for him in Cyprus. He had come to Casteloriso by sea-plane.

His stores and his base party were unloaded and the telegraphists got busy erecting a W/T station. There was no food to be had on the island; the inhabitants had barely enough for themselves, and he was delighted to have whatever tinned food we could spare (and crockery, too). We also gave him a White Ensign to fly from the building which he had taken over as Navy House. We fuelled the MLs from the petrol we carried as deck cargo and we landed some of what was left — but not all of it, for the future was so uncertain and the risk of running dry in enemy waters appeared to me greater than the dangers of carrying petrol in drums on deck. Then we went ashore for a talk with Tooms to find out what was going on.

The opinion in Casteloriso was this: there was still fighting in Rhodes between the Germans and the Italians; it was not known which side was going to gain control, but the harbour of Rhodes was certainly in German hands and many Italian ships had fled in the direction of Casteloriso. German aircraft were operating from at least one of the airfields in Rhodes and had made reconnaisance flights over Casteloriso. There was no suggestion that the troops which had been brought to Casteloriso were to be landed in Rhodes, and we were told that that island must be regarded as enemy territory. That meant that as far as we were concerned the Italians and Germans were being left to fight it out and that the outcome was expected to favour the Germans. As we now know, the Italian Commander on Rhodes, with strong German forces already in the city, had said on 11th September (five days earlier) that he wished to have no further contact with the British.

We were told at our briefing with Tooms that other islands of the Dodecanese still had Italian garrisons and no Germans. The attitude of these garrisons was, however, unknown. The fact that the Government in Italy had capitulated did not mean that they had all laid down their arms; they might be pro-Nazi or pro-Allied and they might continue to fight for whatever side they supported. It was essential to get to these islands quickly and before German forces could land. If we could get there first we might win their support and be able to hold those islands against German counter-attacks.

Scouting parties had already gone ahead. A group of small caiques — part of the Levant Schooner Flotilla — under the command of Lieut. Cdr. Seligman RNR and each carrying ten or a dozen Long Range Desert Group (LRDG) or Special Boat Service (SBS) troops, were already in the islands with the object of finding out whether we would be received in a friendly manner or not. This could only be done by setting foot in each island and seeing what happened. ML 349 (Lieut. Cdr. Ball) had sailed from Castleloriso four days before and nothing had been heard from her since. She was expected to return in due course but for all we knew, she might well be sunk or captured.

A signal had come from the Army to say that scouting parties had landed on Leros and the signal just said that reinforcements should be sent as soon as possible. Did this mean that the reception was good or were those who had been landed fighting for their lives? Later in the day a signal came from Cos also asking for reinforcements and another signal from Cairo asked for a party to be landed on Simi as soon as possible. Lieut. Cdr. Tooms had only two MLs available and he had three signals asking for landings in three places. He chose to reinforce those who had already landed and were asking for assistance, and so ML 355 was ordered to Leros and ML 351 was ordered to Cos.

The two MLs each loaded up with 50 fully-armed troops of the

LRDG, plus plenty of spare ammunition, cans of water and 40 gallon drums of petrol. This all amounted to considerable weight (estimated at 2½ tons) and I thought it necessary to stow all we could (but not the petrol!) below decks. It was then that the value of the discipline and training of those troops became obvious and valuable. The crew of ML 355, about 20 of them, were busy getting the ML ready for sea so I told the Officer of the LRDG party that his men would have to load and stow their own gear, weapons and ammunition and that everything possible must go below deck. I showed him where it could go (in our living spaces) and although soldiers are expected to be ill-at-ease on board a ship, these men stowed their gear with speed and efficiency and then settled themselves down in places where they did not get in the way of the crew.

During the afternoon of that day, 16th September, two French *chasseurs* or sloops (the *Commandante Domine* and *La Moqueuse*) came into the harbour and unloaded more troops and stores. While they were there, two Beaufighters circled overhead and that was a comforting sight for us all.

We were only about half-an-hour's flying time from Rhodes but more like an hour from the nearest RAF base in Cyprus. There was no real anti-aircraft defence in Casteloriso; the MLs' 20mm Oerlikons were perhaps the largest guns available, and a German raid on the harbour could be devastating if carried out at a time when the limited resources of the RAF were otherwise occupied.

Ken Hallows (ML 351) and I sat down to consider how we should get to our respective destinations of Cos and Leros. We had no idea what the islands were like, we did not know the conditions on the islands, nor had we any information regarding enemy activity on the way or when we arrived. After all, we had originally been ordered only to Cyprus and Casteloriso; these onward orders came unexpectedly and with no time for preparation.

We came to the conclusion that enemy activity, particularly in the air, was likely to be uncomfortable for us and that we should therefore plan for our movements to be in darkness as far as possible. It was suggested to us that having landed our troops we should attempt to hide in a quiet spot until we saw the chance to return to Casteloriso. I had visions of lying up under some trees for a day or two. We still had no information of other raiding or occupying forces which had been sent on ahead in caiques of the Levant Schooner Flotilla.

The next problem was one of charts. We had nothing of the Aegean beyond Cos. The Army came to our rescue here by producing first a map of Europe on which we could pick out Leros (looking like a pin-point) and secondly, maps of nearly all the islands which we ought to pass on the way to it. We put all these together like a jig-saw puzzle and got some idea of the course we should steer. The islands are in fact so close that daytime navigation is easy, but our Army maps were designed for land movement and gave no particulars of rocks, reefs, wrecks or other navigational dangers of the sea. We would have to press on and trust that the water was generally deep and just consider ourselves unlucky if it was not.

At 19.45 on 16th September we left Casteloriso in company with ML 351, each carrying 50 men in addition to our crew and 2½ tons of stores. It was a fine night but overcast and dark which suited us well. We had been in Casteloriso for only some 12 hours and it had been another very busy and tiring visit.

The channel between Rhodes and the Turkish coast narrows to some seven miles, and if the Germans were organized enough in Rhodes they might well have mounted a patrol at that point to intercept Allied ships which were beginning to infiltrate the Aegean. That channel could be a danger point. Owing to navigational uncertainties, the dangers we expected and last, but by no means least, because all space below was stuffed with stores and men, I spent all the time on the bridge or in the wheelhouse. I watched the heights of Rhodes and then the shoreline creep nearer on our port bow. We edged closer to the rocky and steep slopes of Turkey and well into Turkish territorial waters hoping that by doing so we should escape detection from Rhodes even if they were keeping a radar watch there.

Just at the point where I expected trouble, in the narrowest part of the strait, we sighted a light ahead of us. It was white and it was obviously from a ship which was approaching us. As it was showing a light it was probably a neutral and we should have nothing to worry about, but in those days anything could happen and this was strange territory for us. I altered course towards the Turkish shore hoping to avoid detection by being in the shadow of the cliffs, for I had no desire to fight an action with an ML full of troops, ammunition and petrol.

It soon became clear that the ship approaching us was already close inshore and had probably seen us because she too was going even closer inshore. It was far too dangerous to try to keep inside her on an unknown rocky coast so I altered course again to pass to seaward, which I did with all our guns trained on her in case of trouble. But we could relax: she went peacefully past and was probably a Turkish coasting cargo boat wondering what the devil two MLs with no navigation lights were doing zig-zagging about in front of her.

As we passed Rhodes, we could see very large fires burning in the hills. They were so large that I could hear our crew asking whether there were volcanoes on Rhodes which were in eruption. We did not know what they were and could only think they were caused by battles on the island between the Italian and German forces.

The next marker was Cape Krio at the point of the Turkish isthmus which juts out westward like a finger north of Simi and Rhodes pointing at Cos and Nisseros. There is a lighthouse on the point of the Cape and being in neutral Turkey it was flashing regularly and reassuringly as the navigational charts of peacetime said it should. It seemed to light us up as we passed and much as we enjoyed seeing a lighthouse reminding us of peacetime, we objected to its acting as a searchlight to illuminate those wishing to pass in silence and in darkness.

As first light appeared in the east, we approached Cos and in the growing light we could see Cos harbour and Cos town. We waved goodbye to ML 351 and left him to land his troops there as soon as he could see where to approach and enter the harbour and feel safe to do so without being fired upon by whoever might be in control. We now know that the men of the Special Boat Service (SBS) under the command of David Sutherland who had been landed in Cos on 14th September — three days earlier — had been very well received by the Greek inhabitants and the Italian commander who expressed his desire to co-operate with the British. As we passed Cos and as ML 351 went into the harbour, we did not know this and we were grateful not to hear any sound of gunfire.

It was now daylight and ML 355 pressed on through the strait between Cos and the Turkish coast — the peninsula stretching westward from Bodrum. Steering northeast from here, we set a course for the narrow channel between Kalimnos to the south and Leros to the north. There was no activity in the air or by sea except for two caiques in the distance which looked harmless.

The Kalimnos-Leros strait worried me. It was not deep and could well be mined. I was told later by the Italians that it was indeed a mined area. However, when we were within two miles of the strait a large caique came out of a bay and made to go through westward and a small trawler or fishing boat and a caique came into view having come through the strait from the west.

They were all flying the Italian flag and we had no idea whether they were friendly or hostile Italians. As we went ahead cautiously, the trawler and the caique passed quite close without apparently taking the slightest notice of us — neither shooting at us nor dipping their ensign in a courteous fashion, for either of which we were quite prepared by having the guns manned as well as a man standing by to dip the White Ensign if good manners required it. Grateful that once again a meeting had not proved hostile, we passed on and took the same channel between Kalimnos and Leros as the fishing boat had done and we overhauled the large caique also going westward. This caique seemed to be full of men and women who looked at this solitary ML with some curiosity but without showing enmity or friendliness.

We rounded a small rocky islet and came out into the open sea at the western end of the strait — and I nearly dodged back again into the cover of the cliffs and rocks! For to the southwest and steaming fast on a northerly course to cross our path were two destroyers only about two miles away. I did not at first think they could be anything but German or at best Italian of doubtful friendliness. But examination through binoculars told me that they were definitely of the British *Hunt* class; I felt sure of that, but what were two British destroyers doing in these waters and in broad daylight?

Identification of them was one thing but that still left our own position extremely dangerous even if they were destroyers of the Royal Navy. We did not expect them and they would certainly not expect to see us. It was regrettable but true that in the Aegean at that time, the right hand did not know what the left hand was doing. British destroyers in this situation would be at action stations and would shoot first and ask questions afterwards. We flashed recognition signals madly and went dead slow to avoid being mistaken for MTBs. The rising sun was behind us and there was every chance that we would not be recognised and our signals would not be seen.

To our relief, they appeared to ignore us and carried on at full speed to the north. It soon became clear that they were bound for

Portolago (Port Laki) on the west coast of Leros which was also our destination and so we followed them at our best speed and arrived off the harbour at 0815 on 17th September.

12

Leros Held

I had no idea what Portolago was going to be like and I did not expect anything large or well-equipped. The entrance to the harbour is between two cliffs and rather narrow. It was a surprise to find a double boom across the harbour mouth, batteries of large guns covering the entrance and an immense anchorage inside where several merchant ships could be seen, a floating dock, large cranes, and dockside buildings behind a considerable length of well-built quays and jetties. This was a Portsmouth in the Aegean.

I noted with relief that the coastal guns were not pointing in our direction. The two destroyers, which were *HMS Croome* and *HMS Hurworth*, had arrived just before me and one decided to go into the harbour while the other stayed for a while outside: I suppose they were as uncertain of the situation as I was. There was no one there to give me orders or advice so I followed the first destroyer through the booms into the harbour which is about three miles in length and on average a mile wide, with the quays, workshops and administrative buildings at the far or eastern end.

Soon a small motor boat approached and a very fat Italian with gold rings in all sorts of unexpected places on his uniform waved his arms excitedly and shouted loudly in Italian. We could not understand him but assumed it to be a greeting and we waved back in a friendly fashion. He seemed to regard this as unfriendly and he looked cross and disappointed.

Everything of importance (with the exception of the beautifully uniformed man in the motor boat) was at the eastern end of the harbour. On the southern side off our starboard bow as we approached was a long stretch of quayside behind which, and against the steeply rising ground, clustered barracks and workshops. At the extreme eastern end of this area were the seaplane sheds around a seaplane base and, nearer to us as we approached, an MTB base and a general purpose quay. Lying off these bases and quays were seaplanes at buoys, MS and MAS boats, a destroyer and several small ships. In the steep and rocky slopes behind, there were signs that fuel tanks had been sunk into the hillside.

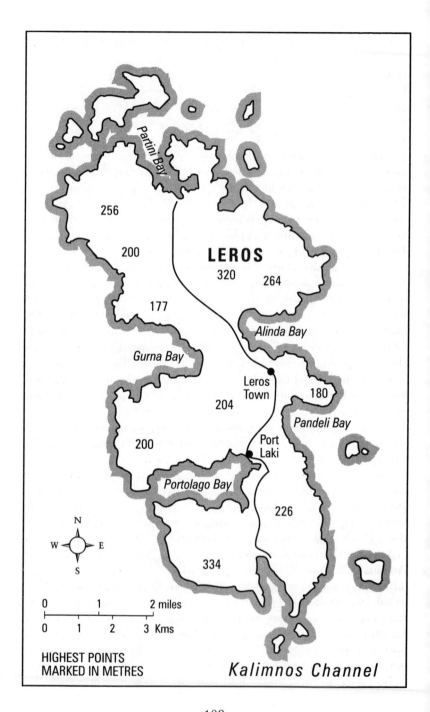

Partini Bay

256
200

LEROS
320   264

177

Alinda Bay

Gurna Bay

Leros
Town

180

204

Pandeli Bay

200

Port
Laki

Portolago Bay

226

N
W   E
S

334

0   1   2 miles

0   1   2   3 Kms

HIGHEST POINTS
MARKED IN METRES

Kalimnos Channel

108

On our port hand, in the northeast corner of this three-mile long stretch of water, was a bay with a well built quayside and cranes bordered by the administrative buildings. Behind these was a hospital and a cluster of houses. This was Port Laki, the main commercial port of the island and also the Naval and Military headquarters. At a buoy just off the quay lay an Italian sloop which was being used as a depot ship.

I put ML 355 towards the Italian MTB base on my starboard side and saw there Lieut. Ramseyer RNVR whom I knew to be on the staff of Raiding Forces, and whom I believed to be on board ML 349. He waved me towards a small jetty but when I went alongside and looked for him so that I could find out what was going on, he had vanished in a characteristic Ramseyer Raiding Forces manner.

It seemed only reasonable to disembark the LRDG troops and this was done with all their guns, ammunition and stores. A crowd of Italian soldiers and sailors, all armed to the teeth, stood around us and watched this strange British craft unloading troops onto their island. There was no sign of any other British anywhere so the Officer in charge of my cargo of LRDG troops and I went along the jetty to see if we really were estatblished on the island and who was in charge of what. We walked by Italians with rifles, Italians with revolvers and Italians with bayonets. This was only nine days after the Italian surrender. Did they all know about it on this island? Had it not been for the sight of a British destroyer dropping anchor in the middle of the harbour, I should have felt like a fly investigating a spider's web.

At last we found someone whose uniform indicated a fairly senior rank. We approached him and asked in bad French and worse Italian for the British headquarters — hoping there was one. He replied in good English and immediately produced trucks to take the LRDG and their stores to the right place.

I then discovered some of the Levant Schooner Flotilla: Lt. Cdr Adrian Seligman RNR, Lt. McLeod RNVR and some others. They had landed troops outside the harbour the previous day and as the Italians had welcomed them, the caiques had sailed into the harbour. So helpful were the Italians that they put their engineering facilities at the immediate disposal of their new allies. The caiques had submitted defect lists and within twenty four hours of arrival one of them was hauled up a slipway to have repairs to her hull.

Both destroyers (*Croome* and *Hurworth*) had now anchored in the harbour. We sent our dinghy over and obtained some much needed stores, for we had been rather too generous in giving away our supplies at Casteloriso and to the troops we had landed. Even crockery was now scarce. We also obtained a bottle of gin for the aid of our Dutch courage. Maybe it was the effect of the bottle of gin because soon after that came aboard, things started to settle down and became, if only for a short time, a little more organized.

The Italian Senior Engineer Officer, a very cheerful and (to us young ones) rather elderly Italian, whose name or nickname appeared to be 'Papa,' came aboard and arranged for our several small defects to be attended to. We investigated the fuel situation and arranged for supplies from the MTB base — all our deck cargo of petrol had by this time been used up.

ML 349 arrived unexpectedly from her 'flag-showing' visits to Cos and Samos and we learned that the destroyers which had arrived in Leros at the same time as ML 355 had brought with them an RN Captain who would act as Senior British Naval Oficer Aegean (SBNOA).

The two destroyers were under orders to return to Alxandria that night and before they left I went aboard *HMS Croome*. Her Captain told me that he was within an ace of opening fire when he saw ML 355 against the sunrise, but had held his hand to give time for identification. He was astounded at the helpfulness of the Italians. His anchor had fouled a mooring buoy and almost before he had realized what had gone wrong, a boatful of divers had come out from the shore and had cleared the anchor from the buoy. This Leros visit was an unexpected venture for him, just as it was for me. *Croome* and *Hurworth* had been on convoy escort duty and only on 14th September (three days before this meeting in Leros) had they been ordered to Haifa to embark troops of the Royal Irish Fusiliers and to transport them to Leros with all speed.

SBNOA (Captain E.H.B. Baker RN) set up his headquarters in the Italian Submarine Depot Ship lying near the administrative buildings in the northeast of Portolago. Sub-Lieut. Harding RNVR, the third officer of ML 349 (which as Senior Officer's boat carrried three officers instead of the normal two) was found to speak fluent Italian so he was immediately transferred to Captain Baker's staff.

There was not much action on the day after our arrival in Leros and we welcomed a day to recover our composure after a long voyage from Alexandria with brief stops only in Paphos and

Casteloriso — and those stops were more exhausting than a night voyage at sea. The following day, however, news came of an engagement at sea to the west when the destroyers *Faulknor*, *Eclipse* and *Queen Olga* (a Greek destroyer) intercepted an enemy convoy between Stampalia (Astypalaia) and Kandeliusa in the early hours of the morning of 18th September. The details were not known to us then but we now know that two merchant ships, *Paula* and *Pluto*, were sunk and their escort ship was badly damaged.

I was with SBNOA in his cabin when a deputation of two or three Italian officers arrived. They had received a signal from the Italian garrison of Stampalia saying that the Germans were invading the island. Precise information was not given: that seemed to be quite normal in these Italian signals, and a fog of misunderstanding and uncertainty seemed to surround the staff work of the Italians on this unfortunate island. Someone had to be sent to Stampalia: firstly to find out what was going on there and, if there really was a battle raging, to encourage the Italians to hold out until British reinforcements could be sent.

This incident was an excellent example of our situation. We were stoking up a fire and putting our fingers into it to try to extract a chestnut or two.

It was in the forenoon when this news arrived. It was some 40 miles to Stampalia and the journey in daylight was considered too dangerous because the Germans dominated the air. Help must be sent by night and I was ordered to take a troop of the LRDG as soon as darkness fell. Three Italian MAS boats which were capable of 30 knots were, however, ordered to go at once and in daylight, in the belief that their speed would give them a reasonable chance of getting there without attack from the air.

Late afternoon more news came in; bad news. Speed had not saved the Italian MAS boats — two had been sunk by air attacks and the third had been damaged and was beached in a bay in Stampalia. Soon after that we had another report. The Germans who were thought to be invading Stampalia were in fact survivors from the action between the two British and one Greek destroyer and the German convoy. The badly-damaged German escort vessel had, it was said, managed to reach one of the bays of Stampalia and the crew had gone ashore for shelter and were quite prepared to surrender. There must have been some panic on the island to mistake them for invaders.

The Italian Chief of Staff in Leros briefed me himself, showing

111

me exactly where the German ship was, according to his information (which was wrong, of course). He said he would lend me an Italian signalman for the journey and that the object of that journey was to put a boarding party on the German ship and bring the ship and her crew back to Leros escorting her with ML 355. His information was that the ship was not badly damaged and would do 8 knots (which was wrong, of course) so I ought to get back before daylight.

I asked the Chief of Staff for recognition signals which might help me to approach the island of Stampalia by night without too much risk of being shot at by the Italian garrison. He told me that the recognition signal was 'MA' which should be flashed at whatever post opened fire! He was quite vague as to the position of observation and defence posts in Stampalia and seemed quite happy that I should discover them for myself by waiting until they fired at me.

At dusk I left Leros for Stampalia. I had about thirty LRDG troops on board who were to be landed there. Major Lloyd Owen of the LRDG came just for the ride. At the last moment the Italian signalman came aboard, in fact we had to wait for him. He was a stout little man, very cheerful but not very intelligent. He looked like a farmer and his happy childlike smile soon made him popular with the crew as a good-luck mascot. Perhaps he was an excellent signalman, I doubt it, but I must give him the benefit of the doubt as I was quite unable to test his ability. Good or bad, he soon appeared to be an unnecessary passenger because he spoke no English and we spoke no Italian. At least he added a theatrical, almost comic opera touch to our expedition which helped to make it seem like an improbable adventure story.

It being only 40 miles from Leros to Stampalia, the high cliffs of the southeast corner of the island loomed up ahead of us just before midnight. In Leros I had managed to borrow or steal several Italian charts of the surrounding waters and it was much to my relief that we no longer had to rely on Army maps which were not really intended for the guidance of seafarers. The Italian charts were very detailed and had the appearance of being accurate. As they were all we had, we just had to assume their reliability.

We closed the coast and I kept careful watch for interrogating gunfire. Eventually, at the top of the cliffs I saw a light flashing — perhaps a gunner looking for his ammunition, I thought. The Italian signalman had had too good a supper and he was asleep so I flashed back the letters MA several times. They may or may not have worked — nobody flashed back, nobody fired at us.

Rounding the corner of the island we entered, according to our chart, an area of very small islands, rocks and minefields: a nasty little place which needed cautious navigation. Thanks to the excellent work of my No. 1 Sub-Lieut. Jock Steedman, we at last found the bay where the German ship was said to be. We entered the bay and we circled the bay — nothing there at all!

The problem of 'what next' was not easy. We could go slowly round the coast looking into each little bay in turn but that put a heavy strain on Jock Steedman who had to see that we did not hit a rock or run ourselves aground. We only had the night hours to work in and time was passing. The decision I made was to go to the main port and town of the island to see what we could find out there. It was probably defended but perhaps the magic signal 'MA' would enable us to make contact with someone.

Threading our way in the dark through more rocks and small islands, we soon saw the main town of Stampalia shining white in the moonlight and lying at the head of a small inlet. I probably became over-bold because flashing MA in all directions we were entering the inlet at a fair speed when there was a bang and a whistle and something passed overhead. Full astern, prepare to turn, the shore was quite close! I gave the Italian signalman a megaphone and told him to shout rather than carry on flashing MA. I don't know what he shouted but soon a light flashed on the waterfront ahead of us and we read 'COME HER.'

A quick discussion: would an Italian or a German be most likely to miss the last E of HERE? If a German force had already landed and had taken over the island, this narrow inlet was a wonderful place for an ambush and they could well try to capture an ML to get themselves home.

Just in case we had to make a quick getaway, I turned ML 355 about and went in stern first and was just able to make out the lines of a small jetty in the dark at the extreme end of the inlet which, being surrounded by high ground, became increasingly black as we went in.

Jock Steedman was on the stern supervising the very dangerous operation, not recommended in any Admiralty Navigation Manual, of taking soundings from the stern (the possibility of fouling the propellers was quite high). Suddenly I saw that the jetty was exceedingly short, — no hope of going alongside, all I could do was to put my stern against it.

The 3-pounder gun on the forecastle was manned and without warning I shouted to them to 'Let go the anchor and veer the cable.' Thanks to the excellent seamanship of Oliver Ford AB (the same one, the ex-truck driver, who had his jaw cracked by one of my Australian crew in Alexandria), the anchor went over immediately and the cable was just being eased out when No. 1 shouted that we had 4 feet of water aft and we were 3 feet from the jetty. Someone jumped on the jetty and took a line (remember that it was around midnight and black as a coal cellar in the shadow of the high ground around us), the anchor held and the engines were cut.

We would have been in some trouble if the anchor had not gone down when it did. I asked Oliver Ford afterwards how it was that he was able to drop the anchor so quickly and he gave me his slow smile and said 'I thought you would need that anchor.' Not bad for a man who had so far spent his life as a lorry driver in Sussex.

Some Italians arrived on the jetty and a plank was provided for disembarkation. The LRDG troops went ashore in double quick time. Major Lloyd Owen and Jock Steedman went ashore to see if anyone knew where we could find the German ship. They soon came back with some very talkative and excited Italians and by signs and shouting we established that: they had been heavily bombed from the air that day, the jetty where we were had been hit and partly destroyed (which explained its shortness and the lack. of depth alongside); some MAS boats had been sunk (this we knew to be true); and finally they expected the planes to return and bomb them again. As they were shouting, gesticulating and jumping up and down, a plane flew quite low overhead and that added confusion and consternation and caused the general conversation level to go up half an octave. I have often wondered whether the bombing was done by the Luftwaffe or the RAF. They were equally hostile to any small ships and an Italian-held island with a German escort vessel in one bay, and a British ML in another, gave both sides a reason to attack.

We were still trying to get an answer to our question: where was the German ship? Eventually, after everyone had had their say and we still remained confused, a young and volatile Italian officer agreed to come with us as a pilot.

Following his directions, we were piloted to a large anchorage in a bay with a chain of small islands completing almost a circle of the seaward side. Booms and obstructions had been placed between the islands so that a protected harbour of considerable size was enclosed.

We approached and found one very small unmanned boom gate. The Italian officer was dancing about in his anxiety as to whether there was width and depth enough for us to get through. I was just as worried too, but I hope I was not so openly demonstrative. Once inside, we saw the escort ship lying close to one of the islands and without more ado we closed on her quickly as time was not on our side and more planes were flying overhead in the moonlight.

She had an anchor down and a considerable list to starboard. I went alongside her starboard aside where, owing to her list, the deck level would be nearly the same as mine. As I went alongside I did my best to assess what sort of affair we were engaged in and what we were taking on.

She looked similar to our corvette class of ships, sturdily built on the lines of a large trawler and carrying a considerable number of guns of the lighter type. The Germans called these ships 'U.J. Class', and they armed them well for escort work in the Aegean where attack by aircraft could be expected. One of them was said to have foundered in a storm owing to the topweight of armament.

Once alongside, I was extremely worried to find her decks crowded with men while others stood silently on the gun platforms around her guns which still looked in good condition.

Not abashed by the crowd of men or the sight of her guns, No. 1 and two hands leapt on board, pistols in hand, and shouldered their way to the bridge. That was good and dramatic stuff but I was very worried that ML 355 herself might be boarded. It was distinctly possible that we could be overwhelmed by weight of numbers and that they would have a nice ML to take them back to Athens. So I posted two stout hands (and I had some good stout hands in 355) on the guard rails with stripped Lewis guns and orders to shoot anyone who came aboard without permission.

Major Lloyd Owen and I went to the guard rails separating us from the crowd of men in the well of the UJ ship. There were several trying to speak to us and I picked out three who looked like officers and brought them aboard. One of them was prepared to do the talking and answered my questions in a fluent and colloquial Glasgow accent. I gathered the following information.

The UJ was badly damaged and could not possibly sail. She might even sink before long. The boiler room was under-water and the decks were badly damaged by shellfire. There were many dead and wounded on board from the UJ crew with about 200 others who were survivors from the sunk German merchant ships. He himself was the captain of one of the merchant ships and explained his Glasgow accent by telling me that he had lived there for some time before the war when he was working on ships trading from that City. So, if he was to be believed, we had a badly damaged ship alongside, with perhaps 300 men aboard, many of whom were wounded. What to do?

Then things really started to happen. No. 1 came back with the Captain of the UJ and four others who appeared to be his Officers. Next, four men in uniform and armed with rifles came aboard ML 355 — and would have been shot by our Lewis gunners if No. 1 had not stopped them — and once aboard announced that they were Italians sent to guard the Germans! My Italian pilot then rushed at me with arms waving imploring me, as far I could understand, to cast off immediately because the guns on the German ship were all in good working order and the crew were preparing to blow us out of the water. The four Italian guards were scared stiff and had come aboard the ML for safety. They had allowed themselves to be jostled about by an overwhelming crowd of Germans who could have knocked them on the head and taken their rifles away at any time.

It was still dark, it was very noisy. In retrospect, we were probably saved by the fact that all those on board the UJ, whether Naval crew or rescued seamen from the merchant ships, were in a state of shock. They had been through a battle, they had dead and wounded on board and I could see what looked like a body hanging from the rigging on the mast. But at the time and in the confusion, I could see that we were outnumbered by over 200 to 20 and by the many guns on the UJ which seemed to be in working order and much bigger than mine. I could not risk the loss of an ML. I decided to accept the view that the ship could not sail and that I should return to Leros with the Captain and officers so that better arrangements could be made to take off the rest of the prisoners during the following day.

We cast off lines and backed away. I was expecting to be followed by a few 88mm shells. Our four Italian guards and the officer clamoured to be taken to a small jetty in the anchorage and, as I regarded them more of a disturbing influence than an asset, I readily agreed.

When we arrived at the jetty I was told that the Governor of

116

the island wished to speak to me. I refused to leave my ship but said I would meet him on board: I had been warned that he had Fascist sympathies and might not be friendly. He came aboard some ten minutes later and was very indignant and voluble because I was not going to take away all his 200 or more prisoners. I told him that if he had wanted them taken away he should have sent a proper report to Leros on the situation. How could he expect me to carry over 200 men — we had been told the UJ could sail — could it or couldn't it, etc. etc. And we parted bad friends at 3.30 in the morning.

It was then that I discovered to my extreme annoyance, that the German captain of the UJ had jumped back on board as we pulled away and that I had only four prisoners on board: his two Officers, a young engineer and a German war correspondent. I was very worried by the action of the German Captain, for while he was on board they had a leader and if they could get the ship going during the next day, who was to stop them leaving the island?

We went back to Leros and I was very tired and very worried. I reported to Captain Baker and was relieved to have a sympathetic hearing. But sympathetic hearing or not, the penalty for not achieving the objective was to be told to try again and when one tries again in war, the element of surprise is lost and the danger and risk of another failure is greater.

On the day after we left, however, the LRDG we had landed on Stampalia were not idle. They soon had the Italian Governor and the shipload of Germans under control and they signalled back to Leros to say that both the Governor and the Germans could be collected as soon as we could send a ship for that purpose.

I prepared to make the trip again that evening and this time took on board both an Italian signalman and an interpreter, having learned from the previous experience what I ought to have known from the start: that one was useless without the other. This interpreter was an extremely helpful and intelligent Italian Officer from the staff of the Rear Admiral Mascherpa who was not only an Admiral but also the Governor of Leros.

For this second trip I also took on board 24 men and an Officer from an infantry regiment, probably the Royal Irish Fusiliers. I have no doubt that they were good soldiers and excellent infantry but as passengers on an ML the difference between them and the LRDG was considerable. They had no experience of ships or this irregular island warfare. They were difficult to embark and disembark and they always found the most awkward place on or below decks to stow themselves and their kit. It was a mistake to employ these regular troops in such unaccustomed surroundings for which they appeared to have had no training. But troops like the LRDG or SBS were limited in numbers and this, after all, was a hastily cobbled together force.

In order to collect all the Germans from Stampalia, it was decided that an Italian auxiliary should sail with ML 355 and this Italian ship would be large enough to carry all the prisoners of the UJ. The Italian auxiliary was lying in Parteni Bay in the north of Leros. Just before nightfall we left our moorings and waited outside Portolago for the Italian ship to come from Parteni Bay to join us. It was rather a rough evening and we were rolling quite heavily as we waited.

To exercise the crew, to test the guns and to give us all something to do, I sounded 'Action Stations.' As soon as the guns were closed up, No. 1 shouted 'Fire' to the 3-pounder, 'Fire' to the Oerlikons, 'Fire' to the 20mm Bredas, to the twin 0.5" Brownings and to our two twin Vickers 0.303" in turn and they all fired with enthusiasm into the evening sky with a fine display of tracer shells. The Italian officer standing beside me on the bridge was most impressed I believe, for he rubbed his hands with glee and said words in Italian which I took to be complimentary.

The shooting stopped but before the gun crews could secure and stand down, smoke and flames could be seen coming from the galley which was situated just below the bridge and only separated by a wooden bulkhead from the petrol tanks. This time I shouted 'FIRE', and people ran about with hoses and fire extinguishers until what might have been a dangerous blaze was put out. While all this was going on, the Italian continued to hug himself with glee and shout his praise and delight at what he thought to be the continuation of an exercise put on solely for his benefit.

After waiting and rolling about outside Portolago for nearly two hours, I decided that the Italian ship was late even for an Italian ship, and with the aid of the interpreter and the signalman we sent a signal to the shore to ask very politely what was going on. In reply we were recalled to harbour where we were told that the Italian ship had gone aground as she was leaving Parteni Bay and could not be refloated in time for the Stampalia operation that night. I had a feeling that the Captain of that ship did not like the idea of the Stampalia operation. Plans were made to try again on the following night.

All this time, while ML 355 was trying to deal with the German ship and the German crews in Stampalia life was going on rather quietly and peacefully on the island of Leros. No enemy planes appeared and British destroyers came in every other morning to unload more troops and more stores. And about this time a real cargo ship arrived flying the Red Ensign. This was the *Palopo* and was the only carrier of the Red Ensign I saw in those parts. She went alongside the quay outside the administrative offices at Port Laki and methodically and quietly unloaded her cargo of ammunition, food and clothing. It was a brave voyage for such a ship to make slowly and steadily at her eight knots across a sea dominated by the enemy and where even destroyers disliked staying too long. But for the *Palopo* Leros might not have held out as long as it did and I only hope she returned safely to Beirut, Haifa or Alexandria — we never knew.

More MLs were arriving to join our small force. ML 354 (Lieut. Jim Patterson RNVR), ML 356 (Lieut. Ken Lloyd RNVR who had been my No. 1 previously), ML 836 (Lieut. Bert Clark RNVR), ML 835 (Lieut. Brian Close RANVR who came from Tasmania) and Lieut. Ken Hallows in ML 351 whom we had left in Cos about a week earlier.

During the daytime, the MLs lay at one of the quays in peace and September sunshine. All round us walked Italians in splendid uniforms which had not yet suffered the dirt and agony of fighting. They were well-equipped with small arms, but what resolution lay behind this bright and clean exterior we did not know.

The ML crews were soon playing football with the Italians and enjoying a 'run ashore' into the main Leros town which was about three miles away from Port Laki and nearer to the largest inlet on the eastern side of the island — Alinda Bay. Here they met the Greek population of the island and were made very welcome; indeed, there were certainly women to be seen there and there was also some wine. I have no doubt that there was some song too, but none of my crew were interested in singing.

Italian workmen came on board to attend to any defects; we refuelled at the Italian MAS base with Italian petrol and we took water from the Italian waterboat. As ML 349 was having trouble with one of her engines, it was decided that a new 'head' was necessary and Alexandria was asked to send one. They did so but owing to difficulties and confusion, it arrived in Cos so the No.

1 of ML 349, 'Twig' Livesey, was sent to Cos in an Italian MS boat and came back in an Italian F Lighter especially to collect this new engine head. He reported that the Italian MS boat went like the wind to Cos and its Captain immediately announced that it was broken down beyond repair. Hence the need to find other transport back to Leros with the engine head.

That was the on-going scene in Leros and against this background ML 355 was still involved with the effort to bring the German prisoners back from Stampalia.

We had come to the conclusion that if we relied on help from the Italians we should never get anything done and so Captain Baker agreed to send two MLs to take the Royal Irish Fusiliers whom we had had to bring back from our abortive effort of the previous night and to bring back all the German prisoners we could carry.

I asked for the Italian recognition signal for the night so that I might identify the two MLs when we again approached Stampalia. I was told that 'It is still MA.'

'But,' I pointed out, 'it was MA when we went over the night before last — surely it changes each night?'

'No' was the reply. 'You see MA are the first two letters of the name of the Governor of the island (Rear Admiral Mascherpa) and therefore the recognition signal will not change until we have a new Admiral or new Governor and then only if his name does not begin with M A.' To us this was a new concept on the use of recognition signals. I wonder whether the Germans knew this system? I am sure they knew the name of the Admiral.

We arrived at Stampalia before midnight and entered the little harbour near the main town without being shot at. Knowing the situation, we quickly secured stern first to the damaged and small jetty and landed our Royal Irish Fusiliers with the exception of four men with tommy guns whom we kept on each ML to help us with our cargo of prisoners — I still had the feeling that there was a real danger of the prisoners trying to capture the ML.

The LRDG who were in charge on shore were certainly very much in charge and they brought the prisoners to us in several small caiques and one large one. They were very efficient. We decided to take about thirty on each ML and gave priority to the wounded on grounds of humanity, and to the Officers on grounds of securing the most important captives.

I made certain that this time I had on board the German Captain of the escort ship and that he did not jump off at the last moment as he had done before. He was a tall, lean man about 40 years of age. He had a large bandage round his head to cover a wound and he looked very tired. I was given his name but can only remember that it had a 'von' in it. The LRDG warned me that he had attended the burial of some of his crew earlier in the day and had made a very belligerent speech, but to look on the kinder side of this he had lost his ship and part of his crew: it was his duty to try to raise the morale of the others.

When they were all on board, the Captain seemed to expect to go down below but I insisted that all except the badly wounded should remain on deck where they were guarded by the guns of the four soldiers I had kept on board and the Lewis guns of my crew. Most of them had to be on the forecastle as that was the largest open space, and I am afraid they got rather wet as it was rough on the way back. I would have liked to be more hospitable but I have said before that we were outnumbered about 3 to 1 and who knows whether they had hidden a gun or two in their clothing.

The two MLs arrived at Portolago in Leros at daybreak and I ordered the prisoners to muster on the jetty. The German Captain organized this and I admired his firm but quiet command in very difficult circumstances. They were all very tired and hungry; they had had the shattering experience of being shelled and all but sunk; some of the crew were killed and they had lived for some days in a bloodstained and battered ship (and there was that something in the rigging which I thought to be a dead body or part of it) yet discipline was still so good that they mustered quickly and without argument in tidy ranks and in two groups, — the UJ crew and the survivors of the merchantmen. They had just done so when, at 8 am, the Italian Colours were hoisted and the appropriate music was played and bugles sounded. The Captain called the tired and dispirited men to attention and they stood with straight backs as he saluted the Italian flag. I was moved by such discipline and the observation of the proper courtesies when non-observance would have been well understood.

The wounded were taken to the Italian hospital and Italian guards came up to march the prisoners off to some area of safe custody. The Glaswegian-speaking skipper of one of the merchant ships had done his best to ingratiate himself with me and with our crew and he did his best to assure us that he was a friend of the British and a most unwilling Nazi. When he saw the Italian guards coming to march them off, he left the ranks and came up to me saying:

'Captain, you cannot let us go to an Italian prison, we are prisoners of the British.'

I told him that he had no choice but to be in the charge of Italian gaolers but I expected that he would soon be sent to a British prisoner-of-war camp in Egypt. At that he cheered up and told his friends what I had said. It was the first time I had understood the unhappy feeling between the Germans and the Italians and that there was real fear that German prisoners might be treated badly in Italian hands.

The rest of the prisoners were brought back to Leros during the next night in the large caique which we had seen in Stampalia. It was manned by a mixed crew of Italians and LRDG and I believe the deposed Italian Governor of Stampalia also came back with them.

Soon after the Stampalia incident, I was turning into my bunk one evening at about 11 o'clock when Lieut. Cdr. Ball, SO of the 42nd Flotilla came down into the cabin with an RNVR Lieutenant of the Intelligence Staff, an Italian officer and a British war correspondent. It appears that there was another midnight excitement going on.

An enemy report had been received to the effect that in a small bay near Cape Papas in Ikaria, a German ship had been reported and around it were several small craft leading to the assumption that troops and stores were being unloaded and taken ashore. It had been decided that an attack should be made on the ship and the proposal was that an ML should be sent together with an Italian torpedo boat. ML 355 had been chosen because we had a greater assortment of guns on board than most of the MLs present, and because we had acquired (regrettable perhaps) something of a reputation for landing raiding parties and carrying out operations on enemy coasts. The plan that Lieut. Cdr. Ball outlined was that, on arrival at the bay in Ikaria, we were to attack with guns and make a smoke screen. Then while enemy attention was directed towards ML 355, the Italian would emerge at high speed from the smoke and torpedo the ship. The Italian who had come aboard was the Commanding Officer of the torpedo boat detailed for the operation.

No more details were available and although it all seemed rather a gin-inspired operation based on very vague information, the report could not be ignored. They gave me some more charts to cover the area involved and sailing orders from SBNOA which just told me to go, and requested the RAF for air cover in the day-light hours. I was not encouraged by the last request because I doubted whether the signal would get through to Cos, the nearest place with an airfield and which now had some planes operational. Given the usual confusion always around us, I thought I was more likely to be attacked than protected by the RAF.

I was to leave at such time as would get us to Ikaria by daybreak, then having fired guns, made smoke and seen the German ship duly torpedoed we would return in daylight — that would be the time we would need air cover. 'A piece of cake,' said Alan Ball.

'What size is this German ship,' I asked.

'Oh, pretty small,' said Ball. 'Two or three hundred tons — your 3-pounder will do well on her.'

'What is her armament?'

'Nothing much on that size of ship.'

'And what craft are with her?'

'Just barges, I expect.'

I accepted all that as factual information from a Senior Officer and an Officer of the Intelligence Staff and I turned to the CO of the MS boat to discuss our tactics. I found him looking decidedly white-faced and miserable and trying to gain Dutch courage by attacking a bottle of Cyprus brandy.

'How close do you want the smokescreen?' I asked.

'About 1,000 metres,' he replied.

'Surely that is not near enough? She is only a small ship and you have only two torpedoes.'

That really caused him to explode and it explained his attack on the brandy bottle.

'Small ship? Small ship?' He shouted. 'She is 8,000 tons and one of the largest transports the Germans have in the Aegean. I know her well. She has quadruple pom-pom guns on each side of the bridge, about four 88m/m guns, a much larger gun aft and several 20m/m guns along her side.'

He drew a sketch of the ship and the position of her armament just to make his point absolutely clear.

'And,' he went on, 'those small boats near her are E-boats and R-boats, of course. She would not be allowed to travel without a screen of R-boats. I expect we will be fired on from the shore as well as from all the ships. Ikaria is strongly Fascist and if we are hit we must not run ashore there. I am a traitor in their eyes and I know how they will deal with me.' And he finished his dramatic

123

intervention by making a show of having his throat cut.

His story cast a gloom over what had before been treated as rather an attractive opportunity — 'a piece of cake,' as it had been described. There was some bad staff work or perhaps it should be put down to the usual and to-be-expected shortcomings of the campaign. We just had to do our best and hope for some luck.

So, in darkness in the very early hours of 25th September we set off and I for one had the feeling that we were going to be involved in a disaster. We were going to attack a large and well-armed ship guarded by about four E-boats in a bay on a hostile coast. If I was worried what about the CO and crew of the MS boat who expected to be executed if they were captured? That CO was a brave man to set out on such a wild venture, but even if I laid smoke and made a diversion, would he be brave enough to press his attack home? I did my best to hide my misgivings from my crew.

We did not keep good station on the way there. It was a question of minimum speed for the MS boat against my maximum. He could manage a minimum of 22 knots on two engines and about 13 knots on one. I was trying my best to average 16 knots on two engines. We had a journey of about 55 miles from Leros to Ikaria.

In the event, we did well and could not have timed our arrival better. We came into Ikaria from the west and came down close inshore. We arrived at the western corner of the bay, which was our target, just as first light was breaking. We were in the dark of the west and we were looking towards the lightening east. It was just before life on the troopship and the E-boats would evolve into a new day, when eyes were misty and commands might be retarded by the remains of sleep. Human habits and human frailty cannot be ignored and must be used to advantage in the successful pursuit of war — and everyone knows that the same principles apply in peace.

So, timing perfect, we were set to go. I rounded the head at 18 knots, all set to carry on across the bay. The MS boat was about half a mile astern, increasing speed with a fine bow wave and looking determined to play her part.

The bay was empty.

What a very, very great disappointment. I know that I thought the whole project was likely to be a disaster and I know that I thought we would be lucky to survive; but we had got everything right and were well-set to make a success of it. Disappointment? Of course.

124

We searched the coast for more than ten miles eastward and then it became so steep and rugged that it was clear that we had investigated all the places on the south coast of Ikaria where a ship might lie and, moreover, where a ship might land troops and stores. So with full daylight now upon us, we set off on the four-hour voyage back to Leros. On the way we actually saw two Spitfires and as they did not attack us, I suppose they were our air cover for which we were grateful. We completed our return journey safely and without incident.

While we, thinking only of our own interests were grateful to see these Spitfires, we were not grateful enough. We did not know of the struggle which was going on to hold and maintain the airfield at Antimachia in the centre of the island of Cos.

Cos and Leros were interdependent: Cos had the airfield, Leros had the Naval base. The Army was established in both with some RAF regiment around the airfield. To the south and southeast — between Cos-Leros and our main bases — were German airfields and islands strongly held by German forces. In Greece to the west were strong German Army, Air and Naval forces. Our main bases were as far away as Alexandria, Haifa, Cyprus and Beirut. Would our Cos-Leros position be able to hold out behind the German-held 'Iron Ring' of Crete, Scarpanto and Rhodes, with all the difficulties of reinforcement through being behind enemy lines? It was perhaps possible so long as there was air support to help the Navy and the Army repel attacks.

At the time I was leaving Paphos in Cyprus for Casteloriso on 15th September, ML 349 and several caiques of the Levant Schooner Flotilla were arriving in Cos with some 50 men of the SBS. They were welcomed by the Italian garrison and the Greek inhabitants. The RAF were not left behind in time although inevitably restricted in numbers. Two Beaufighters arrived from Cyprus at dawn on 14th September and landed men to set up a W/T station. On the same evening six Spitfires of No. 7 (South African) Squadron arrived followed by three Dakota planes.

The Italian troops (who were to pay a terrible price for their cooperation) were not well-armed and further troops and equipment were hastily flown in, but the real shortage was of guns of sufficiently large calibre to form an effective anti-aircraft defence. Bofors guns were badly needed but the problems of transporting these larger guns caused delay.

The Spitfires flown into Antimachia had immediately started

daylight patrols over Cos and the nearby islands but on 16th September, the day before ML 355 arrived in Leros with *HMS Croome* and *Hurworth*, the German air attacks on the airfield at Antimachia started. On 17th September the attacks were heavier, some aircraft were destroyed on the ground and the airstrip was damaged by bombs. From then on the use of Antimachia became increasingly difficult and although gallant efforts were made to keep the airfield and the Spitfires serviceable, the possibility of air-cover became less and less.

Our safe passage to Leros on 17th September was only possible because the German Air Force concentrated on other objectives — the destruction of airfields in Cos. The same German strategy had been employed before in 1940. The destruction of airfields in Southern England was planned as the prelude to invasion of Southern England. These airfields were not destroyed, and the invasion of England did not take place. In the Aegean, we were not so fortunate.

Based in Leros from 17th September, we had so far been spared attacks from the air because the enemy had concentrated on Cos. I did not even know of these German attacks on Cos and, protected by the mountains around Portolago, we did not hear the sound of the bombings and the gunfire going on every day some 25 miles to the south of us. We did not know of the extraordinary efforts being made to keep the airfield and the aircraft serviceable, of the shortages of oil, petrol, guns and ammunition. It was all part of the way this campaign had to be fought.

Some notes which I made at the time are much more critical of those in command of our operations. Then I only saw disorganization and realized our lack of strength in a position which was behind the enemy lines. I saw guns being landed in Leros while the gunners were landed in Cos — and *vice versa*. I saw the dependence on Italians who until only weeks before had been our enemies. I saw nothing but muddle and weakness. I wondered why we were there at all. Now I have read the histories and now I understand enough to forgive my Commanders and withdraw my criticisms.

With insufficient forces, General Maitland Wilson was told by Churchill to 'improvise', and that was all he could do. The Allied High Command preferred to reinforce India and the landings on mainland Italy. The enemy's reaction was different: it was Hitler's decision at a conference on 24th September that the 'Iron Ring' of Crete, Scarpanto and Rhodes must be held and that the other Aegean islands must be taken and held.

With this supreme authority and directive, strong German forces were made available to carry out the operation and what we in the Dodecanese now began to feel was the weight of a force gathered together for the single purpose of taking the Aegean islands against which we could only put out hastily improvised forces who were put there to 'see what they could do' and to capture and hold more by bluff than force of arms.

If the reading from now on looks to be a tale of an Allied disaster, remember that I am writing of just that part of the war which I was watching. On the bigger screen, the German Army and Air force were devoting considerable resources to this area. There must have been some balancing benefits on the Russian front and to the Allies in Italy, in southern France and later in Normandy. But it is not easy to be convinced that you are helping the cause when you are being overwhelmed, as we were about to be.

On 26th September, the morning when ML 355 and the Italian torpedo boat returned from the fruitless voyage to Ikaria, two destroyers came into Portolago at about 7 am and secured to buoys in the middle of the harbour. They were *HMS Intrepid* and the Greek destroyer, *Queen Olga*. Several destroyers had been to Leros since *Croome* and *Hurworth* first arrived with ML 355 on 17th September. They all brought troops and guns and stores for every effort was being made to supply Cos and Leros by destroyer, submarine, ML, caique, lighter and the gallant *Palopo*. The passage was by night from Haifa and Alexandria and so far the destroyers had stayed in the harbour by day where they counted on anti-aircraft defences and, if the airfield in Cos could be kept serviceable, on fighter cover too.

That day the old *Palopo*, flying the Red Ensign, was also in Portolago alongside the main quay at Port Laki on the northern side unloading her stores and ammunition. Several MLs were berthed near her. ML 351 was lying at the quay by the Italian workshops on the south side of the harbour and ML 355 tied up alongside ML 351 who had the day before hit an unmarked obstruction in the harbour causing underwater damage so that she was virtually out of action. We were hoping that the workshops might be able to effect repairs. All around on a warm September day the Italians were enjoying the morning sunshine.

Suddenly the peace was broken by the roar of aircraft engines and low over the surrounding hills came a dozen JU 88s dropping bombs on the workshops and firing their machine guns and cannon shells in all directions.

I was in my cabin when it started. The sudden explosions brought me on deck at the rush but as I reached the top rung of the ladder the explosion of a bomb on the jetty beside us made me lose my footing and I went backwards down the hatch again faster than I had come up. Luckily for me, my fall was broken by landing on top of our telegraphist Moran who was following me up the ladder. I did better at the second attempt. There was a confusion of flame and smoke all around and I had a vivid picture of a plane turning low astern of us and rising steeply to clear the hills as another stick of bombs exploded in the water about a hundred yards away from us.

A near miss on *HMS Intrepid* was immediately followed by a cloud of steam escaping from her side. Ugly pieces of masonry from the jetty and the workshops were descending from the air, and I saw a large shell, about a 4-inch, I would say, sailing slowly through the air past us and turning over and over as it went by. I can remember that it was painted yellow.

Some action was called for. I saw our crew flat on their faces on the deck and before I could bring my rather shaken mind into action, ML 351 alongside took the lead by opening fire on a nearby raider with a twin Vickers machine gun. It was Lieut. Hallows who had reached that gun on the bridge and straight away gone into action. No further orders were then needed. Within a very short time all our guns were manned and firing. I took a stripped Lewis gun and was firing in the general direction of the next wave of planes — perhaps a Lewis gun was not very effective but it did my morale a power of good.

The second and third waves of attack concentrated on the two destroyers. The anti-aircraft fire against them was slight and very ragged. It was extreme range for our Oerlikons but I think our 0.5" Brownings were reaching them. I do not think our two MLs on the south jetty could have done more. It was not the time for me to try to assess what others were or were not doing.

With a shattering explosion the stern of the *Queen Olga* blew off. She had a direct hit in the after-magazine. One destroyer sunk, the other was badly damaged. The repair shops, the barracks and the southern jetties were hit with considerable destruction. The German pilots could be proud of their precision but the defences

28th Nov. 1942. The jetties at Benghazi.

28th Nov. 1942. The harbour at Benghazi.

26th January 1943. ML 355 at Latakia, Syria.

5th February 1943. ML358 (Lt. Mitchelson RNZNVR) off Famagusta, Cyprus.

21st Feb. 1943. ML 357 (Lt. R. L. Jones RNVR) off coast of Syria.

March 1943. ML 355 at Tobruk.

6th March 1943. At a Tobruk jetty.

21st March 1943. Benghazi. ML 1046 leaving for night patrol.

18th May 1943. ML 359 (Lt. G. W. Whittam, RNVR) arriving at Derna.

6th June 1943. Church Parade, Benghazi.

17th June 1943. Derna. A minesweeper arriving with about two hundred survivors from a torpedoed troopship.

May 1943. Derna. Sailors from ML 355 and nurses from the hospital.

8th September 1943. ML 355 returning from Crete to North Africa with a party of Cretan resistance fighters.

20th September 1943. Leros. The Portolago jetties and workshops (before the bombing).

26th September 1943. Greek Destroyer Queen Olga sunk by bombing in Portolago harbour, Leros. MLs and small craft picking up survivors.

should have done better. MLs 351 and 355 both claimed hits on the planes but could not claim that any were brought down.

It would be nice to be able to say that when the waves of raiders had disappeared over the hills on the way back to mainland Greece or Rhodes, there was once again peace and quiet. The damage was too great to leave a peaceful scene in that harbour.

The *Queen Olga* had gone down with great loss of life. First there was the explosion itself; then as oil from the ship spread over the water, it ignited and the place where she had been lying at a buoy became a patch of blazing oil around which MLs 836, 356 and 354 circled as they tried to pick up survivors. MLs 356 and 354 had actually been alongside *Queen Olga* when the raid started and had only just cast off in time to avoid destruction themselves. Astern of us, only some fifty yards away, were the smashed remains of two Italian MS boats which had suffered direct hits by bombs. Ashore, the workshops and barracks were on fire and bodies were being carried out.

The dangers for us were not yet over. The blazing oil from the sunken *Queen Olga* was being blown towards us by the wind. We had to get out of our berth as quickly as possible or we would soon be engulfed and on fire ourselves. Had we been on our own, this would have been easy — just cast off and get under way. But there were two problems. Firstly, we were alongside ML 351 and she was there because she had damaged rudders and propellers; she was for all practical purposes immovable under her own power. So Ken Hallows rightly asked and expected me to move ML 351 as well as ML 355. I went to the bridge and told the engine room to start up. There was a horrible pause, some of my hair went grey, or white. Only one engine would start, the other was quite dead and no one knew why. It was probably damaged by the force of nearby explosions in the water and on the jetty.

So here we were: two MLs lashed together, a wind blowing us onto the jetty and a large patch of blazing oil and dense smoke being blown towards us. And we had only one engine between us and that was the outside one on the outside boat.

Onshore, the Italians were running about like ants in a disturbed anthill. They had problems of their own. I went on the jetty and managed to get the help of a man with a small motorboat and he tried really hard to pull our sterns away from the jetty and clear of the bombed MS boat wreckage very close astern. Unfortunately, he had one eye on us and one on the approaching flames and before long he decided that he did not like where he was and what he was trying to do and, courteously wishing us the best of luck while regretfully expressing his view that we were more likely to suffer the worst of luck, he departed to a safer place without achieving the help we so badly wanted. As I stood on the bridge and went ahead and astern on one outside engine in an effort to get clear, I, too, watched the oncoming fire and remember thinking that the Navy was about to lose two MLs.

There was absolutely nothing else to do but continue to try to work us away from the jetty. As I continued, we had a stroke of good fortune. There was a shift in the wind which not only changed the course of the blazing oil but helped me sufficiently to get the two MLs clear of the jetty. Once clear, I went into the open harbour and cruised around with ML 351 still secured alongside until the flames on the sea had gone out and the confusion on the shore had died down. Then we returned to the jetty and began work on the engine which would not start.

It was only then that our dinghy and two of the crew were reported missing and I was told they had last been seen rowing to *HMS Intrepid* to pick up stores. Before long one of them returned and told us what had happened. They had reached *Intrepid* and one had just got onto the deck of the destroyer to take the line from the dinghy and secure it when the air raid started. One of the first bombs was a near miss on the destroyer and a much nearer miss on our dinghy. The bomb had badly damaged the destroyer but it had blown our little boat to pieces, throwing the remaining occupant — Able Seaman Bottomley — high into the air and onto the deck of *Intrepid* with a bad wound in his leg and with considerable shock at such a painful way of going aboard. Bottomley was being cared for with the other casualties on the destroyer.

As the Germans had been so successful in their first raid, it was only to be expected that they would repeat the attack and so the MLs dispersed themselves around the large harbour. ML 355 had, on return from Ikaria and before the air raid started, arranged with the Italians to use their fuelling base. To be caught in an air raid while filling up the ship with petrol is not recommended but on the other hand, we were getting short of fuel and we decided that the appointment must be kept.

In the early afternoon, therefore, and with ML 351 still firmly secured alongside, we went to the small wooden jetty which the Italians used for fuelling their torpedo boats. There seemed to be no Italians there who knew anything about the fuel lines and so we made our own investigations and found that all the pipelines seemed to be out of action, perhaps damaged by the bombing in the morning. A visit to the cheerful Italian Engineer Officer seemed necessary. Hoping that he was still alive and cheerful, Ken Hallows and I went off along the jetty towards the Italian Officers' mess to see if we could find him. We went into the building and were soon engaged in bad Italian and sign language trying to find our man. Then once again the air raid alarms went off, followed immediately by the noise of gunfire and explosions.

The Italians beat most running records out of the back door of the building and into a shelter cut out of the cliffs behind. Our MLs 355 and 351 were tied up at the fuelling jetty about a quarter of a mile away. We went out onto the open jetty and we were each wondering just how fast we could cover that unprotected quarter mile along the jetty when, amid the clatter of guns and shouts and running feet, the first wave of bombers swooped low over the hills coming straight towards us and clearly with destructive intentions directed at the barracks, workshops and other buildings where we were standing.

Without debate or argument, Ken and I decided against being out on the open jetties for a moment longer and equalled the record put up by the Italians for getting into their air raid shelter. It was as well we did so and we had no reason to feel somewhat ashamed of our retreat. They dropped bombs very close and shot at anything moving. The blast of the explosions came into our shelter, my cap blew off and Ken's shirt was blown out of his trousers. In much less than half an hour, the noise died down and we thought it sufficiently quiet to come out. The building we had left was badly damaged and we should have been damaged, too, if we had stayed there.

At the jetty the two MLs opened up at the planes and made a claim to have hit and brought one down. Before many minutes, however, Jock Steedman, my No. 1, decided that the attack was too heavy and that the petrol jetty was no place to be in such circumstances; so he coolly shifted the two MLs into the middle of the harbour and had the situation so well under control that he left a dinghy tied up to the jetty so that Ken and I could row out when things became quieter.

As we walked back along the debris-strewn jetty towards the dinghy, it gave us great heart to see two or three British soldiers with rifles slung over their shoulders standing guard over some stores piled on the jetty. The bombing had moved them no farther from the stores than the nearest arch of a doorway. They exchanged a word and grinned at us with that cheerful-rueful 'what-a-life' expression which carried them through so many difficult and dangerous days.

Ken and I rowed out to our MLs and found them not only happy but quite jubilant because they were convinced they had shot down one of the planes. They were also able to have a good laugh at us because we were covered with the grey cement dust of the jetty and the shelter.

We remained at anchor in the harbour that night but I went ashore to the Italian hospital to see young Bottomley who had been quite badly injured that morning. The hospital was crowded with casualties from the bombing and gunfire and a newly-arrived Army medical team was doing wonderful work in strange surroundings. The doctors had landed from the *Intrepid* that morning as soon as she had arrived and only an hour or so before the first raid when she was hit. They were followed ashore by several hundred casualties from the raid and it can be imagined just how unprepared they were for such numbers and soon.

I found Bottomley very pale and weak from loss of blood, but by no means dejected. I think his wound was cleaned up that night and he was given a blood transfusion but I did not see him again for he was soon shipped back to Alexandria and I expect he went back to the U.K. after that. I wrote to his parents in Lancashire and I hope he recovered fully for he was an excellent man to have alongside you particularly when things got rough. From the hospital I walked back to the jetty in the dark and that was not without its dangers for the Italian sentries were nervous and had their fingers very close to the triggers of their guns.

Alan Ball in ML 349 was still secured at the jetty on the north side of the harbour and close to the administration buildings and the hospital. I went to pay him a visit but on the way I was attracted to what appeared to be a small public meeting at the entrance to the vast complex of air raid shelters and tunnels which led from the jetty area into the side of the hills. At the centre of this meeting I found Lieut. Ramseyer and one or two other officers from SBNOA's staff endeavouring to pursuade the survivors from the Greek destroyer *Queen Olga* to embark for Haifa or Alexandria on a ship leaving that evening.

132

The Greeks, who had had their destroyer sunk under them, were quite demoralized. They sat in a huddle in the mouth of the air raid shelter and refused to leave under any circumstances. The idea of going to sea again was quite ridiculous to them and no pleas, arguments or threats would pursuade them otherwise.

There was a merchant ship leaving that night, perhaps it was the courageous *Palopo* or one of the ex-German or Italian ships in Leros, and there was a small passenger ship they wanted to get away, too. It was hoped to put on board these ships all the survivors and wounded plus those whose presence was not strictly necessary, so that the island might be better organized to receive the bigger air raids which were now expected and should perhaps have been expected before.

Ramseyer made an impassioned speech about the gallant Greeks and our noble allies who were never afraid, always prepared to face danger with a smile, etc. etc. Even this failed to rouse them, probably because they did not understand English rather than from any lack of patriotism or courage. Eventually, however, we did get some to move towards the jetty and had about fifty on board ML 356 (Lt. Ken Lloyd) which was to ferry them out to the merchant ship. Then, without warning, some trigger-happy idiot in the hills above us imagined that he saw a plane in the night sky and he loosed off some rounds of tracer shells across the waters of the harbour. In a few seconds all the fifty were off ML 356 and back inside the tunnels of the air raid shelters. The work of coaxing them out had to begin all over again. I believe they eventually got the Greeks and the others away that night but I did not see the end of it. I found an Italian launch and went back to ML 355 where I fell into my bunk dead-tired and exhausted.

Early next morning, I went ashore again to make contact with SBNOA's headquarters. The weather was absolutely glorious, blue skies with a freshness in the air like the best summer day in England. The rather barren hills of Leros rose steeply from the sea and gave a false impression of arid heat for their brown and barren appearance was caused more by the rock of the soil than the heat of the sun. At headquarters the Army people were planning raids and landings on neighbouring islands. They appeared to be spurred on rather than discouraged by the air raids which we had suffered yesterday. They were still pinning their faith and hopes on the airfield in Cos and the Spitfires there.

Brigadier Turnbull of SBS was in charge of the raiding forces.

His headquarters was in a small house guarded by Italian sentries who presented arms as I passed or saluted in some other way with a varying degree of smartness. The conference at Brigadier Turnbull's headquarters was mainly concerned with the question of which island should be attacked and how soon it could be done. I listened with some misgiving because the suggestions were so optimistic as to be almost fool-hardy when one remembered that they were launched from a very insecure base. I remember Ramseyer speaking strongly in favour of a landing on Amorgos which was about 60 miles away and I thought that getting there, making a good landing for the troops and returning in one night looked rather an unpleasant operation. Could we stay there for a day? Nobody knew.

It was finally decided that as far as I was concerned, my assignment was a landing on Khios some 100 miles to the north and I was to do this in three stages. First, south to Kalimnos, only about 20 miles, where I would embark a patrol of the SBS. Then to Samos, 60 miles, where I would await suitable weather to make the last 60 miles and land the patrol on the south of the island of Khios which was thought to be German-held. I would leave them there for two days and then collect them again from the same beach.

After dark on 27th September, ML 355 left Portolago and directed our course south down the west coast of Kalimnos, rounded the southwest corner of the island and came upon the inlet leading to the main town in the south of the island. It was a very dark night and I well remember going up the ever-narrowing inlet towards the darkened town. At night all fjords or inlets with steep cliffs on both sides look pitch-black to the seafarer and, of course, no light showed from the ship or the shore. I felt that at any moment we would run ourselves onto a beach or crash into the face of an overhanging cliff.

Somewhere ahead of me a breakwater stretched out into the water. Was there at least one gun emplacement which would fire at rather than ask questions of the blacked-out ship which was coming into the harbour on a pitch-black night? In those days and in those islands, there was no reason to think that anyone had sent a signal to warn them of our arrival or, if a signal had been sent, that it had been received. The mountainous nature of the islands often prevented the reception of wireless signals, even if someone realized the need to send a signal in the first place. In the event we did see the breakwater before we hit it and we did find the harbour entrance. Inside we found the only jetty with *Hedgehog* alongside. We berthed stern-first on the other side. The next day we spent in that harbour at Kalimnos.

The island of Cos was only about seven miles away to the south and from the harbour of Kalimnos we were encouraged to see a Spitfire take off from the Antimachia airfield in Cos. Throughout that day we were not disturbed by the sight or sound of any enemy planes and that was a welcome relief after the excitement of yesterday.

I walked into the attractive Greek town and I visited the SBS and LRDG troops who had made the old castle building near the harbour their headquarters. They were using a very attractive villa on the hillside above as a hospital and there some casualties from their island raiding parties were recovering. In the castle were preserved a collection of unusual objects brought up by Kalimnos divers: sponges of unusual size or shape and rocks which appeared to be like coral. This island is famous for its divers who have trained themselves to be able to go to unusual depths without any equipment and they used to travel far into the Mediterranean and beyond to exercise their special skills. The main trade here was sponges. The men from the town came down to the jetty to barter their sponges for food and I obtained and kept for a long time an enormous sponge in exchange for a small quantity of butter. It was interesting to find that corned beef was not thought much of and had little exchange value.

One of our visitors was a rather overdressed — in western city style — and portly man who claimed to be American. I think he was a native of Kalimnos who had emigrated many years ago to the USA, made some money and then returned to retire in the place of his birth, where he was able to live in some style. He spoke with what I believe is called a Bronx accent, was very talkative and highly delighted to see what he thought (and we hoped) were signs of the end of the Italian and German occupation of his native island. He invited us to his house but we did not go for we had not the time to do so. I think it was as well that we refused his invitation for later on the Germans re-occupied the island and perhaps they did not treat kindly those who had welcomed the British with hospitality.

As evening came on we prepared for sea again and took on board as passengers a party of Greek troops bound for Samos, plus a patrol of about twelve men under Captain Milner Barry of the SBS who were the Khios raiding party. The Greek troops were of the Sacred Heart battalion and were commanded as might be expected by a Greek officer. Before we left, Brigadier Turnbull came aboard and asked for the use of my cabin so that he could have a private talk with the Greek officer. The talk lasted some time and, before he left, the Brigadier was kind enough to tell me what it was about.

The Greek officer had some important political connections; he was, I think, related to a former Prime Minister. The island of Samos was now in Greek hands but the Greeks who were in control were referred to by many other Greeks as either 'left wing' or 'communists' or even as 'bandits.' To us, the politics of the Greeks who held Samos did not seem that important; it was sufficient that the Germans were not there and that the Italians had either gone, capitulated or were now 'on our side.' To the Greeks, however, politics were very important and although our Greek troops were supposed to be reinforcements, Brigadier Turnbull had reason to suppose that they might be just as belligerent to Greeks whom they regarded as 'bandits' as they would be to any German forces. Consequently, the Officer in charge of the party from the Sacred Heart battalion was warned that inter-Greek strife in Samos would not be tolerated by the British and that the Germans were far too close to permit arguments between ourselves.

We sailed at nightfall on 28th September. It was not a good night for visibility, for a moon shone above thin, low clouds and there were patches of mist drifting on the surface of the sea. We rounded the southeast coast of Kalimnos and set off northward towards the coast of Turkey.

About midnight when I was on watch peering through the mist ahead, I suddenly saw a small black object almost dead ahead. I took it to be a floating mine or a rock quite close. I ordered hard aport to take me away from the land to starboard but as the bows started to swing, I realized my mistake: it was not a mine or rock quite close, it was the black bow of a caique rather farther away but not far enough away to avoid the likelihood of collision. The caique had seen us and altered course to starboard and we were closing fast — no time to take further avoiding action, I just hoped to cross her bows. In the end she struck ML 355 a glancing blow as she passed down my starboard side and she put a small hole in my planking just above the waterline.

I circled round to come alongside her to see whether she had suffered damage. I expected to be greeted by a stream of abuse in Greek by some frightened fishermen but all I got was a voice asking me in English why the hell didn't I look where I was going. Yes, he was all right, and if only I would take my noisy and smelly boat away they could all settle down to sleep again. Clearly some raiding party returning from some assignment but I never found out who they were or where they came from. We were just two blacked-out ships who did not quite pass on a dark night.

It was daylight when we passed throught the narrow strait that separates Samos from the mainland of Turkey. It seemed a strange strip of water — a dividing line between a world at war and world at peace. In waters like that I expected to be shot at from both sides but we saw no one and we heard nothing as we passed through the rocks which lie like stepping stones between the two shores.

We sailed up the east coast of Samos, rounded the northeast corner and entered the large and attractive bay which opens onto the northern shore of the island. We entered the harbour area which serves the main town of the island and approached the jetty on the port hand as you enter the bay. To my surprise, MLs 349 (Lt. Cdr. Ball) and 354 (Lt. Patterson) were lying alongside the jetty. I had no idea they would be in Samos but it appears that general dispersal was ordered after the day of bombing in Leros and those two had come north bringing stores and troops. To prevent a dangerous concentration of MLs, I anchored in the harbour well away from 349 and 354 after I had landed the Greek troops. Being away from the jetty also helped to conceal my raiding party of SBS. One never knew who on shore might be supporters of the enemy, either by political conviction or by the persuasion of money, and able to pass on information with the aid of a simple wireless transmitter.

The western side of this natural inlet is hilly and green, and partly wooded slopes run right down to the sea. There were few houses there. The town and the harbour area are on the east side. The quay is quite long and well-built: several caiques of various sizes lay alongside it and the shops and houses on the landward side of the quay looked well-kept and gave the appearance of a prosperous and well planned town.

The only armed men to be seen were very villainous-looking irregulars who carried long cartridge belts over their shoulders and had knives and at least one pistol in their waistbands. They seemed to be called 'Andartes' and they had only recently come into the town from positions in the hills from which they had been harrassing the Italians with a guerilla war. It was said that they also harrassed some of the Greeks, so perhaps these were the so-called 'communists' or 'bandits' who might not necessarily get on well with the Sacred Heart battalion we had just landed at the town jetty.

Our raid on Khios was planned to start that evening, 29th September, and during that day the SBS were checking kit and arms and the rubber boats which were to get them ashore. Some of the men had captured German hand-guns and light machine-guns which they preferred to the standard British issue. I was very happy to hear from Captain Milner Barry that his men had told him that they liked ML 355 and had confidence that we would play our part well in getting them on — and off! — the island of Khios.

The hole in our side, caused by the unfortunate incident with the caique, was repaired by screwing the side of a wooden box over it.

The point of the landing was chosen: a small bay in the southwest of the island. This left the party a long trek to Khios town but those who had to go ashore (and also had to make the trek) considered that it would be unwise to try to land any nearer to the centre of population which was thought to be held by the Germans. Lt. Cdr. Ball in 349 arranged a plan by which all three MLs would leave harbour at dusk and set a course east towards Turkey. After dark, ML 355 would detach and turn about to steer west for Khios and after a delay of an hour or two, MLs 349 and 354 would return to Samos. This piece of elaboration was designed to confuse any watchers and spies on the shore and avoid the enemy being given warning of our intention to land on Khios.

The Alan Ball plan was carried out and in due course ML 355 was alone steering west for Khios on a moonlit but cloudy night. Travelling by sea in that part of the Aegean around the Dodecanese is rather like going down a wide city street with the islands representing blocks of buildings. One takes 'first on the left and second on the right' between the islands in much the same way as a taxi driver, and as one goes down the street-like channel one wonders how many people are watching from the islands just like inquisitive neighbours peering around the lace curtains in their windows.

We were now among islands not occupied by friendly faces. We were passing Ikaria to the south of us before we reached Khios on our starboard bow to the northwest. We had already been warned about the unfriendly inhabitants of Ikaria by the Italian MS boat

Captain when we made our fruitless attempt to find a German ship on its southern shore. The channel between Ikaria and Khios is at least 25 miles across but the mountains of each island seemed in the moonlight to tower out of the water much closer than that, and we could imagine unfriendly eyes picking out the wake of our darkened ship as we made our best speed towards the bay for landing. We found the right bay and the right beach and we put the SBS patrol ashore at midnight with the aid of our dinghy and the rubber boats. We arranged to pick them up again forty-eight hours later.

It was the night of 29th/30th September and it seemed a year away from our last visit to land and bring off Army personnel and Cretans from the south coast of Crete. It was in fact only three weeks from our Crete-Tobruk run on the night of 7th/8th September. This Khios landing was just the kind of operation my crew were trained to do and they felt confident and proud veterans of such operations. Conditions should be more favourable for us here — we did not have the 200-mile voyage to and from Crete with its exposure to many hours of daylight. Yet I felt very uneasy.

It was true that the navigational problems in the Dodocanese were much lighter and the enemy forces on the smaller islands were much weaker than those on the 'Iron Ring' of Rhodes, Scarpanto and Crete, but as we turned away from Khios and set course for Samos, I realized the different situation we were in and why I felt uneasy. There was no base nearer than Cyprus or Alexandria which could be considered safe and they were more than 500 miles away. How was I to know whether Samos would still be in our hands when I returned? Perhaps Leros would have been flattened by bombing? Where would I get my next supply of petrol and would we have to sell our clothes to buy food? How could I promise that troop of SBS that I would be back in forty-eight hours? Castles were being built on sand and the tide might wash them away at any time. Operating behind enemy lines is not easy for ships — even for small ships. They have not the facility for concealment that the Army has, and they need more than food and water to keep going.

As daylight came and in a calm sea we approached the north of Samos, my dark thoughts of the night melted away. With a blue sky and morning sun, the white houses stood out on the green fields, so much more fertile than the rocks of Leros. We were surrounded by peace and cheerfulness which with the smell of breakfast being cooked down below brought us happily to our anchorage.

We waited at anchor in the harbour of Samos town to make the return trip to Khios. Enemy air activity was increasing. Several planes went over the harbour but they were quite high and did not appear a menace to us. Nevertheless, I imagined that some of them took photos and I tried to estimate the time it would take for them to get back to Greece, develop the negatives and send off a few planes to deal with the ML seen in Samos harbour. I probably over-estimated our importance or the availability of German planes because no attack was made on us.

For some of the time we lay at the quay alongside the caiques — perhaps they would help to hide our identity — and we were able to walk around the small town. We did business with a wine merchant and purchased some of the Samos wines which we thought to be excellent. When we did get back to Cyprus, our empty bottles of Samos wine caused great excitement among the Cypriots: they were proof that we had been in an island which for four years had been out of contact with them and held by the enemy. The inhabitants of Samos regarded us curiously but they showed no great delight at our presence. In this they showed good sense, for who was to know whether we would stay, or be able to stay, and who might be the next to carry guns in the streets of their town? The obvious lack of strength in our expedition demonstrated to them the likelihood that we were only temporary visitors.

After a rest in autumn sunshine (and the unusual luxury of a night's sleep), we left again for Khios on the evening of 1st October. Again it seemed a lonely and misty voyage past ghostly islands, watched by unfriendly eyes. At midnight we lay off the beach once more with dinghy and rubber boats at the ready as we waited for a signal from the shore. The signal came and the boats set off. Then a strange thing happened: another flashing lamp showed from farther along the bay and one of our boats, with the redoubtable Oliver Ford rowing, made for the second light. The whole of the SBS platoon were embarked from the nearer beach where the first signal was made and Oliver Ford returned to report no one on the farther beach although he heard a voice as he rowed ashore. Who had made the second signal and who was watching us in the darkness? With everyone safely on board we lost no time in getting away, no shots came from the shore and no ambush was laid for us at sea.

Captain Milner Barry told us of an exhausing trek over difficult country, moving only by night and hiding by day. They made a reconnaisance of Khios town and of the German positions there, and had to return at breakneck speed over the same hills and gullies to be able to meet us at the agreed time. He did not think they were pursued but some of the Greek inhabitants must have known of their movements and perhaps it was they who had been hiding in the rocks, half-friendly and half-afraid, to watch our departure.

The next day we spent once again in Samos and it was the day for us all to clean guns. Again, Milner Barry told me how well his men liked working with ML 355 and enjoyed the happy relationship on board.

When night came, we set course south and made an uneventful voyage to Kalimnos, but passage in the dark, through the narrow strait between Samos and Turkey, is an experience not to be forgotten. It seems narrow enough to spit across and there are one or two large slabs of rock protruding from the sea. These make small low islands which, in the dark and in those times of apprehension, looked like German E-boats waiting for us. Adrian Seligman in his excellent book, '*No Stars to Guide*,' also mentions these small islands of rock and the shock they gave him when he also passed through the strait at night.

In view of what was happening in the southern Aegean at that time, it was fortunate that we followed the coast of Turkey southwards during the night and struck westward towards Kalimnos only just before daybreak. We did not know then that a considerable force of German ships had set sail from Greece and was steering eastwards past Naxos. The existence of this force was known to the Navy, and destroyers were north of the Kasos straits between Crete and Scarpanto, hoping to intercept this German force which was wrongly thought to be carrying reinforcements for Rhodes. To be south and west of Kalimnos that night would not have been healthy. Luckily, we were to the east.

In the early morning of 2nd October, 1943 we secured alongside the jetty at Kalimnos and our SBS troops went ashore to their headquarters. Kalimnos was not the peaceful place it was when we left it only a few days before on 28th September. To the south, the island of Cos, and particularly its airstrip at Antimachia, were being bombed; and to the north, the harbour of Portolago in Leros was being bombed. All day German planes were flying overhead on the way to drop their bombs or on the way back to re-load with more bombs. The noise of bombing carried across the water from the north and from the south like a continuous thunderstorm.

We were the only ML in Kalimnos that day. We were a small but an undisguised target and surely one of the planes passing overhead would break off and give us a burst of gunfire even if he had no bombs left to drop on us. Luckily, the orders to the German airmen were to bomb Leros and Cos and they were sufficiently well-disciplined to do just that and fly over us in unbroken formations. Beside us on the jetty there was an Italian post with a 20mm Breda gun and we sat with them all day waiting for an attack which did not come. Twice I left to take a walk into the town but returned to ML 355 at the double as another formation of German aircraft appeared over the hills and flew across the harbour.

The night brought quiet and sleep was possible — and needed — but as the gentle light of dawn crept into the sky, there arose an uniterrupted crash of gunfire, bombs and explosions which brought us all on deck within seconds. This frightening noise was not, as we first thought, all around us; it came from Cos a few miles to the south and as we looked out of the harbour entrance we could see the flash of guns and bombs.

As light increased, we could see ships between us and the shore of Cos — many ships and with aircraft circling over them. We were looking at a German invasion force: the force known to be at sea and wrongly thought to be bound for Rhodes. There were several troop transports, landing craft, two destroyers, E-boats with torpedoes and R-boats with guns, all covered by fighter aircraft. Yesterday's bombing had made sure that no Allied fighters could take off from Cos to challenge them. This was the bitter blow which was to put an end to any hopes of air cover in the Aegean and although we may not have recognized it at the time, we were watching the end of any possibility of success in the present Aegean adventure.

Ramseyer came running down from the Commando headquarters in the old castle: 'What are you going to do?' he asked. 'Can you have a crack at them?'

The decision was entirely mine and there was no time to reflect on it. Whether I went out and 'had a crack at them' or not this was no place to be: bottled up in Kalimnos harbour with a German fleet outside. At any moment part of the German force might be diverted to attack and capture Kalimnos and we would be caught in the harbour. As to an attack: this was a decision which has to be made time after time in warfare. Should one attack a superior force? Yes, if there can be an element of surprise or if the enemy is disorganized. Yes, as a last resort and as an alternative to surrender. There could be no suprise. I would have to make half an hour's dash across open sea in daylight before my guns would come within range. The smaller craft were the only ones I could successfully attack and they were close to the shore of Cos with the larger ships between us. The German fighters overhead would attack me first and if they did not stop me, the destroyers and other larger ships could easily finish me off before I could reach a worthwhile target. An heroic dash would, I decided, promise little reward and certain destruction. The object must be to avoid capture and so I decided to get out of Kalimnos but not to commit suicide. Athough I was sure I was doing the right thing, I nevertheless felt ashamed of myself for not getting involved. A French general said that the charge at Balaclava was 'magnificent but it was not war.' My charge would not have been sensible warfare and I don't think it would even be called magnificent.

The Commando forces decided to evacuate some of their garrison including Brigadier Turnbull, who happened to be in the island, and Lt. Ramseyer. They packed themselves into a large and beautiful Italian motor boat and set off with ML 355 for Leros, hugging the coast as we went and hoping to avoid detection by the planes and the escort ships of the German landing fleet. As we went, I saw an air battle going on as a Beaufighter or perhaps two of them made an attack. They were in turn attacked by Messerschmidts and it appeared to me that one of the Beaufighters was shot down. That did not make me feel happier about leaving.

We were not attacked and arrived at Portolago in Leros in the forenoon of 3rd October. Since we had left on 27th September much had happened there and none of it was good. The boom vessel now appeared to be unmanned. A large vessel was sunk just inside on the port hand and on the other side the wreck of *HMS Intrepid*, badly damaged on 26th September, was beached and abandoned. The jetties, workshops and other buildings around the port had all suffered from further bombing.

The MLs were dispersed to far corners of the harbour. Lt. Cdr. Ball (349) and Jim Patterson (354) were still in Samos so the Leros contingent other than myself was 351 (Lt Hallows), 356 (Lt. Lloyd), 358 (Lt. Mitchelson) and 836 (Lt. Bert Clark). There was no one to give us any berthing instructions, nor were they necessary. I found a small cove on the north side of the large bay and on the seaward (western) side of the main jetties. Lt. Ramseyer and some Army passengers were asleep in the wardroom bunks and so I had no place to put my feet up. I was happy, however, to sit on the side of the bridge watching the scene on quite a pleasant morning and sniffing the sweet smell of a very late breakfast coming up from the galley.

Suddenly — a bang-bang from the hills and over them swept a wave of German bombers dropping down into the vast space of the harbour and each one singling out his target as he came. There was plenty of fire directed at them from the shore batteries and the ships (and of these the MLs were a significant part) but the enemy had the advantage of surprise. I very soon realized that one of the planes had chosen us as his target: he came directly towards us and there was no other target near us which he could be aiming at. He was low and the nose of his plane seemed to have eyes fixed only on us.

Our guns missed him, no doubt about it, and that might have cost us our lives for out of the belly of the plane I saw one large black bomb fall. Within seconds as I watched the descent of this black object — and there was nothing we at anchor could do to avoid it — I knew we were safe: it was going over and feeling very brave, very confident and even nonchalant, I watched it fly overhead and fall about twenty yards directly astern. You could say that I might have read the serial number and maker's name as it went over.

It exploded just under the water and the stern of the ML was lifted up and fell back again with a crash of everything breakable on board. Up from the wardroom hatch came my visitors like rabbits chased out of their burrow by a ferret damanding indignantly to know why they had been so roughly flung out of their bunks.

We had our breakfast in peace but with our ears on the alert for any further sound of aeroplanes. The dinghy was then lowered and I rowed to the main jetty.

The quayside and the surroundings were badly damaged but not so flattened that they did not expect — and get — further attention from the Luftwaffe. All orderliness had gone and any civilians had taken to the hills. The Italians were either at their gun sites or in the vast complex of tunnels dug into the hillside behind the harbour jetties.

An Italian depot ship had been SBNOA's headquarters and I

cannot recall whether on that morning she was still afloat; if she was, then it was not for long that she remained so. She was at some time sunk at her moorings. Naval Headquarters had shifted to a house inland from the harbour and with other ML officers who had come ashore for orders, we were all making our way there when another raid developed. It was the same as any other raid which seems only sound and fury unless you are singled out for attack, but I clearly remember lying on the ground under some trees and watching the circling planes among the burst of anti-aircraft shells. It reminded me that Constance and I had done this in the summer of 1940 in England as we watched and sheltered from the raids on London. Over three years later and I was still doing the same thing. Not much progress, I thought.

There had once been several Italian sea planes moored at the extreme inshore end of the harbour. Former raids had reduced the number and this raid accounted for the last two. Both were now on fire and were ending their days in a spectacular display of fire and smoke. Very many enemy planes passed over us on that uneasy day but most were bound for Cos where the battle for the island was being fought.

As there were no direct attacks in the afternoon, we made a visit to the water boat which had been moored near the boom and then abandoned by its Italian crew. Petty Officer Gardner, our Motor Mechanic, and his fellow engineers — still known as stokers in the Navy although they had nothing to stoke but a petrol engine — had a very interesting time finding out how to work the water pumps and how to connect the hoses, but they fixed things in the end and we filled up with water which caused us no trouble when we drank it. Next to petrol, water was our greatest worry and we were grateful to the Italians for the large stocks of both liquids which they held in Leros.

So much went on in the daytime that the passage of time became unnoticed and every twenty-four hours contained a night's work without a restful day. We had not attacked the German fleet off Cos in the morning of 3rd October, and nobody blamed us for that, but SBNOA did think that when darkness fell we should have a better chance of inflicting some damage without being destroyed ourselves. So, would we please go back to the invasion beaches on the north shore of Cos and see what we could find and, if it was German, shoot at it.

When darkness came, MLs 355 and 836 set off to carry out a

close inshore sweep along the northern and western beaches of Cos, and this we did. The enemy forces had been very efficiently landed during the morning of 3rd October and the shipping which carried them with escorting destroyers (said to be two German-manned ex-Italian ships) and other escorts must have made off quickly towards mainland Greece or Crete or Rhodes, for the shores on which several thousand troops had landed that day were now deserted. Just as we regarded the daytime as dangerous because of the enemy dominance in the air, the Germans probably regarded the night as a bad time to be at sea. Our destroyers from North Africa continued to make night sweeps in the Aegean in the hope of catching an enemy convoy as they had done on the night of 18th September, which led to our adventures in Stampalia on the following nights.

We went in really close to the beaches of Cos in a night of good visibility and had a look at the shore as well as the sea. There was nothing there at all. In the middle of the night, ML 836 came close alongside and asked me on the loud-hailer to check his list of current identification signals. I did this, replying through my loud-hailer and I thought that anyone on shore for several miles away could have heard us giving the identification signal for the day. Had the Germans left a destroyer to guard the beaches, we should not have felt so brave but finding no big ships we searched the length of the coast for a target. We stayed rather too long in our search and were far too far from Leros for my liking when daylight came. But we both returned having neither attacked nor been attacked.

The next event was of a different kind. There were to be some changes in command. The first step in these was rather dramatic. Lieut. Norman Stallworthy RNVR (who had at one time been my No. 1 in ML 355) arrived from Casteloriso in an Italian sea plane and in daylight! It was, he told me, a hair-raising ride with the pilot wave-hopping and hedge-hopping at almost zero height and the eyes of all on board swivelling around on the look-out for Messerschmidts. He arrived in a cloud of spray and anxiety in the harbour with orders to take over command of ML 354 from Lieut. Jim Patterson. Patterson was to take over ML 355 from me and I was to take over ML 349 from Lt. Cdr Ball who was ordered to return to Alexandria.

This move was a very sad one for me. I had been in command of ML 355 since taking her over from Lieut. Rob Young in Alexandria on 3rd July 1942. I had the greatest respect for my crew.

I regarded them all as my friends and no one could ask for a finer team. The Coxswain, P.O. Blythe, was a tower of strength and was awarded the DSM for his work with me in 355.

Also, to reinforce a good crew ML 355 had acquired, by the enterprise of the crew and quite unofficially, more armament than the other MLs — two Italian Breda 20mm guns and two Browning 0.5″ machine guns in addition to an ML's normal armament at that time. Against the sadness of this change, I had the satisfacton of promotion to Senior Officer of the 42nd ML Flotilla which carried with it the extra half-stripe of a Lieut. Commander. Promotion is not to be regarded as a bad thing even if there were no pay days for us in Leros.

It was my immediate task as a newly-promoted Senior Officer to review with SBNOA the operational effectiveness of the MLs now present and based on Leros.

The harbour facilities had been so badly damaged by the bombing that repairs to the MLs, which at first had been so willingly and so well done in the Italian workshops, were now impossible and the skilled men all seemed to have disappeared. With continued bombing and scarce supplies of fuel, it was agreed that keeping in Leros any ML which was not fully operational made no sense. It would be better to send them back to Cyprus or Beirut for repairs and hope for their speedy return to relieve those who remained and who in turn would need repairs and rest.

So ML 355 (now with Lt. Patterson in command) left in the first week of October towing ML 351 (Lt. Ken Hallows) whose propeller shafts had never recovered from striking an uncharted and probably very recent wreck in the harbour.

I watched the departure of 355 with sadness. To me this ML had a personality: she had been a home to me for over a year.

ML 355 towed ML 351 over 600 miles all the way back to Alexandria via Kapi cove, Casteloriso and Paphos in Cyprus. The tow parted twice and was replaced in the night while passing enemy-held Cos and Rhodes but they were not detected or attacked.

ML 356 (Lt. Lloyd) and ML 358 (Lt. Mitchelson) also with engine defects followed soon afterwards and I was left in Leros with ML 349, in which I had Sub. Lieut. Livesey as my No. 1, ML 354 with the newly-arrived Lt. Stallworthy in command, and ML 836 with the experienced and unflappable Lt. Bert Clark in command and Sub. Lt. Warne as his No. 1.

I learned when I took over 349, that Alan Ball was a sick man and had been recalled for medical treatment. I had not seen much of him in the past as I was detached from his Flotilla but I know he was a well-liked and highly respected seaman: everyone spoke of his skill in ship handling. I have a letter from A.B. Cheetham who was in ML 353 when she was sunk off Tobruk: ML 349 picked up the survivors and although heavily attacked from the air brought them back to Alexandria. Cheetham wrote to say that 'we all owed our lives to Lt. Cdr. Ball.'

For at least some weeks before I took over, Alan Ball must have been very ill. I can imagine few things worse than being seriously ill when in command of a ship which is under attack from the air nearly every day and on patrol at sea nearly every night. However good the other officers and crew, it is the Commanding Officer who by his actions and his leadership establishes the efficiency and personality of the ship. He controls the heart of the ship. If the heart is not strong, morale suffers and ML 349 was not the easiest ML to take over and it was not the easiest time to do so, either.

The invasion of Cos started at daybreak on 3rd October and by nightfall the island was overrun except for a few small pockets of resistance. Most of the British and Italian troops were captured and I believe that some Italian Officers were treated as traitors and executed by firing squad. Those Italians who joined forces with the Allies paid dearly for it and I hope that nothing I have written appears to throw any doubt on Italian courage or resolution. To change one's allegiance is a brave and determined thing to do, which over the centuries has brought terrible retribution to those who have not been successful in defeating their former masters or allies. Many Italians accepted these risks and fought bravely with their new allies. Who can blame those who preferred to keep a low profile and to feel that the war was over for them on 8th September when Italy capitulated.

Some of the Allied troops managed to hide from the Germans for many days after all organized resistance had ceased on Cos. By various means, but mainly by caiques manned by the SBS and the Levant Schooner Flotilla, these troops were evacuated and landed in Turkey. Once in Turkey, they were well treated by the Turks, gathered into small parties and transported to Casteloriso by caiques and other small boats, and then on by larger ships to Cyprus. Captain Milner Barry, whom I had just brought back from his reconnaisance in Khios, was engaged for many nights with his SBS troops in running caiques from Kalimnos to Cos and from

Cos to Turkey on this rescue service.

A few days after the fall of Cos and soon after I had taken command of ML 349, I was ordered to go by night to Bodrum in Turkey to collect a party of Durham Light Infantry who, I was told, had escaped by swimming the eight miles from Cos to Turkey. I wondered whether they did get across by swimming, but the water was warm and somewhere near the middle is a large rock showing just above water where it might have been possible to a have a rest if you could find it in the dark — so the story might have been true.

I left Leros in the evening and went through the Cos strait keeping a good look-out for the rock on the port side and German-held Cos on the starboard side. I had not seen Bodrum in daylight and have not seen it again since. There seemed to be a long appraoch channel until one reached a quayside with the town behind it and a large castle overlooking the harbour. Very conscious that this was neutral Turkey and that they might well disapprove of a foreign warship entering the harbour of one of their important towns on that coast, I switched on my navigation lights and lighted up the ship to show peaceful intentions.

I had been told that the Durham Light Infantry party would be all ready to embark. It was near midnight, all was quiet, very quiet, all was very dark and nothing moved. It looked a deserted town — rather a ghostly town. Feeling a bit of an idiot, I put the ML slowly along the length of the quay and back while using the loud-hailer to ask (in English) if there were any British troops there, and using the searchlight to light up the quayside as we passed. The noise echoed round the hills and the light was startling in the surrounding darkness.

What a liberty! To come into a neutral port at midnight shouting over a loud-hailer and flashing a searchlight about! But nobody answered, nobody even swore at us and no window showed a light. So we backed off and I dropped anchor in the middle of the harbour and waited for daylight. We were up before dawn to see what awaited us: it could have been hostile and angry Turks. We looked around the almost land-locked harbour we were in. There must have been an Army camp near for the hills behind the town were alive with soldiers running up and down the sides with guns, packs and other martial equipment in mock battles or exercises.

Just as I was wondering whether anyone was going to take any notice of us or whether I should have to do some more shouting at the deserted quayside, a motor boat put out from the shore with

Turkish soldiers on board and a smartly dressed officer in charge. He came aboard and I was grateful to find that he could speak quite good English. I told him why I had come to Bodrum and he told me that there had been some British soldiers there but that they had departed in another boat the day before I had arrived. I thanked him and asked his permission to stay in Bodrum until nightfall when I promised to depart. He agreed — all very friendly. Then perhaps I made a mistake because I asked whether I could do anything for him — thinking that he might perhaps suggest that he liked gin or whisky, of which we still had a bottle or two left. Instead of suggesting that, he burst out laughing and he looked around the ML — paintwork dirty, rust on the metal parts, the crew rather scruffily dressed and so on — and he said, 'Perhaps I could do more for you than you can for me.'

I certainly felt ashamed. I have explained why ML 349 was not in good shape when I took over and it certainly showed. I told my No. 1, Twig Livesey, that hard work was the answer — it would get the ship clean and improve morale at the same time. He soon had the crew scrubbing and polishing everything in sight. ML 349 had been in the Aegean away from a base and suffering enemy attacks for over a month. The crew were short of food and drinking water and relying of the sea for washing facilities. Yet the crew and the ship were more unwashed than they need have been, and morale and efficiency required that I should put that right.

We stayed in Bodrum during daylight hours as it would have been asking for trouble to go through the Cos strait before nightfall. When we left after dark we passed quite close to Cos harbour and, as this was only a few days after the capture of Cos by the Germans, we did not know what, if anything, was in the harbour although it would certainly be strongly defended.

Lieut. Ramseyer of the raiding forces had come on this expedition with ML 349 and he said to me as we passed Cos in the darkness: 'Let's go into the harbour and shoot it up.' That seemed to me to be an extremely foolish idea. We did not know the harbour and we did not know what was there. While we looked around with our searchlight, we would make an excellent target. I also thought that the port was probably being used for the embarkation of British and Italian prisoners of war — would I be shooting at them? So we did not enter and attack Cos harbour and Lieut. Ramsayer agreed with my decision.

Back at Leros, Port Laki and Portolago harbour had now been

abandoned by the MLs as a base and by most other ships, too. It was the main target for German air attacks which now came every day and several times each day, and by 20th October only one crane was left operational on the quays. The capture of Cos not only made more German planes available to attack other targets, but it gave them an airfield only some fifty miles away. Italian records give the number of air raids on Leros in the 35 days between 26th September and 31st October as 140 by nearly 1200 aircraft. On 7th October, for example, there were seven raids recorded involving 80 aircraft. There were only the Italian anti-aircraft guns and the guns of ships — now almost solely the MLs who were unlucky enough to be in harbour — to oppose them. The Italian guns were said to be poorly sited with crews very exposed to bombing and to machine-gun and cannon fire. Their gun sites were an early target for the planes and most of them were soon made ineffective.

There are three main harbours in Leros. Port Laki is in the harbour of Protolago which I have already described. Up to the end of September it was the main base for our ships and for destroyers and submarines bringing in troops and supplies. This harbour opens seaward to the west. On the north side is Parteni Bay which was used by some of the Italian ships. It did not suffer in the early days but came in for attention towards the end of September. On 1st October, the Italian destroyer *Euro* was bombed and sank in this bay. On the east coast is Alinda Bay which is quite close to the main town of Leros. Its port facilities were poor; it appeared to be used in peace time mainly for Greek coastal trade in caiques of various sizes. It had no attractions for Naval ships in the early days, but as the facilities in Port Laki were pounded to pieces by bombs and were the main target for continued raids, Alinda Bay was the chosen alternative.

A word seems appropriate about the Italian Naval Forces which were based in Leros and which after 8th September elected to fight with us.

Leros was the base for the 5th Submarine Flotilla of four submarines but none of them was in Leros at the time of Italy's capitulation and they did not return to their base there. The 4th Destroyer Squadron had only one destroyer there, the *Euro*, and she was bombed and sunk on 1st October. Two other destroyers of this squadron were taken over by the Germans in Pireas and used very effectively against us in the invasions of Cos and later of Leros. Eight boats of the 3rd MAS Flotilla were in Leros but they were destroyed one by one with, I believe, only one surviving boat which eventually escaped to Turkey. The 39th Minesweeping Flotilla and some naval auxiliaries were based there, mainly in Parteni Bay, but there were not more than about four ships involved. Finally, there was the 147th Air Force Squadron with Cant Z501 sea planes of which seven were originally serviceable and one by one they were all lost — some in the air but most by cannon fire while anchored at Port Laki. This squadron, however, performed well considering that it was no match for the Luftwaffe, and I was told that its losses in airmen were very heavy.

I visited the headquarters of this Italian Cant Squadron in the early days of October. The headquarters building was at the head of Portolago harbour near the main Italian military buildings and overlooking the sea-plane base. By the time I went there, the building had been bombed and was likely to be bombed again; there was one sea-plane left, the rest were burnt out wrecks. It was a distressing visit. Morale was not only low, it had almost disappeared. The young pilots had no fighting equipment left and they had nothing to do but sit and be bombed and speculate on a very depressing future. They had plenty of wine and there were several women in the mess too, but there was no song and an Italian without a song is a very demoralised Italian. My visit to that defeated mess is an experience I have never forgotten because I was looking at men who had lost heart and hope.

When we returned from our visit to Bodrum we found that Captain Baker, the Senior British Naval Officer Aegean (SBNOA), had set up his headquarters in a small house on the hill at the back of Alinda Bay. The only forces he had in Leros were the MLs and caiques of the Levant Schooner Flotilla. Now that the fighting in Cos was over, it was expected that Leros would be the next target. I believe the evacuation of Leros was considered by the Allied Commander, but it was decided to hold on and hope the island could be defended through the winter. In the spring, the whole future of Aegean operations could be reconsidered. I also understand that the Germans considered holding off their invasion and letting us stay in Leros through the winter but that Hitler himself demanded that Leros should be taken.

During the day, the Luftwaffe ruled the skies; at the end of September and beginning of October some cover was given by long-range fighters from U.S. squadrons in Libya, but this cover ceased on 9th October when the aircraft were ordered to concentrate on operations in the Western Mediterranean. The Beaufighter squadrons based in Cyprus did their best to cover the Naval ships south of Rhodes and in the vicinity of Casteloriso, but were too few and it was too far to give us any help in Leros. By night, the Royal Navy and Allied Greek and Polish destroyers could make a dash into the Aegean, hope to find German shipping and then race south again to get as near to Alexandria as possible before daylight came. In fact, they took great risks in the daylight hours and suffered severe losses. The cruisers *Penelope*, *Carlisle*, *Sirius* and *Aurora* were all bombed and badly damaged during October. In addition to the *Intrepid* and *Queen Olga*, which were sunk in Port Laki harbour, the destroyers *Panther*, *Hurworth* and *Eclipse* were sunk at sea in October and the *Dulverton* in early November. The destoyers *Belvoir*, *Hursley*, *Rockwood* and *Penn* were damaged, and *Adrias* had her bows blown off in that period; three submarines were lost and four damaged. All these fine ships were the supply line and the outer screen, and their loss or damage was suffered in the attempt to prevent a German invasion of islands which for a short time we held with poorly equipped forces. It was largely the German air force which did the damage by daylight bombing, but three destroyers and probably two submarines were the victims of mines.

The inner anti-invasion screen for Leros was the ML flotilla. Every night we were at sea around Leros on the look-out for enemy shipping and to give the first warning of the approach of an invasion fleet. We had no hope of fighting it off, but we could act as a kind of trip wire and at least make a loud noise to alert those onshore. When the invasion finally came on 12th November, it was two MLs who made the first attack and gave the first warning — ML 456 (Lieut. Cdr. Monckton RNR) was hit by gunfire but managed to reach Turkey; ML 358 (Lieut. Lander and Sub. Lieut. Shute) was destroyed by gunfire and only a few of the crew managed to reach shore to become prisoners of war.

On our first visit to our new headquarters in Alinda Bay, not having realized the scale of air attacks now being made even there, we were caught in a heavy raid. I was not at anchor and endeavoured to manoeuvre the ship around to put off the enemy bomb aimer, but found no response from the wheelhouse. On going off the open bridge into the wheelhouse, I found the helmsman lying flat on the wheelhouse floor. Thinking he was dead or wounded, I took the wheel at which he got up saying politely,

'That's my job, sir!' He had panicked and just gone flat on the deck — an example of the morale in my new command which called for some firm words when the raiders had passed.

Whatever I said must have had its effect, for next day we were caught again at Alinda when a Stuka raid developed. They are frightening affairs as the planes scream down to release their bombs as they level out at almost mast height. We made for the harbour entrance as one ugly attacker decided that we were to be his target. All the crew worked splendidly, the bombs missed and as he levelled out just above us, our Rolls gun forward scored a hit on his underside. I saw the flash, and the plane went off eastward towards Turkey making smoke and losing height. We could at least claim a 'probable.' There were many Stukas in that raid and the noise and commotion was considerable. I was looking where we were going and could only see what the Rolls gunner on the foc'sle ahead of me was doing, but I was more than surprised when I found afterwards that we had expended a great quantity of ammunition and the twin Vickers on either side of me, and only a few feet away, had emptied several magazines without my being aware of it. Perhaps we hit more than one plane. I was pleased with the crew and felt we could now give a good account of ourselves; morale went up and the incident of the frightened helmsman was forgotten.

In these few days after the fall of Cos, the heavy air raids sank most of the remaining Italian ships in Portolago and Partheni Bay: the mine-layer *Legnano*, the cargo and support vessels *Prode*, *Porto di Roma* and *Ivorea* and two torpedo boats.

On 7th October there was a German attack on the island of Simi, to the northeast of Rhodes, which had so far been held by a small British force since early September.

While we were fully concerned with our own affairs in Leros, we did not know that a very significant attack had been made on an enemy convoy steaming in our direction. This convoy was first attacked by the submarine *Unruly* and then in the night of 6th/7th October by the cruisers *Penelope* and *Sirius* with the destroyers *Faulknor* and *Fury*.

It was generally expected that Leros would be invaded about 8th or 9th October, and the Royal Navy stepped up patrols to the west of Cos and Leros at great risk and loss to themselves. Up to 9th October when they were withdrawn, the U.S. Air Force Lightnings from Libya did their best to cover the Navy and attacked the German airfield on Cos. The 10th MTB Flotilla under Lieut.

154

Cdr Peter Evensen was brought into the action and on the night of 7th/8th October attacked shipping in Cos harbour.

So on one side there were fierce German air attacks on Leros and attempts by the Germans to build up an invasion fleet. On the other side, the Allies threw in considerable naval forces to find and destroy any invasion fleet and for a short time drew on long-range fighter support from the U.S. Air Force. The result was to cause the Germans to pause and question their plans for the Leros invasion until, at the highest level, it was decided to proceed. We had at least bought time but at a heavy cost.

As a pawn in the defence of Leros, I was not aware of the greater events going on outside. The pattern of life was this: unless some special duty arose, all MLs would be expected to patrol the waters around Leros each night. By day the bombing raids made it necessary for each ML to find a place to hide. Hiding a ship, even one as small as a 112-foot long ML, is not easy, but luckily the coasts of Leros and of the rocky islands nearby provided some opportunities. We tried to find a cliff or narrow inlet with precipitous sides and if an ML could berth alongside an almost sheer face of rock, it would not be easy to see from the air and rather difficult to attack. The Army supplied us with camouflage netting and instructions showing us how to use it to best advantage. The netting spread over us plus a few branches of trees and bushes placed around the deck and a berth alongside a steep cliff were the best we could do to become inconspicuous. It was a very great deal safer than staying in the main harbours of Leros where there was now hardly anything left afloat. The CO of each ML found his own favourite hiding place from which he emerged when night fell and to which he returned as daylight approached.

Communications were not easy. In theory, we could pass coded messages by radio but it was one of the constant troubles in the Aegean that the mountainous islands and high land surrounding the region caused breaks in the ability to receive signals and this was so much worse if one was sheltering under a cliff. So, frequently, orders had to be obtained by coming to Alinda Bay at dawn or dusk to receive instruction by word of mouth.

The SBNOA, Captain Baker, was now at his headquarters in a small house overlooking Alinda Bay and I was instructed as Senior Officer of the Flotilla to be with him at that H.Q. during the day. So ML 349 used to bring me into the bay in the morning before going off to conceal herself for the day and then pick me up in the evening for the night patrol.

At the headquarters, Captain Baker had a very small staff including representatives of the Army and of the raiding forces. When the German planes came over on their raids, we would all evacuate the house, which stood almost alone on the hillside and looked very conspicuous, and dive into a fairly deep ditch in the field alongside. Unfortunately the nearest building, almost the only other building anywhere near, was a small Greek church which stood close to this ditch. I use the word 'unfortunately' because the church was used, as one would expect, for burial services. That would not have been a problem had not the air attacks caused gravediggers to take to the hills; but that did not stop people bringing their dead to the church where they lay untended and unburied for so long that the area around the church became most unpleasant.

The Levant Schooner Flotilla carried on their cloak and dagger operations in the surrounding islands and Lieut. Cdr. Adrian Seligman also visited the Alinda headquarters. The old coastal puffer *Hedgehog* which Lieut. Brian Coleman had brought up from Casteloriso in the early days with stores and troops had also been in Leros but in recent days had been sent off on a mission to the island of Levitha with Sub-Lieut. Harding in command. In the Alinda Bay headquarters one morning, we received a signal from him just saying *'Hedgehog* dying' and later in the day another signal saying '*Hedgehog* dead.' Later on we had news that, perhaps because her engine had failed, *Hedgehog* had been sunk in Levitha and Harding and the crew had been captured.

Contact had to be maintained with Port Laki on the other side of the island and we had a jeep to make the journey. Sometimes I went and it was not an enjoyable ride. On one occasion we found a bomb lying in the middle of the road; we had no idea how it could have got there or how long it had been there and we had no intention of playing about with it. It was worrying enough going very slowly as quietly as possible round the side of it.

On another such ride we were caught on the road in an air attack and the man who was driving was so keen on watching the planes that he drove into a ditch. That left us pushing and shoving a ditched jeep alongside a treeless open road with hostile planes passing over: it was not a comfortable few minutes but they left us alone and we rescued the jeep.

The ML force was now being changed in a reasonably orderly fashion. ML 355 (Lt. Patterson) had left on 3rd October towing

351 (Lt. Hallows) and she was followed a few days later by 356 (Lt. Lloyd) and 358 (Lt. Mitchelson). All these MLs had some damage and were bound for Alexandria or Beirut for repair. In replacement, ML 835 (Lt. Close, a Tasmanian VR) arrived and, on 12th October, ML 359 arrived (Lt. Geoff Whittam). Others were expected from the 24th ML Flotilla which had recently arrived from the UK after making the long and hazardous passage from the UK via Gibralter and Malta under the expert navigation of their Senior Officer, Lt. Cdr. Monckton RNR.

On the night of the 8th/9th October, which was at one time expected to be the date of the German invasion of Leros, and on a night of nervousness and apprehension, occurred the extraordinary incident of the *Alessandro Volta*. The eastern side of Leros was that night being patrolled by three MLs. The northern one was ML 835, ML 836 was the centre boat and I was with ML 349 at the south end of the line of three. We did not know it at the time but the sea to the west of Leros was being covered by the cruiser *Carlisle* and some destroyers, so seriously was the invasion expected that night. It was when returning from that night's work that the destroyer *Panther* was sunk and the long career of the *Carlisle* was ended by the heavy damage she received from the continued air attacks. Meanwhile, we three MLs on the eastern side patrolled slowly up and down, being as far as we knew the only guardians of Leros and rather puzzled as to why we had been assigned to patrol that side of the island.

Suddenly, in the early hours of the morning, a radio call came from ML 835 to say that he was engaging a large enemy ship. That meant only one thing — he needed help! So joining ML 836, we set off hastily northward to find ML 835 and as we did so, we had a further signal from Lt. Close to say that the enemy ship had run aground on a small island and he was standing by.

When we reached the place, there was indeed a large ship with its bows well up on the side of what was more like a large rock than a small island. It was still dark but I could make out guns on the deck including one fairly large one, about 4-inch, aft. The guns, however, did not seem to be trained on us and were in a neat fore and aft position.

Telling MLs 835 and 836 to stand by, I started to close in, watching those guns very carefully! We had a motor mechanic on board who was a German Jew trained in the Mercedes works at Stuttgart, so I brought him up out of the engine room and as I

157

closed in to a few hundred yards, I put him on our loud-hailer and told him to ask, 'Do you surrender?' in German and if no reply was received to say, 'Send your captain over in your boat.'

No reply to the question or the instruction! No movement at all! There was light beginning to show in the eastern sky, we could not be caught out in daylight. Surely the beached ship would have sent word to the Germans of its plight and the next thing we could expect would be the Luftwaffe. 'Right,' I said, 'No. 1, prepare a boarding party' and for the second time in a few weeks (the first being in Stampalia on 18th October) I had ranged on deck my No. 1 with steel helmet and revolver and the six largest of our crew, also with steel helmets and side arms, while all others available stood by the machine guns and Oerlikons.

The stern of the target ship was lower in the water, the bows being on the rock, and I judged that water deep enough for us could only be guaranteed at the stern. I went in fast alongside the stern and then rang down full astern as soon as we touched. The boarding party went over the side and onto the deck of the ship with a traditional shout to encourage themselves and discourage the enemy.

Then a most extraordinary thing happened — as our boarding party hit the deck on the port side, the crew of the ship jumped over into the water on the starboard side where they swam the few yards to the shore and clambered up the rocks.

Back came my No. 1, Livesey, with the revelation that the ship and crew were not German but Italian. It was the submarine depot ship *Alessandro Volta* which had sailed out of Partheni Bay and appeared to be making for the Turkish coast or Samos. As we had not been informed, it is probable that they sailed without orders and, a German invasion being expected, just decided to 'Get to hell out of it.' It was bad luck that they encountered ML 835 whom they assumed to be part of the German invasion fleet. The assumption that our MLs were German naval ships was, to them, confirmed when my motor mechanic ordered them to surrender in his fluent German. They had no wish to confront a ruthless German boarding party which explained their hasty departure over the far side when we came aboard.

By now it was getting light. To stay to try to sort things out would take time and time spent at sea in the daylight meant almost certain attack from the air. I ordered the MLs back to Leros at full speed. I was landed at Alinda Bay and the MLs did their best to hide themselves in rocky inlets nearby.

I was not at all popular at the base. The Captain of *Alessandro Volta* had already radioed to protest about the attack on his ship, the boarding of his ship and the looting and damage caused by our crew. And, of course, he was angry beyond measure at being left sitting on a large rock in the Aegean.

As a kind of punishment I was ordered to return in daylight to the aforesaid rock to escort a small Italian ship which would bring back the captain and his crew to Leros. I suppose we had to do our best to remain on good terms with, and to encourage our new Italian allies and so we had to treat with utmost respect the complaints of the captain of the *Alessandro Volta* and in no way suggest to him that he was suffering from his own unauthorized dash to escape from Leros while it was still possible. Even so, I thought my mission to go back to the ship in daylight was almost suicidal and that we were sacrificing an ML in order to placate the Italians who could well have waited until nightfall for their rescue from their Valkyrian rock.

We were very lucky. It was on that day that great battles were being fought to the south of us. All the planes that the Germans had available were attacking the *Carlisle* and the *Panther* as they tried to return to Alexandria from their sweep to the west of Leros on the preceding night. The Beaufighters from Cyprus and the US Lightnings from Libya were trying to protect these ships and to attack the airfields from which the Luftwaffe were making their attacks. These were great battles with heavy losses on both sides and nobody noticed a small ship and an ML bringing back an Italian crew from a wreck on a large rock to the north of Leros.

We brought them all back to Alinda Bay in full daylight. I was sad to see that some of the Italians were quite badly wounded by the gunfire from ML 835: they were landed and taken to the Leros hospital. My crew had taken the opportunity to 'acquire' a typewriter and some binoculars while they were aboard the *Volta* and these were duly returned to the captain of that ship. On the next day, the Luftwaffe did come over and made sure that the *Alessandro Volta* was completely destroyed.

That incident over, we were back to the patrols by night and my spending agitated days at the cottage on the hill above Alinda Bay with hourly visits to the ditch near the church where the disgusting smell of decomposing flesh grew stronger every day. There was quite a fascination in watching bombs drop out of planes

159

as one lay in the ditch and feeling fairly confident that there was hardly any chance that direct hit would be registered on that ditch.

A night or two after the *Alessandro Volta* incident, MLs 349 and 836 were on patrol to the north of Leros on a bright moonlit night when two planes came over and then turned back, obviously to have another look at us. They were not very high and I put them down as Wellington bombers and therefore friendly. However, it soon appeared that one was manoeuvering to pass right over us and the next thing we knew was a bomb or two landing rather too close. Having started on us, he came back and had another run while I zig-zagged about hoping to make him miss which he duly did. I was so sure that he was 'one of ours' that I did not fire at him, I just assumed he was making a mistake and if I fired back that would double the number of mistakes.

ML 836 was pursued and bombed by the other plane and he got so tired of it that he did open fire quite effectively and discouraged further action.

On reporting next morning, I was shown a signal which should have arrived the evening before and if it had would have stopped our sailing that night. The signal said that RAF patrols would be out in strength and would attack all shipping seen in the Aegean that night — all Allied ships should, therefore, stay in harbour. I have said before that communications in this campaign were, for us, very bad indeed. Sometimes it was because wireless reception was unreliable in the islands and sometimes it was due to error, confusion or enemy action. Most of the time we MLs had no idea what the rest of the Navy was doing and the activities of the Air Force and the Army were equally unknown unless we could see them with our own eyes.

On 11th October we lost ML 835. I found the details difficult to obtain because I did not have the opportunity to see Lt. Close, the CO of ML 835 before he went back to Cyprus after the ML was lost. Strangely enough, the most detailed account I had was published in the *Evening Standard* of 17th December, 1943, a copy of which was kept for me by my family and given to me on my return to the UK. From this report, ML 835 was attacked by Junkers 88's at sea. He reached an anchorage but was attacked again. The engines were put out of action and their ammunition exhausted. They were still trying to get the engines to work when they were hit by machine gun and cannon fire and eventually blew up. ML 836 rescued the crew; Lt. Close and motor mechanic

Chandler were wounded but not too seriously.

Just after this loss, ML 359 arrived in Leros. On that night ML 349 was berthed against some rocks under a cliff near the entrance to Alinda Bay. We must have been having a night's rest which was unusual. A look-out posted on the rocks reported a boat approaching the bay and it was soon clear that it was coming into the bay. Had it been hostile we were in an ideal position to have shot it to pieces as we were hidden against the cliff and the newcomer was clearly visible against the night sky. But we had no reason to get excited as it could easily be identified as an ML and as she passed us only about 100 yards away, we just gave her a hail and said 'What ship?' Having identified each other, she came alongside and Geoff Whittam was delighted to have found a friendly face so quickly.

I told him what went on and what he would be expected to do. Afterwards he told me that I warned him to expect 'some air activity' and he thought I had made the understatement of the year (or of the war). He had camouflage nets and I told him that as soon as there was daylight he must find a berth beside a cliff, put nets over himself, keep quiet and wait for orders.

This hiding under camouflage during the day gave our COs an interesting problem of morale. Some thought that the ML should be abandoned for the day — put the nets over, go ashore into the rocks and sleep because the ML was an indefensible target which could not really fight off an air attack. Others thought that it would be bad for morale to take this view: we should always be prepared to defend the ship and we should always believe that it could be defended even when immobile alongside a rock. I took the view that the crew must be prepared to stay with and defend their ship, and I always saw to it that the guns would not be hampered by the netting and bushes we put on board to disguise ourselves.

The conditions in which we lived and worked did not permit the Commanding Officers to discuss such matters and as Senior Officer I was unable to do any more than act as the assistant to Captain Baker (the SBNOA) in operational matters. After the loss of Cos which saw the start of almost continuous bombing of Leros, there was no opportunity for the COs of MLs to meet and my communication was either via an R/T link when signals had to be kept short and cryptic or by a shouted message in the night if we happened to be near.

I remember that Lt. Mitchelson complained to me later that I did not give him adequate orders or instructions and I have often wondered what more I could have done. We had the briefest of operational orders, little knowledge of what was going on around us and we were left to our own devices to obtain water, food, ammunition and a place to berth the ship during the day.

Unknown to us there were many other actions going on. Up to 12th/13th October caiques were still taking our troops off Cos and landing them in Turkey. The island of Simi was evacuated by British troops as it was felt that the small force, which had already beaten off one attack, would not continue to do so with the growing strength of the Germans now well-established in Cos. The islands of Calchi and Levitha were occupied by German troops on 18th and 19th October. There were still sweeps into the Aegean by cruisers and destroyers from Alexandria and we had no warnings of these. I am glad we did not encounter them. If it was due to the good staff work by SBNOA, then I am grateful to him that we did not have a night encounter with our own forces who in those waters would certainly have shot first and asked questions afterwards.

There was an occasion which I will relate now although I believe it occurred later in the campaign when ML 359 (Lt. Geoff Whittam) encounterd the cruiser *Phoebe* off Rhodes and neither ship knew the other was in the vicinity. ML 359 flashed a recognition signal but, for reasons I do not know, it was the wrong signal. *Phoebe* opened fire but appeared to think ML 359 was a destroyer some distance off instead of an ML quite close. All the fire from the cruiser's guns roared over Whittam's head. He in turn concluded that the cruiser must be the enemy to behave so belligerently when he had given what he thought to be the correct recognition signal. So the ML opened fire on *Phoebe* and his 20mm Oerlikons scored hits on *Phoebe's* bridge. Somehow, the shooting was stopped before lives were lost and the Captain of *Phoebe* was good enough to send in a report saying, 'While I deplore the error in the recognition signals, I admire the spirit with which I was engaged.'

There was a sequel to that story. Geoff Whittam was an artist in civilian life. He illustrated books and undertook advertising contracts and so on. After the war he was asked to supply illustrations for a book to be published (he told me it was called *'Stoker R.N.'*) and on reading the text Geoff Whittam found that the writer was serving in *Phoebe* at the time of her engagement with ML 359. Moreover, one of the duties of that stoker was to look after the ship's bread making machine and he was attending to that machine when an Oerlikon shell from 359 came through the side and put his beloved bread making machine out of action.

On 16th October, ML 354 (Lt. Stallworthy) was attacked and bombed. She was not hit but the near misses caused enough damage for ML 354 to be ordered back to Cyprus and Beirut for repairs. She had been in the Aegean since 12th September and had served in the waters around Leros for 35 difficult days and nights.

New supplies for the garrison and further reinforcements were now restricted because MLs and caiques were the only surface ships to come into Leros. More help was sent by submarine and *HMS Severn* made the underwater journey to land Bofors guns, ammunition, stores and petrol on 21st October.

On the night of 22nd October another severe blow was suffered by the destroyers who were still doing their best to carry out night patrols and avoid daytime exposure by operating from the neutral waters of Turkey. They avoided air attack in this way but the Germans were now laying mines, and on 22nd October the destroyers *Adrias* and *Hurworth* struck mines to the south of Leros. *Hurworth* sank but by a remarkable feat, the Greek *Adrias* which had her bows blown off was able to reach Turkey where she was at first beached and eventually reached Alexandria under her own steam on 6th December.

At last, on 21st October, one of the engines of ML 349 just refused to do any more for us and our turn came to go back for repairs. ML 349 with Lt. Cdr. Ball in command had come into the Aegean on 8th September and I took her back to arrive in Cyprus on 23rd October. This stint of 44 days was, according to my records, the longest tour of duty by an ML in this Leros campaign. It was just four days longer than my own tour of duty there because I had gone into the Aegean in command of ML 355 on 12th September and transferred to ML 349 on 3rd October.

This island seemed to have taken more than 40 days of my life and by its constant incident and drama will always dominate my memories.

13

Leros Lost

On one engine we set a course to Cyprus taking as passenger Major the Lord Jellicoe. We went through the Cos channel without incident, leaving Bodrum to port, then south, rounded Cape Krio with its Turkish lighthouse sending its beam over the sea. As daylight came we anchored in a Turkish bay north of Simi. During the day a single Turkish soldier came along the shore and waved to us. We did not know whether his wave was a friendly or an angry gesture, but we thought it wise not to ignore him so George Jellicoe and I rowed ashore to see him. It appeared that it was just a friendly wave: we did not speak Turkish and he did not speak anything but Turkish, so the communication was limited to smiles and gestures. We did not have any whisky or cigarettes to give him because we had left all such things behind for those staying in Leros, but he appeared to like a rather nice penknife which I had with me and was delighted when I gave it to him. After that we were assured of a peaceful day.

At night we sailed on again past Rhodes and passing Casteloriso felt bold enough to make the last part of the voyage in daylight, arriving at Paphos in the early afternoon.

Paphos was only about 250 miles from Rhodes and from the enemy forces, but to us on that autumn afternoon it seemed another world of peacefulness. The little town was quiet, the harbour had no signs of warfare and we knew that inland was an Army garrison and an RAF airfield. Black clouds of strain seemed to be lifting from our heads.

I doubt whether we worked hard that afternoon and when evening came half the crew had shore leave. It was the first chance they had for a peaceful 'run ashore' for over six weeks and I cannot imagine how the Coxswain decided who should go or who should remain. Nor can I remember how Twig Livesey (my No. 1) and I divided the duties, but I do know that I went ashore to a local hotel and taverna. There were some other Officers there from the Navy, the Army and the Air Force; we had a meal and a few drinks and suddenly I became very, very tired. I was about to excuse myself and try to make my way back on board when an RAF doctor who was there intervened. He told me that I was almost out on my feet, not through the drinks I had but from plain exhaustion, and he ordered me very firmly to take a room in the hotel and sleep that night in a real bed.

I was in no mood to argue with his orders and I dragged myself upstairs, falling into a bed and going to sleep all in one movement. I slept from about 10 that night till 8 in the morning when they wakened me with a cup of coffee. I shall always remember the joy of that night's sleep and how good the world looked when I awoke.

The next day I had words with Naval Headquarters and there seemed to be some doubt as to our destination. Had we been fully operational I think we would have been ordered to Alexandria, some 300 miles away, but as we had only one engine working we were sent to Beirut which was only some 200 miles.

Beirut had become an important base for Coastal Forces and nearly all the damaged MLs from the Aegean were sent there for repair. It was also a most agreeable place to enjoy some relaxation while one's home — the ML — was being attended to. The sea was warm for swimming and behind the city were snow-capped mountains where, in peacetime, or even in war if one had the equipment, it was possible to ski for many months in the year. In the city were hotels and restaurants where a meal and a drink could be enjoyed in the comfort which was ensured by the former French influence. The atmosphere was quite different from that of Alexandria and seemed to be more friendly, although Lebanon and Syria had been the scene of bitter fighting between the British and the Vichy French forces only two years earlier.

ML 349 was put into the hands of the workshops and I was ordered to report to Commander Courage in Alexandria. I flew to Cairo in a civilian plane piloted by an Egyptian: I believe the service had been taken over by the military and was almost entirely used by the armed forces. From Cairo I went on to Alexandria by train duly reporting to Coastal Force base and being found a berth in the barracks at Ras-el-Tin.

I made my report to Commander Courage who badly wanted to learn at first hand what was going on in Leros. I was then sent for by Vice Admiral Willis who had taken over from Admiral Cunningham as C-in-C Levant on 15th October — less than two weeks before and in the middle of the Aegean naval battles. Admiral Willis received me very courteously and asked me to repeat to

165

him my story of operations in and around Leros. He said at the end of it, 'Well, I won't keep you any longer. I am sure you are keen to get your ship repaired and to get back to Leros.' To be honest, I was not in a hurry to get back to Leros but I thought that a lie in these circumstances might be forgiven so I assured the Admiral that I was indeed eager to get back.

So I flew back to Beirut, this time in an RAF plane from an airfield in the desert. We had some fairly high-ranking officers on board and so I had well-organized transport back to the Beirut Coastal Force base alongside the harbour. There I was told that I could have three days leave as ML 349 was being refitted and accommodation on board was temporarily impossible. I could not remember when I was last told I could have 'leave.' A day ashore perhaps or a few days in harbour but I could not remember something called 'leave' since ML 1007 arrived in Port Suez over two years ago.

Among the other MLs being attended to by the workshops of Beirut was ML 354 whose CO was Lieut. Norman Stallworthy. They had arrived back from Leros about a week ahead of ML 349. Stallworthy had also been told he could have leave, so we agreed to go together into the hills behind Beirut and spend our three days walking in surroundings of quietness and peace. We went inland to a small village in the mountains called Brummana which looked down upon the sea and the city of Beirut below and to the west of it. There we found a place which might perhaps be called a hotel: it was a large building built of thick stone with stone floors and large rooms. It was kept by an Englishwoman, a very gentle person, but someone who could never be ignored: she had the power to impress and even to command without ever appearing to have the wish to do so. At the time we met her, she was perhaps between sixty and seventy years of age. She told us that she had kept that hotel in Brummana since the early years of the century. She had been there through the 1914-1918 war and now she was living there through the war which started in 1939 and would end she knew not when. Her hotel had from time to time been occupied or requisitioned by the Turks, the French and the British: she was inclined to think that the Turks had treated her the best.

It was 9th November, 1943. It was cool in the hills but not really cold. The weather was fine and each day we went for long walks taking with us a lunch of bread, cheese and grapes. As we sat at the roadside one day eating and enjoying this simple meal, a well-dressed young Lebanese man came by and although he said nothing the curl of his lip told us that he regarded us as unwelcome tramps in his beautiful countryside.

Our short leave in the happy and peaceful hills was soon over and we said good-bye to our gracious hostess who had looked after us so well. A taxi took us down the steep roads and as we approached the city it was clear that our driver was becoming agitated. We passed several crowds of men and we took side roads to avoid other crowds. There was some sort of civil disturbance going on: we did not know why and as our driver got us through safely we thought no more about it other than to reflect that our few days of peace were over. The street disturbance we saw that afternoon was probably the shadow cast before them of the terrible and destructive years of conflict which were to drag the beautiful country of Lebanon downhill in the years after the World War of 1939/46 had ended.

On 12th November, 1943 my short leave ended and it was on that day that the German forces invaded Leros. The MLs were on their nightly patrol there when at first light the invasion forces were seen to be approaching in considerable strength. Lieut. Cdr. Monckton in ML 456 was on patrol to the east at Leros when he sighted enemy forces consisting of destroyers and landing craft. He engaged these forces but was soon badly hit, and breaking off the engagement returned to Alinda Bay to land casualties. He then put to sea again and in the heavy fire from the shore batteries and the ships at sea was hit again and seriously damaged. He did, however, manage to reach Turkish waters.

ML 358 (Lieut. Lander and Sub-Lieut. Shute) was also on patrol and being severely hit by shellfire was run aground on the shore of Leros. Those crew members who were still alive attempted to get ashore but they were fired on by the invasion forces and by the defenders and very few survived. In fact, we were told at the time that ML 358 was lost with all hands and it is only recently that I discovered that one of the crew, L. Cheetham, had survived the war. He and only two or three others survived to be captured by the Germans and he spent the rest of the war as a prisoner in Germany.

The German invasion force landed on Leros on 12th November, 1943. They were massively supported from the air. Reinforcements were dropped by parachute and more arrived by sea. The Navy still tried to intercept the build-up of German forces and to give help to the Army on Leros but the cost continued to be heavy.

The destroyer *Dulverton* was sunk by bombing on 13th November (the sixth destroyer to be lost in this short campaign) and *HMS Penn* was damaged by gunfire which could well have been from the Italian coastal batteries on Leros which not unreasonably regarded all ships as part of the German invasion.

After five days of very heavy fighting in that small, rocky and mountainous island, the Allied forces on Leros surrendered on the evening of 16th November. For some days afterwards, small parties of men escaped to Turkey but the great gamble of the Aegean campaign by the Allied forces in autumn of 1943 was over. The Germans held the 'Iron Ring' of Rhodes, Karpathos and Crete and by sea and from the air controlled all the islands in the Aegean.

We who were in Beirut for rest and repairs were expecting to take our turn for another tour of duty in Leros. There was now no Leros to return to. Only the stragglers of a defeated force were coming back. We would be repaired and made sea-worthy but what were our next orders to be?

14

The Waters of Southern Turkey

In November it was not revealed to us and perhaps it was not even decided what part we MLs were to play in the days ahead. We were, however, receiving a significant addition to our armament. The ancient and almost useless 3-pounder gun which some of us carried on our fore-deck and the modern but, by comparison with the armament of our enemy, inadequate Rolls gun which others carried were to be replaced by a 40mm Bofors. This was a great step forward: the Bofors gun was a formidable weapon equally useful against aircraft or surface targets. Morale was raised considerably by this improvement in our fire power and it was an indication that Coastal Forces were thought to have done quite a good job in the Leros campaign.

As each ML was refitted, engines overhauled and new guns installed, I was made responsible for establishing ourselves as a flotilla rather than a number of individuals which we had inevitably become during the previous three months and even before that when we were spread along the coast from Turkey to Tripolitania.

We carried out gunnery exercises and smoke-laying exercises. We sailed in formation and perfected our signals. Most of our exercises were carried out between Beirut and Cyprus, using Famagusta and Limassol. MLs 359, 356, 836, 351 and 354 were involved with ML 349 at this time. Some had returned to Port Said or Alexandria, perhaps for repair, perhaps for operational reasons.

I paid another visit to Alexandria for a briefing session. This time I went to Cairo in an RAF plane and I remember being told 'Don't travel in a Lockheed Lodestar, they have had several crashes with those planes recently.'

When I arrived at Beirut Airport I was, of course, told that my transport was to be a Lockheed Lodestar.

'Oh,' I said, 'I thought they were grounded because of too many accidents recently.'

'Don't worry,' they replied. 'Yours is a daylight flight, they only crash at night.''

Off we went, two in the crew and a couple of passengers. After an hour, one of the crew said to the other, 'Did you pick up the mail?'

'No,' said the other, 'I thought you did.'

'Better go back for it.'

So they turned round and went back to Beirut, collected the mail and set off again some three hours late for Cairo. Not serious, except that it now became a night flight and a night landing. But we landed safely.

I returned as a passenger in an MTB which I found to be a most uncomfortable way of travelling especially in the very bad weather we had for the voyage. The motion of an MTB with its almost flat bottom beating down on the waves is very different from the roll of an ML with its conventional shape of hull.

One of the problems of a stay in Limassol in the south of Cyprus is the nearness of the alcohol trade. Limassol seemed to be a production or gathering centre and in peacetime would have been a main shipping port for wine and brandy. Cyprus brandy was for sale there at two shillings a bottle — if you could provide your own bottle as these were almost unobtainable on the island. Local beer was about the same price and so those of the crew who were inexperienced in the drinking of anything other than beer went ashore with the idea that one bottle of brandy equalled one bottle of beer and they regulated the quantity of their drinking accordingly. This tended to cause fights.

Army headquarters in Cyprus were also responsible for the defence of Casteloriso which was now our farthest outpost and nearest to the enemy. At the end of November 1943, I was ordered to embark the General Officer Commanding 25th Corps and take him on a visit of inspection to Casteloriso. He came aboard with three of his staff and we transported them there by night. They spent the day on Casteloriso while we laid up in Turkish waters. The Luftwaffe were making routine visits to the island in daylight, sometimes to bomb and sometimes just to look. So ships did not stay in the harbour any more but went across to Turkey where there was an excellent anchorage in a long and narrow sheltered inlet with a small port and town at the end of it called, as many of these ports were called, Port Vathi.

In the evening we embarked our passengers again but before returning, the GOC asked us to make a circuit of the island and as we were leaving Casteloriso in the darkness I heard the sound of engines and saw the bow wave of a fast-moving boat on our starboard bow. I decided quickly that he was coming across our bows and that to alter course could invite a disaster, so I slowed down but kept straight on and sure enough a British MTB went across our bows at about 20 knots and much too close for comfort. The GOC and a Brigadier were on the bridge beside me and from their language I understood that they found the incident rather alarming. So did I, but I did not tell them so and put on a good pretence, I hope, of having the situation well in hand. To tell the truth, we were very lucky not to have had a serious collision.

I think the General and his staff found our quarters rather cramped and were astonished at our feeding arrangements by which a seaman brought the food from the galley (probably sausages and baked beans) along the cold and windy deck on a plate, manoeuvred himself cleverly down the hatch to the wardroom, banged the plates on the table and produced knives and forks out of his trouser pocket. I offered them some red Cyprus wine called 'Commandaria' but the General excused himself politely by saying, 'Do you mind if I don't have that? I am rather good at red wine.'

On the way back he tried to come on deck and opened the hatch with the wardroom light on, breaking all the rules of keeping a darkened ship. Whereupon the conscientious gunner on deck said, 'Close that bloody hatch', and did so himself, giving the General a nasty bump on the head as he tried to emerge from the light inside into the darkness outside. However, I think he had no hard feelings for he sent me a very appreciative letter thanking me for the trip and for all I did for his party — and he sent his best wishes to me and to the crew. I also had an invitation to spend a few days leave in the Army mess but unfortunately I never had the chance to take up this offer.

During December our future operational role was decided. In the later stages of the Leros campaign we had found from experience that neutral Turkey would not make trouble if British ships unobtrusively used Turkish waters as a sheltering place during daylight hours, and so far the Germans had respected Turkish neutrality. International law permitted the temporary use of neutral ports for repairs and in wartime most naval ships needed repairs most of the time.

Destroyers had tried to protect Leros by operating at night from these neutral waters. The remarkable Greek destroyer *Adrias* had beached herself in Turkey after having her bows blown off by a mine and had eventually made her way slowly back along the

Turkish coast to Cyprus and then on to Alexandria still with her bows missing up to the bridge.

Many of the defenders of Leros had escaped to Turkey and then found their way back to Casteloriso and Cyprus. Major the Lord Jellicoe had done this with most of his SBS force and the tale he told me is worth repeating. He was defending a position in Leros and went down to Army Headquarters to report on the fifth morning of the battle following the German invasion. As he approached the building used as an HQ, he was startled to see German sentries at the door. He might have turned and run for it but he kept straight on, passed the sentries who saluted smartly, and into the main room. There he found the O.C. British and Allied troops in the act of signing the surrender.

George Jellicoe pointed out to the German General that the SBS troops under Jellicoe's command were scattered in the hills and he asked permission to inform them of the surrender otherwise, he said, they would continue to fight. Permission was granted. So he went back to the hills and said to his troops:

'Those stupid bastards down there have surrendered. Let's get out of here fast.'

They found a small boat or two and rowed or sailed across to Turkey and eventually made their way back to Cyprus.

The use of Turkish waters in defence and in defeat gave us the idea that they could still be used to our advantage in the future.

The strategy which evolved after the Leros defeat and the loss of the Aegean to German forces could be described as a strategy of making life uncomfortable for those forces and keeping them engaged. The previous policy hastily decided upon in the early days of the September was based on the instruction — said to have come from Winston Churchill — of 'Improvise and Dare.' Those instructions had been carried out and losses had been heavy. Certainly, no advances had been maintained in enemy-held territory but the Germans had committed large numbers of troops and aircraft to the battle and those must have been drawn from other theatres of the war. Some of the aicraft were said to have been diverted from the Russian front and some of the troops might otherwise have been engaged in Italy.

Having induced the Germans to deploy these forces to capture the Aegean islands, the next best thing we could do towards the Allied war effort would be to keep them there, and this meant maintaining threats against those islands and their supply routes.

This was not a job for large forces and indeed large forces were not available. We had not been strong enough when the Leros campaign was started and now we had been driven out, a large part of the Army, Navy and Air Force was diverted to other operations — particularly to the Western Mediterranean.

The threats we could continue to make against German-held islands could now only come from Army raiding parties and from small naval forces consisting of MTBs, MLs and the Levant Schooner Flotilla. The Coastal Force base in Alexandria was named *HMS Mosquito* and the operations we were about to carry out in the Aegean were very like those of a stinging insect annoying a rather large animal.

In December, 1943, I had my orders. The 42nd ML Flotilla was assigned to Aegean raiding duties with its main base at Beirut and forward bases in Cyprus and Casteloriso. I was to concentrate on the direction of Flotilla operations and in order to enable me to do this I was to relinquish command of ML 349. I could then 'fly my flag' in which ever ML I chose, or direct operations from a shore base.

I handed over ML 349 to Lieut. Peter Newman on 27th December 1943, took up residence in ML 351 which was commanded by Lieut. Ken Hallows and at 19.00 on the same day I sailed from Beirut with MLs 351, 356, 359 and 836 to start our new Aegean operation. I had had briefings in Alexandria and Beirut. The Naval authorities were very interested in this new expedition and we had an official 'send-off' by the Commodore Levant at Beirut. I hoped there was not too much publicity; however good it was for morale, it was certainly not good for security.

We had spent our 1943 Christmas and New Year in Beirut and by the first days of January 1944 we were in the Aegean once again. From Beirut we went to Casteloriso where I left MLs 356 and 836 and pressed on with MLs 351 and 359, intending to stop during daylight in a small inlet on the coast of Turkey just north of the port of Rhodes. We had been ordered to enter this small and deserted inlet in the rocky coast in order to make contact with Lieut. Cdr. Peter Evenson, SO of the 10th MTB Flotilla who was using this uninhabited place as his headquarters. The two MLs crept into the narrow inlet in pitch darkness and there seemed to be a good chance that if the MTBs were there they would fire on us. With a few loud shouts we announced our arrival and our identity. The MTBs were lying alongside the rocks and they said that the water was also deep enough for us, so we found our own rock, went alongside and secured our lines to it.

There was always a good chance of suffering damage when trying to berth alongside rocks in the darkness. It was risky to conceal ourselves in this way but it was more risky not to do so. Peter Evenson had chosen this place because it was the nearest he could get to Rhodes and in daylight he could keep a watch on the port. He expected, however, to operate only at night as German aircraft were constantly active in the day. I asked him what he would do if he saw a large German ship off Rhodes in daylight. He replied, 'I would drink half a bottle of whisky and then have a go!'

The next night we moved on to another Turkish bay which we had been ordered to visit and to use firstly as a headquarters and secondly as a re-fuelling site.

Re-fuelling had been organised by way of Greek caiques which would sail up from Cyprus loaded with large drums of petrol and wait for us in certain designated Turkish bays. The bay we were told to use was easy enough to find but turned out to be quite unsatisfactory and dangerous.

It was directly below the lighthouse at the point of Cape Krio at the western end of the Dorian isthmus. It is about 15 miles south of the eastern end of the island of Cos and about the same distance from the island of Nissiros to the west. Shipping from Rhodes and Simi must round this point on their way to Cos, Leros and the islands to the north. Cape Krio is certainly a vantage point for watching shipping movements in that southeastern region of the Aegean. But just as one could see very well from there, one could also be seen very clearly by those at sea and in the air, because the bay was only enclosed by a low rocky reef to seaward, while having on the landward side a steep cliff with the lighthouse at the top of it. This lighthouse, being Turkish and neutral, continued to flash its warning light and illuminate the bay throughout the hours of darkness.

The two MLs entered Cape Krio bay before dawn relying on our echo sounder and a leadsman in the bows, and hoping there were no unexpected rocks. We dropped anchor near the centre of the small bay because its sides were obviously too shallow to give a berthing place alongside the shore. A caique with its deck full of drums was already there with its bows anchored and a line to the shore from its stern. That was our re-fuelling ship.

There was a strong wind blowing round the headland and the

bottom of the bay was rocky. Soon it was clear that the anchors were not holding well. Attempts were made to drop anchor in a place with better holding but with no more success. While we were doing our best to find a secure anchorage daylight had broken and we had just decided to have breakfast while we tested the holding power of the latest cast of anchor, when two ships appeared close inshore crossing the entrance of our small bay.

They were German gunboats of the type usually described as R-boats, being designed to carry guns rather than torpedoes. They were not unlike an ML but were rather lower in the water, diesel engined and, had it not been for our Bofors, carried more fire power. They came close in right across the opening of the bay just a few hundred yards away. They had men on deck who stared at us and in return we stared at them and their Nazi swastika flag. They did not appear to aim a gun at us and we did not aim a gun at them. It was a good test of the neutrality of Turkish waters and neutrality survived.

Such confrontations were bad for the nerves. I decided that the Cape Krio bay was a bad anchorage, far too public, and placed a strain on the concept of Turkish neutrality which one day might not survive the pressure of a finger on a trigger and end with a bloodbath in very narrow waters. So we re-fuelled and, seeking local advice from Greeks on the caique, we left Cape Krio that night and set up our nightly resting place and re-fuelling centre in a bay to the north of Simi which appeared to be known as Penzik Bay.

A word on the re-fuelling caique. When we first went alongside in the early hours of the morning, Greek hospitality was such that we all had to drink a glass of raki before operations could start. Raki before breakfast is not recommended for good health or long life but we had to keep our relationship good with the caique crew. The second peculiarity we noticed was that while sitting on several thousand gallons of aviation fuel, they continued to smoke cigarettes. Fire precautions were a subject we in MLs took very, very seriously and re-fuelling was a time of danger, particularly when it had to be done in a rather primitive style of hand pumping from drums. We did manage to stop the Greeks smoking while they pumped the drums through a leaky pipe into our tanks, but they clearly thought we were a nervous and fussy lot of people. Someone from another ML swore that he saw a Greek put out his cigarette by plunging it into an open container of petrol. I am told that you can perform this trick if you do it quickly as it is the gas and not the petrol which would be ignited by a cigarette. I would rather not be around when it is done.

The bay at the foot of Cape Krio seemed so unsatisfactory that I did not use it again. I did not know that my decision to go elsewhere caused some annoyance in high circles in Alexandria. I found this out when I returned to Alexandria in March and was sent for by a Colonel of Marines who was in charge of Intelligence at Naval Headquarters there. He told me that the lighthouse keeper had been paid with golden sovereigns to keep a watch for enemy shipping and had been instructed to come down the cliff path from his lighthouse to the bay below to give us a report on what he had seen. He said that my refusal to stay in the bay had wasted good money and deprived me of useful information on shipping movements. I told him that the bay was a bad anchorage because the seabed was too rocky for anchors to hold, and that while the lighthouse keeper could see other shipping, that other shipping could also see us in that exposed place. He could not argue with my decision which was based on the safety of the ship in a poor anchorage, but he was rather cross that his planning had been upset.

The inlet on the Turkish coast which we called Penzik Bay was an excellent place to be. It was quite large and surrounded by hills with a large rock, more like a small island guarding the entrance. This rock looked, in the darkness, very like a large warship at anchor just outside the bay and it became known to us as Battleship Rock. There is a town or village of Pencik or Bencik between the head of the inlet and the northern coast of the isthmus, but no habitation could be seen from the bay itself and the wooded hills looked deserted. Another finger of Turkish land stretched to the south and could be seen beyond Battleship Rock; there were some small villages there, one of which was probably Turgut.

When we left this anchorage we steered west between these two fingers of Turkey. The southern finger is the shorter one and gives way to a channel between its western end and the Island of Simi on which there was a German garrison.

We had set our patrol area as the sea bounded by Cos in the north, the islands of Nissiros and Tilos to the west, Calchi, Alimnia and coast of Rhodes to the south and Simi to the east. We aimed in this way to cover the approaches to Rhodes and traffic between Cos, Simi and Rhodes. The pattern of our operations was simple: each night we went out into the patrol area and each day we returned to Penzik to carry out routine maintenance in the morning

176

and to sleep in the afternoon.

On 10th January, 1944 we were lucky and two ships making for Rhodes were unlucky. I was with Lieut. Ken Hallows in ML 351 and with 356 we were patrolling at slow speed east of Nissiros when a keen-eyed look-out saw sails at some distance to the east in the direction of Rhodes. We set off after them and soon caught up with two very large caiques making for Rhodes under power assisted by their sails which were fully hoisted (without their sails we would probably not have seen them).

We went alongside and a boarding party went over led by Sub-Lieut Peter Osborne. He found a Greek crew and one German armed with a machine gun. The German decided that he was out-numbered and surrendered without trouble. We took the Greeks and the German on board and examined the ships. They carried an assorted cargo of stores, mainly food and a large number of live sheep.

The alternatives before us were either to tow the caiques into Turkish waters and beach them — towing to Casteloriso was out of the question in view of the distance — or else to sink them. There was always a chance that a fast German-manned ex-Italian destroyer might come out of Rhodes and re-capture the ships; perhaps they had sent a radio call for help? So I decided on sinking and Peter Osborne was told to see that no one was left aboard as we were going to sink the ships. He shouted back, 'You can't do that, what about all these sheep?' I, too, hated to drown the animals but time was passing and we were loitering in enemy waters, so I was rather rude to Peter Osborne and told him to obey orders.

Unnecessary gunfire was to be avoided so it was decided to break the caiques up with a depth charge. We ran past at speed and dropped a charge set at 50 feet. This blew the bottoms out of them and at that short setting, it shook us up too. I found out afterwards that we had dropped two depth charges 'just to make sure.' It is not surprising that we were short of crockery after that.

We now had a German prisoner on board and some Greeks who protested that they had been forced to work for the Germans. It meant a trip back to Casteloriso to hand them over to someone who would take them back 'down the line' to Beirut or Alexandria. We went straight back to Peter Evensen and his MTBs in their anchorage opposite to Rhodes; it was as far as we could get before daybreak.

During the day we interrogated the prisoners and Peter Evensen joined us. We wanted to find out all we could about enemy shipping movements but our prisoner insisted that he knew little about it: he said he had just been told to act as a guard on these two ships from Pireas to Rhodes and he knew nothing about the movement of other ships. I think he was telling the truth. He told us he was a steel worker from Mannheim who had been drafted into the Army and he did not have the bearing of a regular German soldier. The interrogation was conducted through a German-speaking member of the crew; I have forgotten his background but I remember that his family had suffered at the hands of the Germans, and I believe his questions were not phrased in the most kindly way. He did admit to me that he took some pleasure in telling the prisoner that the Germans were retreating in Russia and here I believe his phrasing was 'Running like hell.'

Our prisoner had few personal belongings other than a wallet with his normal Army papers and photos of his wife and family. I insisted that these photos were returned to him and he seemed extraordinarily grateful for this. We held him under armed guard on board not because he seemed dangerous, but because both our interpreter and one of our ratings from the Channel Islands were said to be making threats against him in retaliation for the sufferings of their families.

In dealing with the captured Greeks, we sought the advice of Colonel Londos of the Greek Army who happened to be passing through in one of Adrian Seligman's caiques on a raiding mission. Londos was a tough and formidable commando leader and his view was uncompromising: he said these Greeks were traitors and not to be trusted in any way. He made a gesture indicating that their throats should be cut. We took them all back to Casteloriso and transferred them to a ship going back to Cyprus. The Cox'n saw them safely away and then came down to the cabin: 'I have a message from the German prisoner of war,' he said. 'He wishes to tell you that the officers on board this ship are gentlemen.' Why should I have been so proud of that? But I was and I am.

I received a signal from C-in-C congratulating 42nd ML Flotilla on a good start to their operations which had only begun about ten days ago before.

It was now mid-January 1944. Casteloriso had changed very much since I first saw it some four months earlier. It had been bombed many times by the Luftwaffe, and because it could be bombed again at any time, all ships were cleared out of the harbour in daylight hours and anchored in the long and narrow inlet on the coast of Turkey only a few miles away to the north. Port Vathi, best described as a large village, lies at the head of the inlet which would be called a fjord had it been in Norway. It had very high mountains on its northern side and steep hills of quite a fair size on the finger of land protecting the anchorage on the southern flank. The anchorage normally held a few MLs, some caiques, an RAF rescue boat and perhaps an MTB. The weather in January was cold and became even colder when a northerly wind swept down off the mountains.

There was, of course, a garrison in Casteloriso and Naval Headquarters. It was not a happy place to be. The town had suffered badly as a result of bombs and fires. It was said that most of the inhabitants now lived in the hills. There was a well-known 'secret' signal at the gun site on the port side of the harbour entrance: a highly-coloured carpet was hung over the protecting wall of the gun site to show that the island was still held by the British; if there was no carpet, the presumption was to be that the Germans had taken over. As we now only went in and out of the harbour in dusk or darkness, we had to take on trust a continued friendly reception.

Lieut. Cdr. Tooms had been replaced as the Naval Officer in Charge. The present NOIC had only just recovered from a nervous breakdown and this was a dangerous and depressing appointment for him. He seemed in good heart, however, and after a drink or two he would wave his discharge paper from the psychiatric hospital and declare that he was the only Naval Officer able to carry a certificate to say that he was sane.

He had on his base staff a Canadian Lieutenant whose name, I believe, was Fuller. Out of the kindness of his heart and as some return for their co-operation, he wished to do something for the inhabitants of Port Vathi, and without much consultation with those inhabitants he decided that their roads needed improvement. There was, for instance, only a track from the village to the shore. Our ambitious Canadian Lieutenant was also horrified to find that the villages along this mountainous southern coast of Turkey were only connected by difficult mountain paths and that, consequently, the principal inter-communication was by sea.

So perhaps having some civilian knowledge of road building, and having found some explosives, he set about a scheme of road improvement making up for lack of manpower by liberal use of dynamite. He probably did a good job but as usual with such things, ambition went too far. He sent a signal to Alexandria for more dynamite, some road equipment and a jeep to use on the excellent road he was making. When their Lordships of the Admiralty realized that he was engaged in blowing up rocks and building roads in Turkey, they expressed their displeasure and ordered that the work should cease. There were those unkind enough to suggest that the people of Port Vathi were relieved to hear this news.

In the operations we were now engaged upon, we had to rely on the friendliness of the villages in or near the bays where we anchored. Petrol for our engines was supplied by the caiques but water, of which we only carried a very limited amount, had to be obtained from springs and streams on the shore. We carried 'Jerricans' (ex-German) to gather water supplies each day. We carried on board plenty of tinned food, but there was the chance to obtain fresh meat or fish by bartering. What the villagers were most keen to have in exchange for their food was clothing and anyone with a spare pair of trousers soon found that they had been exchanged for half a sheep.

MLs were not normally expected to be away from a port for more than a couple of days, and so they were not designed to carry much water for drinking or washing. Hence the need in our present surroundings to go ashore to find water as often as we could. We always seemed to keep up a daily shave and there were few requests to grow a beard, but general cleanliness was not that easy. In September, it was normal to jump into the water for a swim which also served as a bath albeit without soap. But we were now in winter. There were some who put personal hygiene above the fear of cold water and jumped over the side in January: but to do it twice was unusual.

Our good relations with the Turks nearly came to an end one night in our anchorage at Port Vathi. Late in the evening during one of my brief stays there, a small Turkish boat came alongside and delivered three Unites States' airmen. They explained that they had taken part in a bombing raid on the Romanian oilfields in Ploesti. Their aircraft had been damaged and being unable to get back to their base in Libya, they had landed in or close to Turkey and they were now attempting to get back to their base by whatever means they could. As we were giving them some food and a drink, a dinghy from another ML came alongside. They warned us that Turkish police were touring the anchorage looking for the American airmen whom they wished to arrest for some misdemeanors they were alleged to have committed while travelling through Turkey. It was said that they had become involved with some Turkish women who had lodged a complaint, but I have no idea whether that was the true story. Anyway we decided that we were not going to let the airmen be arrested. So all that evening they were moved from one ship to another around the bay, all the time keeping one jump ahead of the police, who went away tired and angry after searching every ship in turn. Eventually the airmen were taken to Cyprus and then back to their base and our only contact with them was on that rather disturbed night which could have soured relations with the Turks had the airmen been found on board.

By 20th January I was back in our patrol area and lying up by day in Penzik bay.

I suppose one was lucky to fight a war (starting with the assumption that one had to fight a war) in the Mediterranean. The weather by land and sea was for most of the time very much better than that experienced in other theatres of war. The Mediterranean Sea does have one very dangerous characteristic: the occurrence of sudden and violent storms. Back to Biblical days and long beyond, ships were lost in such storms. There was that one I encountered off Alexandria which nearly wrecked us on the rocks. In a patrol in late January 1944, I encountered another. I was still 'flying my flag' — if that is not too glamorous a phrase for the senior officer of an ML Flotilla — in ML 351 and it was probably with ML 356 that we were steering in an easterly direction some five miles south of Cape Krio. Suddenly we seemed to run into a dense cloud on the surface of the sea. Visibility dropped so suddenly and so much that we could not see from the bridge to the bows or the stern and heavy rain was lashing at us. At the same time the compass went mad, the needle going round and round quite out of control. Green lights appeared running up and down the mast and the mast halyards while the masthead glowed like phosphorous.

We could see nothing and had nothing to steer by. We were safe from running ashore for at least half an hour but where was the other ML? A collision was quite possible. She should be following, so we broke all rules and showed our searchlight and an aldis lamp astern. They scarcely carried their light beyond our stern but they did what we wanted. Close astern, far too close astern, we saw an answering searchlight. And so we kept on slow ahead for perhaps an hour with only the length of an ML between us and dependent on the strongest light each could shine in the direction of the other. Within an hour the storm passed as quickly as it had come, the clouds passed; and very wet, very cold and very shaken by an extraordinary experience, we continued our night's patrol.

On another night we decided, with only one ML, to go to the east of Nissiros. This was outside our normal patrol area but we had had many nights without any sightings since our original chance interception of the two supply caiques bound for Rhodes. We were lying in a calm sea in a moonless dark night, with engines stopped, keeping a listening watch on the Asdic equipment and as much of a visual watch as was possible in the surrounding blackness. Suddenly, there was a roaring noise, starting softly and growing second by second. In the brief time it took to increase from a murmur to a shattering blast of noise, possibilities passed through our minds: E-boats? A submarine blowing tanks? A destroyer about to ram us? Then with almost a rush of air rather than a sound, an aeroplane flying only just above the waves passed so closely above us that we could see the outline clearly as it went over and appeared to miss our mast by only a few feet. We had guns manned but I gave no order to fire. I paused because through my mind were passing all kinds of possibilities: why should a German plane fly so dangerously low in an area safe for German aircraft? Was it a British plane on a secret mission flying low to avoid detection? I paused for only a few seconds but that was long enough for the plane to be lost in the darkness, and if we had wanted to shoot it down we had lost our chance. On reflection, and I have reflected many times on that incident, I am inclined to think that the plane was 'one of ours' and that my pause (or lack of decision) saved us from ruining (assuming we might have damaged the plane) one of our own side's deep-laid plans. I shall never know whether it was a German General or a British General who was saved.

About every two weeks we returned to Port Vathi for a couple of days in order to take on food supplies from Casteloriso and to report to the Naval Officer in charge more fully than was desirable by way of radio. On one such trip back, and because we made the voyage at the end of night patrol, we had to find sanctuary well short of Casteloriso when daylight came. Just to the northeast of Rhodes we found a delightful little anchorage which appeared on our charts to have the name of Kapi Cove. It had a rather long serpentine entrance channel and at the end doubled back towards the sea into a tiny circle of an anchorage surrounded by unusually verdant hills, so that we felt quite enclosed in a private paradise. Ashore and partially overgrown, was a very small monument or perhaps a temple in the Greek style. There were no other signs of buildings or people, and to stay there for a day was like a day in another world where there was nothing but peacefulness.

On most of the beaches around the little bays where we sheltered during daylight along this south coast of Turkey, we could find quantities of broken pottery left by previous inhabitants. We were not knowledgeable enough to say how old these remains were, but they added a little romance to this extraordinary phase of my wartime experiences.

During my briefing in Alexandria before I left on this expedition along the Turkish coast into the Aegean, I was given a camera by the RAF reconnaissance unit. This was no ordinary camera: it was about 12-inches high and 24-inches long and it was heavy. It was said to take detailed photographs at considerable range and I was encouraged to use it whenever I could to obtain information of shipping moving in the areas in which I was ordered to operate. I do not think I ever took a photo which was likely to be of any use to our Intelligence units. As we operated only at night, the camera could not be used while we were at sea. In the day we could indeed take photos of the coastline and we livened this up by taking pictures of the crew and of bathing parties in the cold Aegean waters. As we had no swimming trunks, these photos must have been most interesting to the WRNS' photographic development crews.

This camera was partly responsible for an incident which could have been dangerous for me and could even have caused trouble between Turkey and those who were taking advantage of her neutral status. I was with ML 351 at the time and we were spending the day in Penzik Bay. It was a fine clear day in early February 1944 and Ken Hallows (CO of ML 351) and I decided that it would do us good to stretch our legs on the shore for an hour. I have already said that it looked quite deserted around that bay, and the low hills were covered with thick green vegetation even at that time in the winter.

We took the dinghy and rowed ashore and I took the RAF camera with me. We hauled the dinghy up the beach and we set out on a track through the undergrowth and trees which appeared to lead to the top of one of the hills. We reached the summit and admired the view over the land and to the sea beyond. As we looked around, however, our peaceful enjoyment of the scene was suddenly disturbed: along a track from the landward side leading to the hill where we stood, we saw half a dozen Turkish soldiers coming in our direction 'at the double', and with rifles held in the position of the charge.

Ken and I decided without debate that we should retreat at once, and also 'at the double' we went down the seaward side of the hill back towards our dinghy. We got aboard and started to row as fast as we could back to the ML, but we had only covered about fifty yards from the shore when the soldiers arrived on the beach. They at once took up a kneeling position and aimed their rifles at us.

This was no time for taking chances on the aim of the soldiers even if they had been running, so we put our hands in the air as a token of surrender and then rowed the dinghy back ashore. The sergeant in charge indicated that we should follow him, and the soldiers reinforced his message by prodding us in the back with their rifles.

We walked uncomfortably in this fashion for perhaps a mile or so until we came to a small isolated building which was the headquarters of this small Turkish outpost. There were only about three rooms in the building. There was a kind of office and two rooms which were probably used for sleeping. We were pushed into one of them and our beautiful camera, which they regarded with great suspicion, was confiscated. The sergeant then tried to use a telephone which was on his desk in the office outside our bedroom-cell. The telephone was extremely primitive, literally two jam jars of acid to provide battery power and a tapping device for sending messages in Morse code. The sergeant and two of his riflemen spent about two hours trying to make contact with his commander in the nearest town of Marmaris. It was clear to us, however, that contact was not being made and he could not report our arrest and could not obtain instructions on what to do with us.

Meanwhile, we had not been sitting idly by. Considering that we spoke no Turkish and they spoke no English, we managed to communicate remarkably well. We understood two important things: firstly, they were short of ammunition and, secondly, they liked whisky. They were very interested when we explained that we could supply both ammunition and whisky if only we could be allowed back on board. They were frustrated by, and angry with their telephone after some two hours of effort. They were attracted by our offer of bullets and whisky.

In a more friendly atmosphere, with no rifles in our backs this time, we all set off back to the beach. The sergeant and one of his men came back with us in the dinghy and was duly rewarded with some ammunition for his troops' rifles and for his own revolver, and a bottle or two of our gin and whisky. Our camera was returned and it is likely that it was this large piece of apparatus which caused us to be treated more like foreign spies than relatively harmless sailors who had been taking an innocent walk ashore. So ended happily something which could well have ended very unhappily. We found out, too, that Ken Hallows' No. 1 and the crew had watched our capture and, but for the danger of killing us too, were seriously considering opening fire on the Turks. What an international incident that would have been!

The way in which I organized our operations was to keep two MLs west of Rhodes on patrol duties and two back in Turkish waters north of Casteloriso. In these early days, I had decided to spend January and February with the two forward MLs. After that I would probably 'have a rest' (if a rest could be had) back in Casteloriso.

About the end of January or early February I was on board ML 356 commanded by Lieut. Ken Lloyd. We were out one night in the vicinity of the island of Tilos and as we approached the main bay and anchorage of the island we saw a small cargo ship of about 500 tons entering the harbour. We stopped and the second ML came alongside. We decided to wait for a short time so that the ship could anchor or go alongside a jetty, then we would enter the bay on one side in the darkness of high cliffs at slow speed, increase to full speed across the bay and attack the ship with gunfire. We did not know what defences there were on the shore or on the ship, and we hoped these tactics might at least give us the advantage of surprise to offset what might be heavier gunfire from the ship and shore defences.

As soon as we increased speed to close the ship which had anchored near the shore, we came under fire. We had not approached unobserved as we had hoped and they were ready for us. But the fire was all from the shore and not from the ship and there did not seem to be anything heavier than machine gun fire aimed at us. We came in really close to the ship and while the Oerlikons shot up the bridge and upperworks, we tried to damage the hull with the Bofors. At one stage I was sure I saw a fire inside the hull but it did not take hold and I felt frustrated at our lack of power to do the ship serious damage. Remembering our affair with the caiques, I decided to try depth charges and dropped one right alongside set at 50 feet. Nothing happened. Our fellow ML repeated the treatment. Nothing happened. It must have been too shallow. Theoretically, we could have set a time fuse into the depth charge primer but it was not the sort of thing which I felt like doing: it meant messing about with detonators on a dark night while still being shot at. So we spent a lot of Bofors ammunition on the ship's hull and having reported our action to Alexandria and the presence of this now damaged ship, we departed from the harbour.

One of our crew had been hit by a bullet in the fleshy part of his bottom and our woodwork had some scars from the gunfire directed at us. I had not noticed anything near me but later on I found that our searchlight mounted on the bridge had two bullet holes through it. During the action I was standing beside the searchlight.

Although I sent my enemy report to Alexandria, I neglected to request that it should be repeated to Peter Evenson and his MTBs, so he was not informed of the presence of this ship which would have made an excellent torpedo target. I have often wondered why Alexandria did not think it was their duty and responsibility to pass the information to the MTBs.

Dawn was getting all too close when we left our scene of action and we had no chance of reaching Penzik without considerable risk of reprisals from the Luftwaffe. So we made for the nearest part of the Turkish coast a few miles to the east of Cape Krio which avoided passing enemy-held Simi in daylight. We found a suitable bay and dropped anchor but no sooner had we done so than our look-out reported two or three craft 'like R-boats' approaching from the east — that is, from the direction of Simi.

There were indeed four small craft in line ahead and steering directly toward us. Were they German boats sent to take revenge for the attack we had just made in Tilos harbour? For a few minutes it was panic stations — we had been caught at anchor and were sitting targets for an attack. Some of the crew strained to raise anchor, others manned the guns. Then just at the last moment before entering our bay, the four boats turned ninety degrees and headed southwest along the coast and when they came broadside on with the wind spreading their flag, we saw that they were not Germans but Turkish coastal patrol boats who had probably come to see who we were and had then been kind enough to leave us alone.

We relaxed, dropped the anchor again and aimed to have some breakfast. But the day's adventure had not ended. Soon a soldier or two came onto the beach and as they seemed to want to talk, I took the dinghy ashore with the No. 1 of ML 356. They seemed friendly enough but indicated that they wanted me to go with them to a small town which was not more than a mile or so away.

We walked there and when we arrived, we were shown into the office of someone who appeared to be of great importance in the town. He could have been the mayor, the chief of police or the senior customs' officer. A Turkish Army officer and some other civilians were with him. They only spoke a few words of English, they looked rather serious and each was doing his best to be seen to do his duty in front of the others. I suppose they felt they should ask us what we were doing in their bay and what our intentions were. The standard reply in such cases was to say we had put in for repairs or to rectify trouble with our engines; this would justify our use of neutral waters under International Law. The Navy must have had a dreadful record of engine defects in the eyes of the Turks if they believed all the excuses made by our ships using their bays and harbours at that period of the war.

Assuming their questions to be on this subject, I did my best to signify engine trouble and the going was hard until I suddenly had a piece of luck. Above the head of the chief dignitary, was a large framed picture and I recognised it to be the Turkish President. 'Ah,' I said, 'President Inounu' and I stood up as I said it and then sat down again. They all beamed with delight and I am sure they all said to each other in astonishment, 'He recognises our President.' They asked no more questions. They shook us warmly by the hand and saw that we were escorted in a most friendly way back to the beach, the dinghy and our ship.

It was not healthy to go back to Casteloriso too often and it wasted time when we could be on patrol, so we managed to find one of our caiques to take our wounded man back in the care of the Sick Berth Attendant we carried as an additional crew member in this forward base.

The two MLs I now had with me had spent nearly three weeks on these patrol duties and were due for a rest quite apart from the need to replenish food and other stores and carry out maintenance which could not be done while on full operational duties. I was just about to make a switch of boats when a signal arrived for me personally, instructing me to report to Alexandria for onward passage to the UK.

It was quite unexpected and the receipt of such an order after two years nine months' service in the Eastern Mediterranean was an emotional moment. I cannot now remember why I decided to make one last patrol before leaving the area: it is probable that the order fixed a date for my return to Casteloriso.

So we sailed from Penzik for another patrol but not feeling in best operational order because one ML reported that its Bofors was defective and liable to jam, while the other reported similar troubles with one of the Oerlikons. It was very bright moonlight with not a cloud in the sky. As we made a sweep south of Simi, we saw in the distance and very close to the northern shore of Rhodes a convoy of several vessels. There appeared to be a coaster — and we jumped to the conclusion, perhaps wrongly, that it was the ship we had tried to sink in Tilos — escorted by a German U.J. auxiliary escort ship, which was similar to one of our armed trawlers, and about four R-boats.

Our tactical situation was not good. Coming in from the north we had the moon behind us: we could be seen clearly and they were in the shadow of the land. They were so close inshore that we could not approach them from the south which would put them in the moonlight and us in the shadow. It was so very bright that attack from the air was a real possibility and we were very close to the Rhodes airfields. In brief, we were outgunned by a larger force and there could be no element of surprise.

I decided not to attack as I judged success to be unlikely: if we could not sink the coaster when she was at anchor, what chance did we have when she was escorted by five warships? I suppose one of the most difficult decisions in war is to know when to attack and when to turn away. If one is defending, then one has no option but to fight. When one is attacking, one weighs the odds of success and failure. I believed the risk of our own defeat and destruction to be large and I thought the chance of inflicting significant damage on the enemy to be small. I would have liked to leave the Mediterranean with a spectacular victory, but in this I could only see a miserable defeat.

Nevertheless, I have often questioned myself closely in an attempt to convince myself that my decision was not influenced by the knowledge that this was my last patrol before I returned home to see a wife I had not seen for three years and a son whom I had not seen at all.

The following night we returned to Casteloriso, the MLs stayed with the Aegean force and I went back to Alexandria to report to Captain Courage, Commander Coastal Forces Eastern Mediterranean and to find out how I was to be transported back to the UK.

15

Back to the U.K.

In Alexandria, the Coastal Force base was concentrating its thoughts on the Aegean operations which I had just left. New officers had arrived from the UK so there would be some changes and more MLs were being prepared to go 'up the line.' I was surprised to find that I was regarded as an expert and a veteran of these operations, but I had been there since September 1943 and had started the present round of activity following the fall of Leros. I was asked by Commander Courage to brief all the officers who were expected to operate there and to advise them on all aspects of the operations from food to gunnery. I spent about two weeks at *HMS Mosquito* on these duties and was consulted by Commander Courage and his secretary regarding the officers and crews of the MLs of the 42nd Flotilla whose Senior Officer I had now ceased to be.

There seemed to be silence regarding my passage back to the UK and I was warned not to make a nuisance of myself on the subject. There was a story of one man who did so and an overworked and harrassed secretary made a note of his name on a piece of paper which happened at that moment to be in front of him on his desk. Unfortunately, that piece of paper was a list of bomb and mine disposal experts urgently needed in Malta. So he was immediately transported to Malta by submarine to the disgust of everyone concerned when they found he could not make bombs safe, and he found he was not in the UK and unlikely to find any means of getting there.

After about three weeks I was told that I was to command a large landing craft and take it to Italy where I might be involved in operations there. Getting back to the UK seemed to have been forgotten.

That evening I went to a dance organised by the WRNS in Alexandria and while there I met Commander Courage. 'What are you doing here?' he asked. 'I thought I had sent you back home.' I explained the situation to him and he just said 'Come and see me in the morning.'

As early as I could, I attended his office and repeated my story about taking a landing craft to Italy. He picked up the telephone and asked for a certain officer on the C-in-C's staff. 'Look here,' he said, 'about this chap Searle. We had an order to send him home and I agreed to do that. Now some bloody fool is sending him to Italy. I want you to understand that he has been out here a long time, he's done a very good job here and I want him sent back to the UK just as soon as possible. No more messing about with Italy or any other place — just straight to the UK. Is that clearly understood?' There was a sort of gasping noise from the other end of the phone. Commander Courage had an uncompromising way of giving orders which absolutely stopped any possible argument or question. The reply had to be either 'Yes, Sir!' or a gasp of submission.

That same afternoon I was ordered to report to transport office at first light next morning, where I would be taken to an RAF station for immediate transit by air to the UK. There was only one disadvantage to this welcome invitation. I could only go in the clothes I wore and carry a very small bag to contain my shaving gear and toothbrush and perhaps a few small personal belongings as well.

By the time I had organised myself for the journey, I was wearing two sets of underwear, and all the other clothing I could put on under my heaviest and newest uniform. With a great-coat on top I must have weighed fifteen stones and I moved ponderously like a tired elephant. All my other clothing and belongings I packed into two large and heavy suitcases which I bought in the Alexandria bazaar. I addressed them to my home in Horley, Surrey, handed them in to the Naval people who dealt with the mail, and expected never to see them again. In fact they arrived home quite safely and, as I will later relate, I heard of their safe arrival while on the way to the invasion of Normandy about three months later.

At daybreak on a day in early March 1944 a party of some twenty or so Service personnel reported to the transport depot and were loaded into an enclosed truck. There were only two Navy people, An RN Commander and myself. Some of the others were Army officers and the majority were RAF. We travelled for about an hour to the airfield and by the time we arrived we were all quite ill. There was a leak in the exhaust so that the inside of the enclosed truck became thick with fumes and we all boarded the aircraft feeling sick and with headaches.

The aircraft was a two-engine Dakota — a DC3 — which put in such wonderful service during and after the war years. The inside of this one was basic — metal seats with canvas sling seats like upright deck chairs. No heating, no air conditioning — how glad I was that I wore two of nearly everything.

We flew along the North African coast to an airstrip in the desert in the south of Algeria. It was an oasis which before the war was being developed as a holiday resort based on one luxury hotel. This luxury hotel was now used as a home for those servicing the airstrip and the aircraft, and as temporary accommodation for those like us who were just on passage. It was a strange and lonely place and I was told that the famous novel, *The Well of Loneliness*, was written there.

After a basic supper, a basic bed and a basic breakfast, we made the fairly short hop to Gibraltar where we spent the day. My excess clothing which had been so welcome in the air was now most uncomfortable in warm Gibraltar.

When darkness came we re-boarded. In the case of the RAF, they were re-loaded because most of them were very drunk. They proclaimed loudly that the next leg of our flight was 'far too bloody dangerous' and they needed an anaesthetic to face it. It was indeed a long and probably dangerous flight because we went west from Gibraltar far out over the Atlantic to avoid the coast of Spain and Portugal, then turned north keeping well clear of the west coast of France where Luftwaffe patrols operated.

As daylight came we sighted the Scilly Isles and before midday we landed at an RAF station in the west country. We were all quite closely questioned on arrival. My collection of war-time Mediterranean photographs caused some excitement but I had had them all stamped by the Naval Censor in Alexandria, and but for that they would have been confiscated.

There was only one casualty on this long trip. The RN Commander had bought a large and gorgeous cream-decorated cake from Groppi's in Alexandria who were famous for their confectionery. He nursed it on his lap all the way home but as he boarded the transport to take us from the airfield to catch a train to London, he dropped it. He was devastated but I do hope that although the decorations must have suffered, it was still a sufficiently gorgeous cake to give pleasure to his family who had not seen a cream cake (or that RN Commander) for some years.

On arriving tired and scruffy at Paddington, the Commander

and I went to the Admiralty to report our arrival to a not very interested clerk and having left our UK addresses, we parted company. I set off to Victoria and caught a train to Horley after making a telephone call to my wife who was living with my parents, to tell her that I was now within 25 miles and, if all went well with the Southern Railway, I hoped to see her again for the first time in nearly three years.

As the train slowed down to stop at Horley I looked out of the window and saw Constance and beside her a very small boy of about 2½ years — my son whom Constance had been caring for so well in those difficult days when my absence must have seemed endless. I have a mental photograph printed into my mind of those two standing at the foot of the unromantic metal stairway leading down to the platform, and it is not surprising that a picture of such an emotional moment remains with me so many years afterwards.

I had supposed that after nearly three years away, I might have the pleasure of a reasonably long leave. The general impression was that one could expect a week's leave for every year spent overseas and that was the extent of my expectation of 'long leave'.

All the time I had been away, Constance and our son John had been living with my parents in Horley. The house had been very badly damaged by a bomb which landed in the garden during the air raids of 1941, but it had been repaired quite well and was a comfortable home once again. At the time of the bombing, the family except my father, had been in the well-built air raid shelter which had been sunk into the garden and they were unhurt. My father, who was not in the shelter, was badly shaken by the explosion.

The weather that March was quite good and I relaxed by doing jobs in the garden. I was half-way through mowing the lawns (with a hand-pushed mower — there was no petrol for a motorized one) when Constance came from the house with a telegram. I had been only ten days at home with her but the telegram she handed me demanded my immediate return to duty. I was to report to Hayling Island for a 'course'.

16

The Invasion of Normandy, ML 490

So to Hayling Island I went and found that the course I was to undergo related to the use and maintenance of certain navigational equipment which then went by the code name of QH. This device became standard equipment for shipping in post-war years but when I went to Hayling Island it was new and secret. Its importance in the invasion of Normandy was immense and I believe that not sufficient tribute has been paid to all those involved in the invention, the development and the decision to use QH. I do not know how we would have located the invasion beaches so accurately in small ships after a slow and rough night passage through the tidal waters of the English Channel unless we had had QH to guide us.

What was involved was briefly this: stations had been set up along the south coast of England which emitted signals. Each ship had a receiving apparatus which culminated in a screen very like the present-day television screen. This screen showed a map of the region and the signals from the shore stations were translated into lines on the screen. The position of the ship was at the crossing point of two or more lines on the screen and one navigated by keeping this crossing point moving steadily towards one's destination.

I joined a class of some two dozen officers and spent two weeks engaged in intensive instruction mainly in classrooms, with an occasional short sea trip in a boat fitted with the equipment. It felt strange to be going back to school again. It was only about four years since I had been at *HMS King Alfred* on Officer Training classes followed by courses on Asdic and Navigation. I now felt like an old man by comparison with those days. I had seen a lot and done a lot and learned a lot and I now felt rather out of place, not so much in the course itself but in returning to the life of a student.

I was billeted in a house on Hayling Island with about half a dozen others; we shared bedrooms and a living room and the kind landlady cooked us a breakfast before a truck came to collect us each morning. We worked late and there was nothing to do in the evening when we finished.

After two weeks, we all received postings and mine was to join ML 490 at Brightlingsea in Essex. I managed to travel there by way of Horley (I was surprised how well the railway system still worked) and to steal a day's leave on the way. After all, I needed some time to deal with such minor matters as clothing. I had only come back from Egypt with the clothes I was wearing and I supplemented that with anything still available from my pre-war stock at home plus whatever I had the time, the money and the clothing coupons to buy.

I arrived at Brightlingsea by train rather late in an early April evening of 1944. Brightlingsea was a centre for the repair and maintenance of small craft and the Naval Headquarters was a large house near the harbour with an RN Commander in charge who was one of the many who had retired from the Navy long before the war broke out and had been recalled to undertake such shore commands as this one in Essex.

He and a lady guest had just finished dinner when I arrived and they were enjoying a glass of port. I felt rather out of place but he hospitably offered me some port — I would have liked a meal but that was over — and as he made it clear that he did not want to be bothered with business that evening, I retired to my allocated bedroom and left tomorrow to reveal what it would reveal.

ML 490 was having a considerable refit. The two major works were firstly, the installation of the QH equipment and secondly, the replacement of the traditional mast by a four-legged metal structure supporting a large perspex dome housing a radar scanner. The rest of the work related to taking things off rather than putting things on, and there were two reasons for this: the radar dome and its supports were very heavy and affected the stability of the ship, so any surplus top weight had to be removed. And the other reason was explained tactlessly and unfeelingly by the foreman of the yard. When I asked for some small carpentry job to be done he said: 'Now look here, this ML is being prepared for the invasion, it is only expected to go one way and I'm not going to waste my time doing anything more than the bare minimum to get you to the other side of the Channel.'

I was joined by my No. 1, David Turner, and by a new crew. Before long we were all living on board and soon the work on the ML was finished and we sailed past the Goodwin Sands, through the Straits of Dover and on to Portsmouth where our radar and our QH apparatus was checked, tested and calibrated.

We were now, on paper at least, ready for the task for which the ML had been refitted — the invasion of occupied France. With the remark of the yard foreman constantly in my mind — that we were only expected to go one way — everything we did now was incidental to and leading towards that invasion. We were preparing for, and filling in the time until, that great event which should lead, one way or the other, to the end of this long war.

I was ordered to report to the U.S. Admiral in command of the U.S. Naval Forces gathered in the ports of Cornwall and Devon. I reported to him in person at Plymouth and was impressed with the courtesy and consideration with which I was received. At the conclusion of our fairly long interview, he did not just dismiss me from his office, but he escorted me down the stairs to the entrance of the building and shook me warmly by the hand as he saw me into the car which he had laid on to take me back to the ML.

The formidable American force which was now gathered in the southwestern ports of the UK was well-equipped with landing craft and larger ships but was deficient in small craft such as MLs which were required to lead the landing craft to the right beaches and act as shepherds to the flock on the way there. The Americans credited us with experience of the conditions in the English Channel (which was an overplaced confidence) and they knew of our navigational equipment. On these two factors plus their undoubted respect for the Royal Navy, they were prepared to trust a British ML to guide and land their forces. It was a frightening responsibility which has worried me more in retrospect than it did at the time.

The 11th ML Flotilla of which I was now Senior Officer consisted of ten B-type MLs. All had two Hall Scott aviation spirit engines, Asdic and depth charges, echo sounders, W/T and R/T gear and five had type 970 radar (the dome on a four-legged structure such as was fitted to ML 490). The gunnery consisted of a 3-pounder, three 20mm Oerlikons (one single and one twin mounting), two twin Vickers .303 mounted machine guns, three Lanchester hand machine guns, three pistols and a rifle. The crew consisted of two officers (I had three most of the time) and eighteen ratings: the number varied from time to time depending on the operations in hand and also the availability of trained men. Later, the 11th ML Flotilla had three HDMLs added to its strength. These three — 1397, 1402 and 1469 — were commissioned in July 1944 after the invasion and although I was responsible for them, in fact I saw very little of them.

I was in command of ML 490 and of the 11th ML Flotilla for only some two months before the invasion of Normandy took place, and in that busy time I was unable to work up any firm relationship with the other MLs in the Flotilla. Our base was at Falmouth and I was the last to arrive there. I was delighted to find that the CO of ML 118 was my old friend Alex Wallace, who had travelled out to the Eastern Mediterranean with me in 1941, and who has appeared before in this narrative. Apart from Alex Wallace, all the other COs were new to me and as we were constantly on the move between all the ports and harbours and inlets between Dartmouth and Falmouth, it was not easy for me to get to know them before we were to be tested in a most serious operation.

The U.S. Forces and some of the MLs had been exercising for several months and had practised invasion tactics at Slapton Sands — where they suffered a considerable disaster one night when attacked by German E-boats during an exercise. By the time I arrived, the order to invade France was expected at any time and further exercise and practice was stopped. We were supposed to be fully trained and ready but I had not taken part in any form of preparation. I scarcely knew my fellow COs and I had no time to meet the commanders of the American ships, the Marines and the Army units which formed that part of the invasion fleet I was responsible for guiding across the Channel to France.

Lieut. Wallace went off to attend a briefing meeting for several hundred American officers held in a cinema in Plymouth. To show instant readiness for combat it was usual for the U.S. Marine and Army officers concerned to attend in battle kit with granades and revolvers hanging from their belts. At this meeting, the General in charge laid out to his men exactly what was expected of them and after a tough and rousing speech he said, 'And now, men, we have to face the matter of getting to the other side and I want you to meet Lieut. Wallace of the Royal Navy who has that well in hand. Lieut. Wallace has a ship made especially for the job and he has a well-trained crew to operate it. He himself has years of experience and he knows the English Channel like the back of his hand.'

Now Alex Wallace is a quiet and retiring man, much more terrified of appearing on a stage to talk to several hundred armed and belligerent-looking troops than of the operation they expected him to carry out. He said to me afterwards, 'You know, Geoff, I felt a right fool up there after that introduction: you see, just like you, I had only taken over my ML a few weeks earlier. I hardly know my crew and I have never been in the English Channel before.'

The whole of the south coast of England had become, for security reasons, a restricted area: meaning that for a distance of about five miles from the sea all movement was controlled. If you lived there, you stayed there; if you lived outside the area, you were not allowed in without a permit. From about Dartmouth westward every creek and harbour was filled with U.S. landing and associated craft. No doubt the coast to the east was similarly filled with British invasion craft — but my duties were with the Americans.

The American headquarters at Falmouth were at the Greenbank Hotel. The ML base was close to Penryn on the narrow inlet branching north-westward from Falmouth and its main harbour. The massive build-up of landing craft must have been well-known to the enemy. There had not to my knowledge been any sea-borne attacks since the E-boat attack on the U.S. landing craft exercising by night off Slapton Sands, but air attacks were not uncommon. These were of the hit and run type, with fighter-bombers coming in fast and low, dropping bombs with machine gun and cannon fire and getting out again fast. We were protected from heavier attacks by the radar warning systems and the power of the RAF and US Air Force. Nevertheless, the bombing did inflict considerable damage mainly to the towns and ports rather than to the shipping in the harbours.

One night there was a raid on Penryn and I was woken by the noise of one of our Oerlikon guns firing. Now the orders were that we were not to fire at night unless directly attacked — the theory being that firing gave away our position when otherwise we might be unnoticed in a narrow creek and in blacked-out countryside. Nevertheless, with an enemy circling overhead and dropping bombs, it hardly seemed sensible to sit behind a gun and not fire it. Our sentry that night evidently thought like that for without orders he manned the Oerlikon and loosed off in the general direction of the circling plane. Bombs had been dropped and a fire had been started nearby so I could not bring myself to reprimand him for taking immediate action on his own initiative. Able Seaman Parker was the rating involved. He called himslf a Canadian and wore a 'Canada' sign stitched onto his sleeve. I don't think he was a Canadian — he came from Norfolk — but the 'Canada' sign gave him some advantage with the girls.

October 1943. MLs hiding during daylight. Leros and islands nearby.

October 1943. ML camouflaged alongside cliffs on Dodecanese island.

October 1943. ML trying to be inconspicuous alongside rocks near Leros.

30th January 1944. Lt. Ken Hallows. Vicinity of Penzik, Turkey. In sight of German held Simi.

30th January 1944. Geoffrey Searle on hills above Penzik anchorage.

Geoffrey Searle, Alexandria, 1943.

21st January 1944. Geoffrey Searle. Port Vathi in Turkey, north of Casteloriso.

9th February 1944. Casteloriso.

February 1944. Finding a berth in a narrow creek.

1944. ML 490.

1st Nov. 1944. From ML 490 at head of landing craft sailing from Ostend to invade Walcheren at the mouth of River Scheldt.

August 1945. MLs 118, 448 and 119 astern of ML 490.

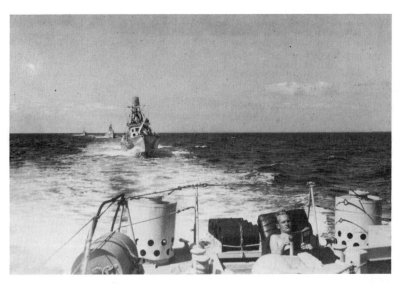

August 1945. Returning from Denmark to UK. MLs 118, 448 and 119 astern of ML 490. Lt. David Turner off watch.

In the first days of June 1944 I was ordered to attend the US headquarters in Plymouth together with several other senior officers. We were ushered into a briefing room and there on the wall was a map of part of the coast of Normandy showing the invasion beaches. We all know now where the invasion took place and we forget that up to June 1944 the beaches chosen for the invasion were the most secret of secrets, and rightly regarded as the information the Germans would most like to have. And so it was a subject we did not speak about and hoped for our sakes that only a very few people were permitted to know the chosen site. It was, therefore, a shock to see on the wall a large-scale map showing the coast of France from the Cherbourg Peninsula to the port of Le Havre — the Côte de Nacre. And for us in particular there was an enlargement of the east coast of the Cherbourg Peninsula and the beaches to the seaward of Carentan between Sainte-Mère-Eglise and Grandcamp. These were to be known to us as the Utah beaches on which we had to land our troops. I had the feeling that I should not be looking at such secret information and at first I only took furtive glances at the map when I thought no one was looking.

We were given a briefing — and it was a very concentrated and short briefing — on what we had to do and what was expected of us. We were told that more information would follow in the form of maps and written instructions. I returned to Falmouth and passed the orders I had been given to those officers who had not been to Plymouth with me. That night a sack — yes, a whole large Father Christmas style sack — of books and papers arrived on board.

That sack contained all we needed to know and a great deal which we did not need to know about the invasion. There were well-prepared books giving information on radio communications, tides, landing beaches, depth of water, recognition signals, ship and aircraft identification and particulars of enemy forces ranged against us, of which the most chilling was a detailed map of enemy gun sites showing the calibre and the range of the guns with their arcs of fire. The beaches and the sea approaches we were to use appeared to be not only covered but doubly covered by on-shore gun emplacements.

We had already been given personally the information necessary for us to navigate to the appointed beach by means of QH signals. We had also been given a radar 'picture' of the beach which we could put over the front of our radar screen in order to check the radar echoes we were getting from the shore and help us identify our position. These were the most important pieces of information and of the two the QH instructions were by far the most significant for the success of our navigation.

We had orders to sail next morning to Salcombe with three other MLs. The rest of my flotilla were attached to other units of the US landing forces and started from other ports. For example, Lieut. Colin Beever in command of ML 304 was attached to the US Forces who were to land by scaling cliffs to the eastward of our beaches. He was decorated for his part in this action.

We arrived in Salcombe in the evening of 2nd June and reported to the US Naval Headquarters at the buildings adjacent to the Ferry Boat Inn.

I had never been to Salcombe before. My two impressions were firstly the natural beauty of the estuary and secondly the unnatural number of US landing and landing-support craft in the estuary. The force which we were to lead consisted mainly of small landing craft each designed to be beached and put ashore about twenty men. There were some bigger landing craft carrying tanks and even bigger command and control ships. They had for the most part been based in Salcombe for some months and had set up workshops and repair facilities on the eastern shore of the harbour. They had been bombed while they were there, but most of the casualties were civilians in the town which, for a small town, had suffered quite badly. The present war memorial bears witness to the many civilians who died in Salcombe and whose numbers are not so very many less than those Salcombe men and women who lost their lives while serving in the Armed Forces.

We spent no more than a night and a day at anchor in the middle of the estuary. Everyone knew that we were only waiting for the word to go and there was an air of nervous expectancy. We all expected a very rough and dangerous time. At the shore bases there were several officers to be seen who were there 'to replace casualties.' It might have been better for morale if they had been kept farther away from us rather than to have them standing on the quayside so obviously and keenly waiting for a place to fill.

There seemed to us little chance of the end of this war without achieving a successful invasion and fighting the enemy on the fields of Europe, and so I think it right to say that our enthusiasm to make a significant move which should open the way to peace, far outweighed our natural anxieties about an operation which might be a one-way trip for many of us.

In the afternoon before we left I called the crew together and talked to them on the importance of our mission and the need for total dedication to duty. If ever there was a time for efficiency, it was now. I do not know whether my talk did any good to the crew but it made me feel a lot better.

On the evening of 3rd June, just as light was fading, we sailed from Salcombe. I cleared the boom first at the narrow entrance to the estuary and stood away to eastward watching the long column of ships come out to sea against the fading light in the west. It should have been a glorious sunset to silhouette such an armada but bad weather was blowing up. It was a cloudy and watery sky obscuring the sunset and the sea was beginning to develop an uncomfortable roughness.

There were, I believe (strange to say I never had a list of the flock I was to shepherd to the other side), more than sixty craft, all of US Navy: and to guide them, four British MLs. Most of the craft were small rectangular flat-bottomed craft built to carry and put ashore about twenty infantrymen. They raised in front of them a large bow wave as their engines struggled to push their square flat noses through the waves. With them were the larger tank-carrying craft and in the centre, like mother hens, the even larger control ships.

The real problem of the voyage was one of speed. The small craft could do no more than five knots and that set the speed of the convoy. We, the MLs, could not do less than about eight knots and that was with one engine shut down. Ours were Hall Scott petrol engines which ran on better than 90 octane aviation spirit, and prolonged running at low speed caused trouble with the plugs and the valves and particularly the 'valve inserts' in the engine. Starting up an engine which had been shut down could be difficult and showers of sparks came out of our funnel when revolutions were increased after a period on low power. This firework display was not welcome when trying to move without enemy detection on a dark night.

We tried to ease this problem by making one ML at a time act as the leader of the convoy and the navigator while the others circled the convoy at higher speed. This gave the MLs a chance to clear their engines but the leader at any one time had great trouble in stopping himself from going too fast and losing contact with the convoy during the very dark, rough and rainy night. Any form of guiding lights on the ships was, of course, unthinkable.

All that night we moved slowly across Lyme Bay and, as we did so, the weather became steadily worse and the sea became steadily rougher. In the Channel the tide can run at seven knots or even more at spring tides; and so our five-knots convoy was actually going backwards for part of the time. In the middle of the night, one of the small landing craft caught fire, making itself quite a beacon and lighting up all the ships around it.

We had been given an extra Officer for the operation and he, a young Midshipman, had come on board just before we sailed. Unfortunately he had never been in any small ships before. Indeed I wonder whether he had ever been in any ship before, because we found out as soon as we passed the boom at Salcombe that he could not stand the movement of the ML and he became almost unconscious with sea-sickness. He retired to his bunk and he stayed there throughout the entire operation only putting his head out of the hatch when we came back to the UK after our part in the first wave of the invasion was completed. He was just one of those people who turned green at the sight of a wave: how he ever got into the Navy — or even wanted to get into the Navy — is past my understanding.

It was our original plan to sail towards the south of the Isle of Wight to rendezvous there with other units which had sailed from other ports and then to set course for the Normandy beaches. On arrival off Portland, however, in the early daylight of 4th June and in very rough weather, we were ordered into Portland Harbour. And it seemed to us that everyone else had been ordered into Portland Harbour too. The vast expanse of the harbour was filled with landing craft of all shapes and sizes and all those in charge were going mad in trying to keep some sort of order and discipline.

I went ashore and was told the reason for the unscheduled stop. The landings timed for dawn on 5th June had had to be cancelled because of the very bad weather expected in the Channel on 4th June and the night of 4th/5th June. At my first briefing by those in charge at the Naval Headquarters it was not known whether the operation was cancelled indefinitely or whether it was to be regarded as a short delay.

There was, of course, a considerable confusion. What were we to do? How long would our food and water last? Were all the troops to be kept on board? Remember that the small landing craft were just about the most uncomfortable pieces of metal for twenty soldiers to remain in for any length of time and they had already spent a rough and miserable night in their restricted square box without shelter from the rain and the sea-spray which broke over them. Those in bigger ships could wait more happily, but those who were expected to be at the front end of the landing faced an extended period of discomfort (and that is a mild word for what they had to endure) on top of the serious blow to morale, which is inevitable when a great event for which one has prepared oneself is possibly not going to take place after all. We were all worried, too, about security. How could secrecy now be maintained when so many ships were milling about along the coast and in Portland and other harbours for at least an extra day?

Eventually the orders came through to tell us that the operation was only postponed for 24 hours. We now know the agonizing decision which had to be made on this and the gamble — with respect to the experts in weather prediction — that the seas would become calmer and the winds less windy in that 24 hours.

While waiting during that day ML 490 made several tours of the harbour, partly in an attempt to keep track of our own convoy and partly out of curiosity to see what other craft and convoys were also in Portland. To my surprise, I found that *HMS Centurion* was there. *HMS Centurion* was a dummy battleship. Onto an old battleship hull, they had fitted wooden 15-inch size guns and done everything to make her appear like the real thing. She was not intended to fight — only to deceive.

She was in Alexandria when I left in March and as I could only fly home with the clothes I wore, I had put all my other clothes and gear (including a tennis racquet) into two large suitcases. By good luck they were put on board *Centurion* in the care of some friends of mine from the MLs who had at that time been ordered to join *Centurion* for (so the rumour went) passage back to UK.

The rumour was correct. *Centurion* did indeed make the passage back to UK and here she was in Portland Harbour. I went alongside and was delighted to find some of my Mediterranean friends looking down at me from her enormously high deck. Lieut. Ken Hallows was one of them. They told me they had had a good passage home and were now expected to sail with the invasion fleets in the hope that a battleship — even a dummy battleship — would help to add alarm and confusion in the ranks of the enemy and eventually form part of an artificial harbour.

They also told me that my two suitcases had been safely put ashore and despatched to my home address. That would save me some money and clothing coupons. I still have those two large suitcases in the attic: I bought them in Alexandria and they were well-made of Egyptian leather, very heavy indeed and very durable.

In the afternoon of 5th June we were ordered to resume our voyage to France and to my surprise our convoy and all the others sheltering in Portland left in quite good order. I stayed till last in the harbour to round up any stragglers. I found no 'lost' ships but I did find one man on the jetty who had missed his ship. He appeared to be of Chinese origin and, as one would expect, was a cook. I took him on board and set off at best speed after the convoy.

I found the ship of the Chinese cook and with some difficulty managed to put him back on board where he was no doubt received with delight by all those who wanted more than bread and water on the voyage. I thought it strange that here was a Chinese cook sailing from Britain to France with a crew of American servicemen in order to fight the Germans.

We kept our flock clear of the Portland Race which in the rough seas was throwing up water spouts of turbulence. We set our QH equipment to the desired course pattern and ploughed and rolled slowly onward in low cloud, high wind and heavy rain. The soldiers in the small craft (and even in the larger craft) must have been very miserable indeed, but the weather was ideal for secrecy.

Our heavy radar equipment made us roll more than any other ML. I never heard of a radar-equipped ML capsizing like the *Mary Rose* off Portsmouth nearly 400 years earlier, but I was always conscious of the possibility, and did all I could to avoid being caught broadside on to a heavy sea. We suffered all the while from the problems of slow speed — the landing craft making five knots and the escorts having to zigzag or go in circles to keep down to it. The tide now took us westward or eastward of our course as it ebbed or flowed and navigation would have been a nightmare without our QH guidance.

On such a pitch black night with rain squalls and with not the smallest light permitted, this convoy of ships of many different sizes did well to keep together and not to collide by keeping too close. At one time we were ahead of schedule but we lost time on one over-elaborate zigzag, which the leading ML at the time decided to do, much to my annoyance. Towards the end we had to push on as fast as we could make our flock go, and we arrived at our designated gathering zone about one mile off the beach a little, but not seriously, behind time.

The convoys in that gathering zone had as escorts and navigational leaders some seven Royal Navy MLs and one US Navy PT boat. As soon as we reached the gathering zone — it was still quite dark and before the first faint light of dawn — these eight craft detached themselves to form a line from the gathering zone to the beach. It was along this guiding line that the landing craft would go when light came and the order to invade was given.

As the senior boat I took the centre of the line about 800 yards from shore. I anchored in darkness on the information of my QH and my radar picture of the shore line. The other MLs took station on me at two hundred yard intervals and the US Navy PT boat had insisted that he should take the innermost berth which was only two hundred yards from the beach. So, before daylight came there were eight of us strung out like a line of living buoys from the beach to an area more than a mile offshore where the great force of our landing and support craft waited their time to invade Utah Beach.

We sat there with our lifebelts and steel helmets on, at our guns, our radar sets, our W/T sets and even at our galley stoves cooking a breakfast. The sea was much calmer and we now had the shelter of the Cherbourg peninsula to the west of us. As daylight slowly came on a damp and cloudy morning, I was able to identify churches and other landmarks on the shore. It was with relief and with thankfulness for our navigational equipment that I calculated that I had anchored within two hundred yards of the spot which was designated as my objective in the plans.

I have read subsequently that the Utah Beach invasion force did not land at the right place on the Utah beaches. It has also been said that it was an advantage for them to have landed where they did, rather than where they should have landed, and so they profited from an error. Nevertheless, and despite the advantage they gained, I feel professionally upset to read that an error was made, especially when my own bearings taken from identifiable objects on the shore told me that ML 490 had anchored in the dark within two hundred yards of the appointed place. My explanation of the error is this. I was the central marker on which all the other MLs and the PT boat took station. The line led from a mile offshore to about two hundred yards from the beach and it is possible that while I could have been close to the right place at the centre or axis of the approach, the line might have swung on that axis, and the inshore end of it could have been much more than two hundred yards off station. This error could also have been exaggerated by the small landing craft being carried away from the line by the tide as they hurried to complete the last two hundred yards of the seaborne part of the attack.

Let me return to the events of the day. It was pitch dark when we anchored and the MLs ahead and astern of me took station on me to form the line of approach. Behind us and out to sea larger ships with larger guns were firing over our heads at unseen targets onshore. Secrecy was now abandoned but each of us still relied on the cover of darkness to avoid becoming a target. I saw no return fire from the German guns which our charts told us covered completely the area of sea in which our force was gathering, and in which we were anchored.

At daylight the first waves of landing craft passed us. The preliminaries were over and the real acts of invasion had started. Guns from the cruisers and destroyers were still firing over our heads but gradually these ceased as the landing craft closed the shore. It was then that we saw a dramatic sight. Coming in from the north with a heavy and continuous roar of engines, appeared a cloud (and that is a reasonable word to describe what I saw) of aircraft. There was a great variety of them, too. Some were towing gliders, some were on bombing missions, and around and above were the fighters. It was an inspiring sight to us and would have been more so to the troops landing and about to land on the beach, but I doubt whether they had time to look upward.

We became aware of some noise from the land but in the grey and misty morning, I could make out nothing through my binoculars. It was as if a stage army had passed by us, the audience, and had disappeared into the wings of the stage there to make noises of distant combat. More waves of troops passed us mostly crouching silently in their small square craft but one at least was more demonstrative. That US craft had hoisted a Confederate flag and at the stern held upright by his fellows in the boat stood a trumpeter sounding what I supposed to be the Charge of the Confederate Cavalry.

Some craft were already starting to come back from the beach with casualties and as they passed we learned that our inmost marker — the US PT boat — had suffered a direct hit with a heavy shell and had sunk with few survivors.

The infantry control ships remained in a circle out to sea well astern of us and directed further waves of troops ashore, but soon the reinforcement stopped. Had our force all landed or were some still held back? Was there a hold-up ashore? We in ML 490 did not know how the battle was going. We just remained there at anchor as the dull and misty early morning grew into a warm day. I did not recall that any of the tank landing craft had passed near me, yet later I knew that they had landed their tanks with fewer casualties than on other beaches. Perhaps they landed more off station than the infantry, and chose their spot regardless of our line of markers. I only remember seeing the infantry go by in their small craft.

The daylight grew on this almost midsummer day. The winds eased; the clouds grew thinner and the day grew warmer. There was an uneasy quietness. Tea came round to the men standing by their guns. Steel helmets came off. Some craft came past us going to and fro between the shore and the bigger ships but they were in no mood to stop and chat. So we stayed at anchor in idleness and ignorance.

I do not recall that I had slept since leaving Salcombe. We had been issued with benzedrine tablets which were supposed to keep us awake for abnormally long periods, but we were worried that when their effect wore off, nothing on this earth could stop us from falling asleep. I always refused to take these tablets because I could not be sure how long I would wish to remain active — what if I needed to be most alert just at the time when the benzedrine effect was wearing off? I must have rested at some time because it was two nights and a day since we set sail, but excitement and responsibility kept me going better than pills, and I felt no tiredness as the events of the day unfolded.

Apart from the tragic loss of the PT boat, we saw no activity from the shore batteries and there were no attacks on us from the air. One solitary Messerschmidt flew fast and low over us and disappeared without any action.

The crew had reacted well to the long hours of duty and of tension but with two exceptions. I was very cross when during the morning our one and only radio operator came up and complained to me that he was being kept on watch too long. There are, in more peaceful times, certain periods of the day and night when one-operator ships keep radio watch, leaving the operator time for rest in between these periods. But during this critical time I had insisted on a continuous watch on the radio, just as the gunners had stood by their guns, and I had stayed on the bridge for an abnormally long period. Our radio operator made his complaint. I told him that he was being asked to do no more than the rest of the crew and far less than the troops who were being landed on the beaches. He returned to duty in a disgruntled state of mind. When we returned to the UK he deserted — he was that kind of man.

The other exception was our young Midshipman. He continued to be rendered almost unconscious by seasickness and from Salcombe to our return he lay groaning in his bunk.

As night approached we were ordered to up anchor and with the other MLs form a screen — against E-boats and submarines — around the larger ships which remained about a mile offshore.

The night was dark and quiet.

Soon after daylight ML 490 was ordered to go to a position off Cherbourg where an enemy plane was reported to have come down in the sea. Cherbourg was still held by the Germans and the position given was not far from the harbour. We sighted a life raft with about five airmen in it who were doing their best to paddle the craft ashore. A gun onshore fired a couple of shots in our direction but they fell nowhere near us. Perhaps they were afraid of hitting the life raft or perhaps they respected our life-saving mission and were only firing as a warning against coming too close to the harbour.

We picked up the German airmen who had no serious injuries and took them to a large Tank Landing Craft (LCT) which, having put its tanks ashore, was given the job of housing prisoners who were being sent from the shore. In fact, so many were being crowded into the LCT that we were told to keep our five airmen and were given about a dozen more prisoners to take back home when we were ordered back to Portsmouth that evening.

During that day of D + 1 (the day of landing having been designated as 'D' Day in our plans) the offshore area had become unbelievably quiet. The sea was calm and the day was warm. There was a cruiser offshore which had played its part by shelling the shore batteries. Now the atmosphere was so relaxed that the enthusiastic First Lieutenant had parties of men painting ship: some were actually on cradles over the side splashing grey paint on with enthusiasm. This was a real case of the mad English dressing for dinner in the jungle.

It was a calm and fast trip back to Portsmouth. We handed over the prisoners we were carrying and awaited orders. We were short of fuel, water and food so there was no rest for the crew. We had no action damage to report but we had collected certain mechanical and electrical defects and the base staff came aboard to put them right. Those men from the base were tired out. Before, during and since the invasion they had worked enthusiastically for long hours, and I well remember seeing one Petty Officer fall asleep on his feet as he was trying to concentrate on a defect in our electrical wiring. Meanwhile, as if to show the differences in mankind, our radio operator deserted.

Without much delay we were ordered to sail to Falmouth which was our Flotilla base and we sailed, I believe, with ML 190 (Lieut. David Bound) which had been in company with us all the way from Salcombe. On arrival at Falmouth, we berthed at the Coastal Force base at Penryn where we found a welcoming party on the quayside anxious to catch sight of those just back from 'the other side.' There was an armed guard, too, awaiting 'our prisoners', and there was some disappointment when they found we had landed them in Portsmouth.

Seeing the welcoming party and their obvious emotion at the return of at least two small ships from a great and hazardous enterprise made me realize that, while we were concentrating busily on our day's work and thinking of nothing but ourselves, there were many, many other people we had never met, who were thinking of us and wishing us well. There had been an emotional build-up to this invasion as well as an assembly of men and equipment. There had been understanding of the supreme importance of success with an awareness of the high risk of defeat. There had been an expectation of heavy casualties whatever the outcome. We saw all this in the faces of those who welcomed us back.

We were very soon sent back to the invasion area carrying people and escorting ships backwards and forwards. The artificial harbour constructed off Sword Beach was now in use, but when Cherbourg was captured we went into the harbour and most unwillingly spent a night there. The port had only just been captured: booby traps had been left on the jetties and mines laid in the harbour. As the tide went out the ships' hulls would touch the mud on the harbour bottom, and just before we arrived one ship had set off a mine when its hull had come to rest on it. The tide was going out and when we were there and during the night we, too, would rest on the mud: I did not sleep well until the tide started to rise again.

The English Channel was full of traffic crossing backwards and forwards and on the English side going from harbour to harbour between Falmouth and Dover, — all to aid the build-up of forces in France and to supply every conceivable item of stores for those forces. All the time we seemed to be travelling urgently and we sometimes passed small landing craft with engines broken down in mid-Channel. They did not seem distressed and we did not stop. I hope someone collected them or towed them to their destinations.

One dark night there was a burst of firing in the sky above us and as we ploughed along on our way to France we saw a parachute drifting down from the low clouds. We were alongside almost as soon as the airman hit the water and we nearly suffered a casualty by being so keen to rescue him. He was swimming in the water still attached to, and surrounded by, his parachute and as some of our crew hung over the side to haul him aboard, he pulled out a signal pistol and fired a star shell which passed between the heads of those trying to rescue him. We were at first angry at such a stupid and unnecessary act but soon changed our minds when we found that he was very badly burned about the face and was probably blind. He was the German pilot of a reconnaisance plane which had taken off from a French airfield and had had the misfortune to meet a night fighter on patrol over the Channel. On reaching the French coast, we put him on board an LCT which had been converted into a hospital and we left with the hope he would get quick and good attention to the terrible injuries to his face.

For our journeys to the Normandy coast we were now using the 'Mulberry harbours' to land our personnel and our supplies. These Mulberries were artificial harbours constructed of large concrete structures and ships deliberately and carefully sunk so as to create a harbour wall enclosing a large area for craft to land and unload in reasonably calm water. Pontoons carried a roadway onto the shore and along these roadways from the jetties made by the sunken ships and the enormous concrete blocks, reinforcements and supplies of all kinds poured onto the shore. Utah Beach, where we first put troops ashore, did not have a Mulberry but the next American beach to the east — Omaha Beach — should have had one at St. Laurent.

Things did not go well with this construction and bad weather caused sufficient damage to the block ships to make it of limited use. Further west off Arromanche in the British sector, the Mulberry was much more successful and, reinforced by some parts intended for the St. Laurent structure, became the major supply port to which we made most of our visits.

All the time we were using our QH equipment. We were now expert at picking up the signals from the stations on the south coast of England, setting the appropriate line of approach on the screen and steering straight along it just by keeping the signals from two stations constantly intersecting on that line. Of course, one could set the wrong line and one of my flotilla, taking a high-ranking Army officer across, was proudly showing him how easy it was to steer 'straight down the line' until they found themselves at the wrong Mulberry harbour, having set the wrong line to be followed.

A week or two after the first landings, when the Army had advanced some way inland, things became relaxed and quiet on the coast: so much so that I allowed some of the crew to go ashore to 'have a look round.' They came back very pleased with themselves because they had walked a mile or two to a farmhouse and had bought a large amount of Camembert cheese (which we had not seen for several years).

On the way back and about mid-Channel in a calm night without wind or rain, we all became aware of a most disgusting smell. At first we thought we were passing through some wreckage, some disaster, with corpses of men or animals putrefying on the surface of the sea. But as we steamed ahead the smell persisted and we seemed to be in a cloud of foul smell which travelled with us.

We had the ship searched and it did not take long to find that the source of the trouble was the large box of Camembert. It was, perhaps, pre-war Camembert and although of a good vintage it had now been taken over by maggots. It was ditched overboard by volunteers detailed for the job and only the fish and the French farmer profited from the incident.

The rest of that summer was a collection of incidents. The war was being bitterly fought in northern France not so many miles from our journeys to and fro. We were always prepared for attacks from the air or from the sea but none came and as the weeks passed, our expectation of attack became the less. How very different from my life six months ago. Then to move in daylight meant almost certain attack from the air. Now we did not see any enemy planes and we moved freely by night and day.

For a month or so after D-Day ML 490 and the 11th ML Flotilla were still attached to the US Forces and our duties took us from Falmouth in the west to Portsmouth, the Isle of Wight and the Normandy beaches in the east.

We helped to guide the US ships along the Channel and on one night went out to find a US tug which, having crossed the Atlantic and made landfall near Penzance, now was fogbound and uncertain of its position somewhere between Plymouth and Start Point. Our radar was of immense advantage in such a situation: by its help we found the tug. The fog was dense and we shone our aldis light astern so that he could follow us with his bow almost over-hanging our stern. Our radar alone enabled us to navigate round Start Point and to the entrance to Dartmouth. It could even pick up buoys in the dead calm sea and we sailed confidently through the boom into Dartmouth Harbour seeing only the boom and the buoys as we passed close to them. The captain of the tug, who had no experience of radar, was amazed at our skilful navigation which he regarded as a kind of witchcraft in a dense fog on a dark night.

In Dartmouth I went alongside an MGB for the night and in the morning found that their Cox'n was someone I remembered well from the 42nd Flotilla and who had been with me in the Aegean. He had come home about three months after I had and was able to give me some news of things that happened after I left. He said one thing to me which gave me much satisfaction. He said: 'I hear you got the DSC, sir, all the boys were pleased about that. They thought that if anyone deserved it, you did.' I suppose that most people who receive an award wonder why they should be so honoured when others unrecognized seem to have done so much more. It gave me great pleasure to know that my crew and the crew of other MLs approved of my recognition. What I had received was only earned with their loyalty and support.

Start Point fogs were no fun even with radar. We were travelling east one day and ran right into one, and just at that time our radar warned us that right ahead was a convoy of ships travelling directly towards us at a fair turn of speed. Worse still, some of them, perhaps the escorts, appeared to be zig-zagging. Should we go right ahead and hope to pass down one of the lanes of ships? Before we could do otherwise, we were among them: noises of propellers and the swish of bow waves all round us. Then something was heard, or almost felt, right ahead on collision course. A 180-degree turn and full ahead! It was the only thing to do and as we settled on a westerly course in place of an easterly one, the bow of a large ship appeared right over our stern.

At that moment my No. 1 came up the after-hatch; it being my watch on deck, he had been sleeping below until the change of speed and the sharpness of our turn woke him up. As he looked out of the hatch he looked up and saw the awful sight of the bows of a ship above him. He was so surprised that he lost his footing and fell back into the cabin. Our turn of speed was just enough to save us from being run down, and another tight turn to starboard saw the large merchant ship pass by. We missed all the rest of the ships by a much wider margin and none but ourselves knew how close we were to losing an ML that day.

Many of the Americans we had to deal with were very new to the Navy, very inexperienced, but keen and enthusiastic to a degree which we found almost theatrical in its application to operations which we considered routine. Perhaps we had become old and tired in our appraoch to the war, particularly to the more boring parts of wartime duties.

We were in Falmouth Harbour one day, it was about noon, and I was visiting and probably having a midday drink with my old friend, Lieut. Alex Wallace, the commanding officer of ML 118. Suddenly our peaceful drink was interrupted by a young officer of the US Navy who cluttered down the ladder into the cabin shouting excitedly, 'Urgent signal for the CO of ML 118'. Alex slowly looked up from his gin.

'Yes, laddie, that's me, what's the bother?'

'Urgent sailing orders, sir'. was the reply.

Alex Wallace, my companion in the Mediterranean and now with five years wartime sea-going behind him, took the signal, read it in silence and slowly went up the ladder to look out onto the deck. He came back, again at leisure, handed the signal back to the young officer and said quietly, 'I can't go.'

The young man jumped up and down in astonishment and enraged bewilderment and said:

'Can't go? Can't go? Why ever not?' Lieut. Wallace looked very quiet and almost sorrowful as he said slowly,

'Well, you see, it's raining.'

That should have ended the scene with a general howl of laughter and another quick gin all round, but the slow Scottish humour passed right over the head of the young officer who, red in the face with indignation, drew himself up and like an avenging schoolmaster said:

'Don't you know there is a war on?' Unsmiling and outraged, he threw the signal on the deck and left. I wonder if he reported us to the US Naval Headquarters.

As the weeks moved on into July and August and the beachheads were consolidated by the Army which slowly fought its way eastward, so we too moved eastward. We left the west country and the seas off Cornwall and Devon and became for a while based at *HMS Hornet*, the Coastal Force base at Portsmouth.

Before we left the west, I did by chance have the opportunity to go back to Salcombe where for me the great 'D'-Day' adventure began. We were part of the escort of a convoy of cargo ships going westward from Portsmouth and as we reached Start Point the already foul weather deteriorated into a Force 9 southwesterly gale. This sort of weather is hard going for an ML and makes it a poor sort of escort. An Asdic watch is next to useless and the inability to fire guns with any degree of accuracy reduces their effectiveness to that of just noise-making.

There were two corvettes also escorting the convoy so I requested permission from the Senior Officer to shelter from the storm. My request was granted and, turning north against a heavy beam sea, I struggled over the bar into the Salcombe estuary. I anchored once more off the Ferry Boat Inn. How quiet and peaceful it looked. The tumult and the shouting had died. The Captains and the Kings had departed. Across the water in France many had made the sacrifice.

It was a moment of reflection and, for us, of thankfulness.

But for all that, we had our fun, too, and in this visit to Salcombe we played a rather cruel practical joke on our Third Officer, Sub. Lieut. Dickie Bales who was designated our Navigating Officer. When we left the convoy, my No. 1, Lieut David Turner, and I were on the bridge. Dickie Bales was below, off watch, and although the ML was being tossed about like a cork, he was undoubtedly fast asleep.

David Turner and I decided we did not need the help of our Navigating Officer to get into Salcombe and we also decided that when we were safely anchored and he had awakened, we would deny all knowledge of where we were. And we told the crew not to reveal that we were in Salcombe. Sure enough, Dickie Bales' head soon appeared out of the hatch; he looked round in amazement at the hills around the estuary and the attractive town alongside us and said: 'Where the hell are we?'

The answer from all of us was: 'You are the Navigating Officer, — if you don't know where we have anchored, how should we know!'

So after stamping round the deck in frustrated rage he lowered the dinghy and rowed ashore to the Inn to ask where we were. It did the reputation of the Navy no good at all but it was great fun for all except poor Dickie Bales. But you don't play jokes like that on someone who will not laugh with you afterwards and we thought enough of Dickie to know he would do just that.

In Portsmouth one summer day, I was summoned to the Senior Officer Operations and told that I was to place myself under the orders of Colonel Bill Browne of the Royal Engineers and, with such MLs of my Flotilla as were available in Portsmouth, carry out an operation which Col. Browne would reveal to me.

Col. Browne, a tall and impressive New Zealander, came aboard and with the COs of some six other MLs of the Flotilla gave us the detail of the unusual operation he wanted us to carry out.

The object was this: although the maps of England and France were in themselves excellent, the British Isles were not correctly placed in relation to the coast of the Continent. Consequently, when, for example, our aeroplanes over France were being directed by radar bearings from stations in England, those directions were not accurate enough. Bombing raids directed solely by radar were ineffective when it should have been possible to achieve a fine degree of accuracy at such comparatively short range. The maps had to be correctly co-ordinated and this was to be done by having observers on church towers and steeples in France and England taking sights on objects in mid-Channel. The objects in mid-Channel were to be balloons tethered to the decks of our MLs!

At that time the Army had not progressed much beyond Le Havre or perhaps Fecamp on the coast of France, and the nearest point on the English coast to the north of that was in the region of Brighton and Newhaven. On a day when the weather was clear and fine our six MLs steamed out to mid-Channel to a point somewhere south of Brighton and sat there bravely flying our balloons in an east-west line. I wonder what the enemy thought we were doing if they ever took any notice. At least the balloons should have made us safe from low flying aircraft, but we saw nothing high or low or on the surface for the whole of that cloudless and sunny day.

Col. Browne lived on board ML 490 for about a week while we were planning the operation, testing the equipment and then doing our balloon-flying in the Channel. In peace time he had been the Chief Surveyor for the Anglo-Iranian Oil Company, and among other assignments had spent many years in Iran mapping the

215

concession areas which the company had negotiated in that country. He was a keen yachtsman and he enjoyed his time on board ML 490. Before he left he asked me what I intended to do after the war. I said, 'Look for a job.' He told me that Anglo-Iranian was a good company to work for and he promised to give me a letter of introduction to the director to whom he had been, in peace time, responsible. This letter and his personal intervention did in fact get me a job with AIOC (now BP) when the war ended, but that is another story and follows almost two years after these events in mid-1944.

I received a very kind letter of thanks from Col. Browne who told me that the operation was successful but, he had to admit, was overtaken by events, because by the time all the new calculations had been worked out, the Army had moved on and either better sightings had been made from Dover to Cape Gris Nez, or radar control for aircraft over northern France had become unnecesary. Perhaps our work has been of some help to those constructing the Channel Tunnel.

Among the COs of MLs in Portsmouth at that time was Lieut. Cyril Brown of ML 153. A very efficient and careful officer who for that reason became the target of another of those practical jokes. One or two of the jokers (it shows perhaps that we were having an easier time in Portsmouth) enlisted the aid of someone in the operations office and caused a signal to be sent to Lieut. Brown. The signal spelt out in some detail that, owing to the evacuation of civilians from the towns in Normandy, the troops were suffering from an absence of women. Consequently, High Command had decided that women must be provided from England. Lieut. Brown was therefore instructed (by this entirely false but apparently official signal) to transport fifty prostitutes across the Channel and the girls would arrive on board ML 153 at noon the following day.

Lieut. Brown was horrified but his dedication to duty was absolute. He set about making elaborate arrangements and caused signals to be sent in all directions for such things as medical inspection of the women before they came aboard his ship, for doctors and medical orderlies to travel with them, for arrangements to separate the women from his crew (whether by barbed wire or Marines fixed with bayonets, I do not know).

The joke was in danger of getting out of hand within half an hour of its launching and had to be explained and abandoned before the dedication to duty and efficiency of Lieut. Brown caused the affair to come to the notice of those with the ability to make things very uncomfortable for us.

These games we played to enliven the hours while we awaited our next orders may make it appear that we were all relaxed and happy. But it was during this spell when we were based on Portsmouth, and the progress of the invasion meant that for a few weeks we were not worked so hard and had some time to reflect, that I began to question my health. I felt tired and I felt nervous. At sea I was not sleeping well and felt that I ought always to be on the bridge. I was, without justification, losing confidence in my fellow officers and my crew, and unless I was involved in everything, I was sure things would go wrong.

After all I had been at sea for five years and with very little leave. I had been in command of an ML for about four of those five years and in that time had had only ten days leave with my wife and family.

I dwelt on this, I brooded on it and became worried. So I went to see the Medical Officer and was seen by a Surgeon Commander. He listened to me, examined me, then he looked hard at me and said I had nothing wrong with me. He said this so coldly, so devoid of any sympathy and understanding that I was sure he regarded me as just another malingerer trying to persuade him to prescribe some extra leave.

I thanked him and left immediately. If there was anything wrong with me, I must cure it myself. I faced my nervousness head-on and told myself to be sensible. Helped perhaps by a rather easier time and less arduous duties, I think the phase slowly passed. And as this phase of mental strain passed, so did my period of operations in the English Channel between the coasts of France and England.

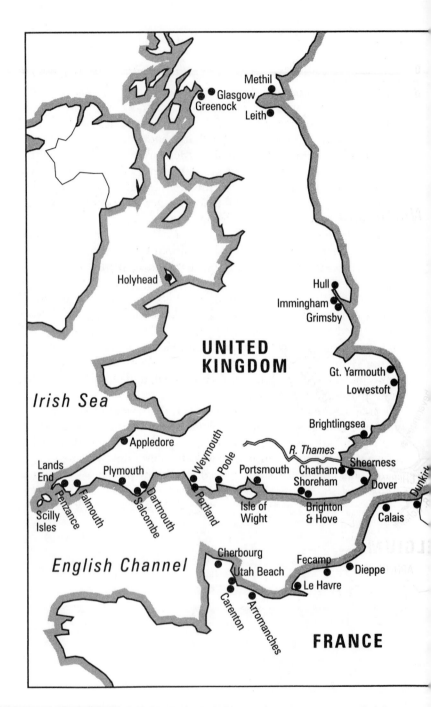

Methil
Glasgow
Greenock
Leith

Holyhead

Hull
Immingham
Grimsby

UNITED
KINGDOM

Gt. Yarmouth
Lowestoft

Irish Sea

Brightlingsea

Appledore

Weymouth
Poole
Portsmouth
Chatham
Sheerness
Shoreham
Dover

Lands
End
Plymouth

R. Thames

Penzance
Falmouth
Salcombe
Dartmouth
Portland
Isle of
Wight
Brighton
& Hove

Dunkirk

Scilly
Isles

Calais

Cherbourg
Utah Beach
Fecamp
Dieppe

English Channel

Carenton
Arromanches
Le Havre

FRANCE

17

The North Sea — Winter of 1944/45

In the autumn of 1944, the flotilla was ordered to Grimsby on the east coast. We sailed in twos and threes from Portsmouth to Dover and when I arrived there, the German batteries near Cape Gris Nez on the French coast were busily shelling the harbour and town. The Allied armies were approaching the German gun positions, Boulogne and Calais were soon to fall to the Allies and the German gun positions would be captured. So the Germans were using their last hours before retreat or capture to expend their arsenal of shells and were firing them at the nearest point of England. I berthed alongside Dover harbour wall together with an assortment of MLs and MTBs. Every now and again there was a loud bang as a large shell from France landed in the region of the harbour.

I went to the operations office for orders regarding the rest of our voyage to Grimsby. A sweet young WREN told me that I would be given orders to sail tomorrow. Hearing another loud bang somewhere not too far away, I said, 'Can't I sail now?'

'No,' she said, clearly enjoying the situation, 'you stay in the harbour tonight and sail tomorrow.'

'What time?' I said.

'Nine o'clock,' she replied.

'Why not at first light, say about 5 am?' I asked.

'All right,' she said, 'what about 7 am?'

'Done,' I replied, thus ending a most extraordinary bargaining session. I have often wondered at the policy which kept us unnecessarily long in a harbour being shelled. I suspect that there was more than a little of the feeling 'We have to put up with this all the time, why not teach these softies from Portsmouth what it is like to be the target of those bloody guns in France.'

No one could say that the shelling was intense and the chance of being hit was very small. Nevertheless, I did not sleep well. We sailed very smartly on time. Northward across the Thames estuary after carefully keeping clear of the Goodwin sands.

The idea of sending us to the East Coast had several facets. In the long term we were bound for Germany. High Command were optimistic of a speedy end to the war and we were to be prepared for occupation duties in German ports and even to sail up the Rhine to the industrial cities when they had been captured.

At Grimsby the hulls of our MLs were to be covered with copper sheeting as protection from marine parasites and the fungus which plain wood would gather in fresh water. After that we would go to Yarmouth for special training in the duties of an occupying force and to learn the elements of land warfare and street fighting, coupled with an ability to mount a ceremonial parade. All this would take some time for the whole flotilla had to be made ready. Meanwhile, Germany was still fighting with determination and we were held in operational readiness to assist those Coastal Forces who night after night were protecting the East Coast and acting offensively against German E-boats which continued to lay mines and threaten Allied shipping using the channels up and down the East Coast.

At Grimsby, two of us were kept at readiness every night. Our berth was at a jetty alongside the railway sidings. It may seem unbelievable but our only communication with Naval Headquarters, and the only channel through which orders might come, was by way of the railway siding's telephone. The terminal of this vital telephone link was in the night watchman's hut — a small wooden structure like a sentry box — situated about a hundred yards from the jetty where the MLs were secured.

I did my turn at telephone watch duty and spent many hours sitting with the railwayman in his hut, keeping ourselves warm — for it was now winter — by a small brazier which he kept glowing in a metal bucket with holes in it placed at the entrance of the hut.

He was a fine man. To me he seemed very old, perhaps he was nearing sixty, and we passed the hours pleasantly talking of many things. One of his stories has always remained with me. In 1940, he said, while he was at work he heard of the victories of the German armies, the evacuation of the British Army from Dunkirk, capitulation of France and so on. And one evening at the depths of the bad news when everything seemed black and all seemed lost, he went home to his wife.

'Have you heard the news?' he said.

'Yes,' she replied, and they sat down in silence for a while.

'Do you want your supper?' she asked.

'No,' he replied, 'I don't feel hungry.'

'Neither do I,' she said and so they sat again in silence. They switched on the wireless for the news and it was the evening when

Churchill broadcast one of his greatest speeches to the nation. He described and did not minimise the disasters; he promised nothing but blood, sweat and tears but we would fight on. We would fight on the beaches, we would fight in the fields . . . his words are now history but one can perhaps imagine those two elderly, sad and lonely people sitting in their kitchen in the fading light of evening, listening intently to every word and drawing strength from the oratory of a great leader. When the speech was ended, there was silence in the kitchen and then, the night watchman told me, he turned to his wife and said: 'I would like some supper now.'

'So would I,' she replied.

I never did get a call to go to sea over that railway telephone but I enjoyed the companionship of the night watchman for many midnight hours.

We nearly came to grief at that jetty and it was perhaps only the experience of several years of sleeping in an ML that warned me of trouble and roused me from my bunk. A gale had sprung up. That should not have worried us being, I thought, safely tied up alongside a jetty in the harbour. But when I went on deck I could see that it was a very high tide, we were no longer protected by the jetty and were being blown violently away from it secured by only two ropes which were both under very great strain. The ropes should have been doubled up but this precaution had been neglected.

Just as I got on deck and asked our watchman what he thought he was doing, one of the ropes parted, leaving us like a dog on a leash straining at one line only from our stern. The crew were called on deck. Engines were started and we hauled ourselves closer until someone could jump ashore. Then we used all the lines we could find to secure ourselves properly this time and, having sworn heartily at all those responsible (and at several who were not responsible) for our near disaster, we doubled the sentries and retired again to our bunks.

Having been copper-bottomed at Grimsby, we were ordered to Great Yarmouth, which was one of the major Coastal Force bases on the East Coast. On the way down from Grimsby we were involved in an alarm relating to a reported midget submarine. We spent some hours in a search but neither heard nor sighted anything.

At Great Yarmouth we (that is, the whole 11th ML Flotilla) were supposed to 'work up' and train to become part of the occupying forces in a post-war Germany. There is a saying to the effect that he who sold the lion's skin before he caught the lion was killed in trying to get it. And so it was premature to organise the occupation of an enemy who still had much fighting spirit left.

Nevertheless, we did our land-based training. We spent hours at the ranges firing pistols, rifles, Lewis and Bren guns. We spent hours marching in ceremonial parades — officers with drawn swords and so on.

At the end of several weeks, we were inspected by a formidable RN Captain. He thought nothing of our ceremonial marching. He was appalled at the inability of the officers to hit anything with their pistols, but he was delighted with the members of our crew who put up a really remarkable exhibition of target shooting with Lewis and Bren guns. We were therefore passed as fit to occupy Germany and we awaited the orders to do so. The fable of the man who sold the lion's skin before he killed the lion and the saying about counting chickens before they are hatched, remained with us. The war on land did not progress speedily that winter and before the final advance was made, the reverse of Arnhem and the near disaster of the German Ardennes' offensive had to be suffered.

So the 11th ML Flotilla was gathered together for normal Coastal Force sea-going duties and was ordered to the Belgian port of Ostend which was then the farthest port to the east which had been captured. Beyond Ostend eastwards, lay the river Scheldt and the cities of Flushing and Antwerp, still German-held. To the west lay the port of Dunkirk which had been by-passed by the Army and remained as a German-occupied bastion in our rear.

Ostend was filled with MTBs, MGBs and MLs. It was in those days a frontier town. It had been 'liberated' by the Allies but the population knew that the Germans were still not far away. Signs of jubilation were not in evidence and perhaps some of the residents were not keen to show favours to the Allies in case the Germans should return and call them to account for their pro-Allied support. It was, in that cold and dreary winter, a cheerless town and if there were delights to be found in it we did not have the time to seek them out, for we were kept busy, and when not busy then always in a state of readiness.

From Ostend to the Norfolk coast of England was the sea frontier. From the harbours in Holland, German E-boats would come out by night on offensive patrols and on mine-laying missions. The MTBs and MGBs from Ostend in Belgium and from Yarmouth and Lowestoft in England would be there to engage them and drive them off. The MLs generally formed an inshore screen. We spent night after night patrolling or, if the sea was calm, lying with engines stopped just outside Ostend listening on hydrophones for the sound of high speed engines, which would be E-boats, or a less obvious noise which a midget submarine might make as it tried to make its way into Ostend or farther west.

We listened on our R/T sets to the quite exciting dramas going on farther out to sea. The Navy usually placed some larger ships such as frigates or corvettes in positions in the southern North Sea where they could keep a radar watch on marine activity off the coast of Holland and North Germany. MTBs and MGBs would lie near these ships in groups of three or four boats.

As we lay a mile or so off Ostend at night, we would hear the mother ship report 'Four E-boats leaving Scheveningen steering 280 degrees, speed 25 knots.' The leader of a group of MTBs (or MGBs) would reply. 'Setting course to intercept.' Then would follow a series of reports and instructions from the mother ship giving the changing courses and speeds of the E-boats and guiding the MTBs to meet them. Eventually would come the shout from the British boats that they could see the enemy. Then almost always came the disappointment — 'E-boats turning away, increasing their speed to 35 knots, losing contact.' For the E-boat diesel engines could drive their boats at this speed and more, while the petrol engines of the British boats could only reach about 30 knots, and so if the Germans wanted to avoid a fight — which they normally did — they could easily do so.

I often wondered why those German E-boats often avoided action rather than joined battle. They had the speed advantage; they had diesel engines against the more inflammable petrol engines of the British; and they had as many guns as an MTB, although less than an MGB. Probably their objective was to lay mines and if they could not achieve that, then their orders were to turn for home.

For the most part, we MLs stayed inshore and watched and waited. One night there was the roar of engines approaching but before we could sight anything, the craft, presumably an E-boat, turned away from us and the roar died away too. On another night, during a gentle patrol along the coast, an Asdic contact was reported in rather shallow water. We made a spirited attack and at the same time that I gave the order to drop two depth charges, I sighted an object right under our bows. We just missed a collision and as it passed down our side, I saw it was not the conning tower of a

224

midget submarine but a large buoy. I knew then that our contact had been its anchor cable or perhaps its concrete mooring slab. Anyway we did our best to blow it all up, but this vandalism was prevented because our depth charges, which were activated by water pressure, had a minimum setting of 50 feet and the water was too shallow to trigger their explosion. Somewhere off the Belgian coast there may still be a buoy with two rusty but perhaps dangerous depth charges alongside its moorings.

One morning, at the end of October 1944, all available MLs were summoned to a briefing. This was the first we had heard of an invasion which was being mounted on the island of Walcheren which guards the approaches to the River Scheldt and the port of Antwerp. The island was, of course, heavily defended by the Gremans and the advance of the Army through Belgium and Holland would be greatly helped if the coastal region could be cleared of enemy and the important waterway of the Scheldt opened up as a means of supplying the Army, whose land supply lines were now stretched a long way from the ports of Calais and Ostend.

It appeared to me that the Walcheren invasion was somewhat hastily mounted. The Army and Marine landing forces were to be conveyed in the small beach landing craft which each held about twenty men. These craft were mostly the survivors from the Normandy landings. There were also tank landing craft and the shore defences were to be engaged by LCRs (Landing Ship Rockets) and LCGs (Landing Ship Guns). Attacks by RAF bombers and fighters were planned to take place on the gun emplacements which lined the low shore line of this flat and rather featureless island.

At the briefing those in command of the Naval units were assigned their duties. The MLs were to provide escort for the landing craft until those craft formed a line to attack and land on the shore. Some of the MLs then had to act as beacons to mark certain areas of attack — one was ordered to anchor to mark a shallow sand bank on which landing craft might run aground. This bank was very close inshore, and to anchor there appeared suicidal unless the shore guns had been silenced. The ML selected for this job was decided by the Naval officer in charge of the briefing. The CO of this ML was sitting next to me and it seemed that the briefing officer had just pointed to one of us at random. On such things does one's life depend.

ML 490 was ordered to attend on the large landing craft chosen to act as the command boat and carrying the Senior Officers in charge of the operations. My duties were not otherwise defined: I was the spare number available for any job required as the attack unfolded.

We sailed from Ostend on a miserable day with rain and low, dense cloud. It was such an unfavourable day that support from the air was considered impossible, and the RAF part of the operation was cancelled. The attack on the heavily defended coastline was for the Navy and Army alone.

The force arrived on time and in good order in the early morning of 1st November, 1944, and the attack began in the first daylight of a dull and rainy day. The small landing craft strung themselves out facing the coast like a line of infantry. Perhaps the invasion area was about a mile long. Behind this disciplined line were ranging the LCRs and LCGs.

An LCR was a flat-bottomed tank landing craft converted as a rocket launcher. On its flat deck were mounted row upon row of tubes from which rockets would be electrically fired. The crew were aft and could not stay on deck because of the heat and flame generated when the rockets were fired. They retired behind armour-plate and steered and fired by the aid of radar screens in their protected quarters. The LCGs were similar ships but in place of rockets they carried three or four Naval 4.7-inch or 4-inch guns each operated by a gun crew and directed from the gunnery control on the bridge aft.

It was planned that the LCRs would hold their fire until the line of invasion craft had reached a few hundred yards from the shore and then, firing over the landing craft, would saturate the defended and mined beaches with their exposive rockets. The LCGs would cruise slowly, parallel to the beach, engaging with their guns the enemy gun emplacements which could be clearly seen on the low and flat landscape of the island. Except for a township in the distance and the defences near the beach, the landscape looked deserted and largely without trees or habitation.

The line of landing craft set off, the LCRs formed up behind; the LCGs started to close the shore. Shells began to fall from the shore batteries. Then came a tragedy. The landing craft were coming into range of enemy small arms' fire and the time had come to saturate the beach defences with rocket fire.

On the LCRs the radar images of the low and flat beach did not show up well, but what did appear well as a firm and positive line, was the well-disciplined and straight formation of infantry landing craft approaching the beach. We were told afterwards that some of the LCRs took this line as their target, thinking it to be the beach, and the first wave of our own troops was struck by part of the shower of exploding rockets. By this bad error, the enemy defences escaped and our own troops suffered. But most still remained to fight their way ashore and not all the rockets were ill-directed.

The LCGs were superb. They cruised along the beach exchanging shot for shot with the shore batteries. Their losses were heavy but they were firing to good effect. Further waves of Army went ahore and as the hours went by, the firing from the shore batteries declined.

At sea we were not having a happy time. The ML detailed to mark the sandbank was hit by a large shell which went through the bridge, killing the CO and all who were there with him. She cut loose her anchor and came hell for leather past me, bridge destroyed, blood running off her deck and down her side as she made for the depot ship to off-load dead and wounded and retire from the action.

As many of the ships attempted to close the shore, we found we were in a minefield. Two of the larger landing craft near me went up in a cloud of water and pieces of metal. I saw a man thrown above the spray and debris high into the air as if fired from a gun.

There were wrecks around me from mines and shell fire, there were men alive and dead in the water. There were so many to be rescued that I knew it was impossible to save them all. Should I go to this group or to that? I remember the despair of the decision, knowing that by going one way to save some struggling men I must leave others in the water who would not be there when I had time to go back in their direction.

The chance on which life or death depends was once more shown to me. The briefing officer had seemingly at random pointed to the Commanding Officer of the ML who was to anchor on the sandbank and die there. Now by rescuing some men I had to leave others to drown. A man's life and a man's death depended on my decision. There was an awful desire to do nothing because I could not do everything. We saved all we could but there were many we could not.

Commander Sellar in charge of the LCGs had two LCGs sunk under him but slowly the LCGs won the day. The enemy fire ceased and the beach was secured by the Army.

By the afternoon the battle was won. Walcheren was captured and the forces of the Army which had landed linked up with Allied forces fighting their way northward along the landward side of the Scheldt estuary. Among those forces was my cousin, Captain Dennis Grant, MC.

The successful but badly-battered Naval force made its way back to Ostend and a bloody operation which has had little publicity was over.

It was a hard winter in Ostend. The North Sea is a rough, cold place at that time of year. I remember Lieut. R. K. Stracey of ML 347 coming in from a night patrol, berthing alongside and stepping into the cabin of ML 490 to report. His eyebrows were covered with ice and his oilskins were white and shiny with frozen spray. It was always a strict rule with us that we never drank alcohol at sea but on those cold dark days it was not long before the spirits cupboard was opened when harbour was reached.

The capture of Walcheren meant that we could extend our patrols farther to the east, and one of the weapons of the enemy which we had to watch for was the one-man submarine. These were launched from north German and Dutch harbours and attempted to make their way towards the port of Ostend and westward to the Channel and the east coast of England. We were told to try to capture one of these midget submarines if we found one. It was generally believed that an attcmpt to do this was the cause of the explosion which destroyed with all hands an ML from another flotilla when it was on patrol off the Dutch coast. These submarines were nothing more than a torpedo with a space made amidships for a man who could steer and control the speed of the machine. The explosion could have been caused accidentally or even deliberately by the driver in order to avoid capture at the cost of his life and the lives of those attempting to take the submarine in tow.

Some weeks later, we were ordered to go to the assistance of another ML which had detected and captured a midget submarine and was attempting to tow it back to Ostend despite the fatal outcome of the earlier attempt. By the time we sighted them, they had taken the pilot on board and lashed the whole explosive device alongside the ML. It was about half the length of an ML and it was rather a terrifying sight to see the ML steaming slowly back to Ostend with a live torpedo-like object bumping along beside her. She got back to harbour safely, the submarine was detached and moored in a solitary position at an unused jetty where experts started to crawl all over it. The CO of the ML no doubt stopped sweating and had a well-deserved drink. I hope he was at least commended for a very gallant action.

It was not only the enemy who could damage us. After a night patrol, I had gone ashore on the morning of 14th February, 1945 to a small building on the jetty where there were lavatories and washing facilties. There was even a bath there and, if one was in early, there was hot water too. I was lying in this beautiful hot bath, relaxing and without a worry on my mind when there was the father and mother of an explosion outside and the ceiling of the bath house fell in on me.

I grabbed a pair of trousers — the requirements of modesty being stronger than the fear of injury — and rushed out of the doorway which was now without a door. I looked up and there right overhead was a formation of bombers flying at a rather low altitude. I should have known at once, but I did not, that these were US Air Force heavy bombers returning from a raid on Germany. It was absolutely a coincidence that they were flying overhead at that time.

My judgement of the situation was perhaps impaired by the continuation of shattering explosions going on around me. I had ducked back inside the ruins of the wash house when I saw the bombers but it very soon became obvious that it was not bombs exploding around me. The planes had passed. I went out into the open again and found myself in a representation of Hell: flames and smoke, people running and people shouting. There was no obvious reason for the chaos and no sign of where the eye of the storm might be, so that one might go to it if brave or run from it in fear.

To tell the tragic story of this event, some background description of Ostend harbour is necessary. I will describe it as it was then — it may be much the same today.

The central part of the harbour consisted of a deep and wide main estuary leading straight to the sea through harbour walls. Leading off the main estuary on the western side were several inlets or docks which could take a large ship or several smaller ones. The whole of these waterways was tidal, and the rise and fall of the tide was considerable. The western side of the estuary and the sides of all the docks leading off it were built up with perpendicular walls of brick and stone. When the tide was out, a small craft could be some twenty feet below the surface of the dock and the ship could only be reached by a ladder of iron rungs built into the sheer side of the jetty wall.

The fleet of MTBs, MGBs and MLs was moored alongside the western wall of the main harbour or estuary and in the docks leading off through narrow entrances in that western wall. Every night most of this Coastal Force fleet was at sea and in the daytime the crews would be catching up on sleep before preparing the ship for sea on the following night. The whole of this fleet was powered by high octane aviation spirit, highly inflammable to the point of being explosive when confined. It was a danger that all Coastal Force crews had lived with for so long that it was easy for them to disregard or even forget the danger. So long as the fuel was contained in the fuel tanks, everything should be safe and these fuel tanks were covered with a rubber-like subtance which was supposed to make them self-sealing. This meant that if a bullet or shell splinter pierced the tank, the rubber would close up the hole behind it so that leaks were prevented and fire should be avoided.

Fuel leaks did occur however: perhaps when taking on fuel, which one did nearly every day, or from the engine room where feed pipes were rarely secure from the occasional malfunction or the damaging effects of vibration, the pounding of the sea and the concussion of gunfire. If not immediately detected and stopped, these leakages of petrol ended up in the bilges of the craft and mixed with the salt water which accumulated there in the normal course of sea-going activities. Too much water in the bilges affected the performance of the ship and bilges were thereafter regularly pumped out — particularly in craft requiring speed, such as MTBs.

On that tragic morning, the tide was low. The small Coastal Force boats were far below the level of the jetties, resting on stagnant water almost as if they were in a deep pit rather than in a dock open to the estuary at one end. Perhaps no one really knows how the fire started but most of those in Ostend at the time would give this explanation. As a matter of routine some of the boats had pumped out their bilges. Because this was done frequently, nobody paid much attention to it and so nobody noticed that there was enough petrol pumped out with the water to spread an inflammable film over the surface of the water in one of the docks where about a dozen MTBs were berthed. Had the tide been going out rapidly, this film might have been carried out of the small dock and dispersed harmlessly in the wide estuary. But the tide was already low and, although still ebbing did not provide sufficient movement to shift the polluted water from the dock.

As was the custom, most of the crews were below deck sleeping after the long night at sea but some elected to sit chatting above deck and one of those, having smoked the best part of a cigarette, may have thrown the fag-end over the side into what he thought was water. If so he was throwing it into petrol, and within seconds the surface of the water in the dock was on fire—a quickly raging fire.

However the fire had started, there was nothing the crews could do to stop it. They tried to climb up the iron rungs of the ladders in the side of the dock. Some succeeded but the heat and flames and lack of oxygen overcame many before they could reach the top some twenty feet above. Those below deck had no chance at all. Soon the hulls of the ships, wooden hulls, were on fire. The petrol tanks exploded, the ammunition exploded, the compressed air bottles of the torpedoes exploded and the depth charges and torpedo war heads were in danger of following.

I made my way through the heat, smoke and chaos and was at least able to conclude that the whole harbour was in danger. ML 490 was by good fortune berthed with the other MLs alongside the wall of the main estuary. At the moment, they were clear of fire but blazing petrol on the surface of the water was spreading out of the inferno of the dock into the estuary and, their ropes burnt away, blazing hulls of what were once MTBs were also starting to drift like fire ships out of the dock into the main stream where MLs were berthed. Apart from this obvious fire hazard the explosions were sending burning debris into the air and lethal pieces of metal and spent ammunition were flying through the air for considerable distances.

I ran back to the jetty intending to take ML 490 out to sea only to find that my No. 1 had very properly taken that action already. He, with all the other MLs and with those MGBs and MTBs not trapped or on fire were well underway towards the mouth of the harbour where they waited until later in the day when the fires died down and it seemed safe for them to return.

This left me on the jetty and the best I could do was to make my way back to the blazing dock to see whether I could in any way help. I have said that I left the bath-house in only a pair of trousers. In the confusion, I had come across an Army great coat which had a corporal's stripes on the sleeve. In this strange outfit of black trousers, an Army coat and with no hat I ran towards the fire. At the side of the blazing dock from which flames were rising as if from a volcano, with explosions great and small sending flying debris, were standing absolutely heroic firemen playing water from their hoses from the edge of the pit into the raging heat below them. They were Army fire fighting services and, I think, local Belgian civilian services.

They had driven one of their engines so close to the edge of the blazing pit that it was itself on fire with its rubber wheels already burnt off. There was a jeep close to the edge with a live torpedo on top of it — the torpedo had been blown out of the dock below by an explosion and landed on the jeep without itself exploding although it was getting dangerously hot where it had rested.

An Army sergeant saw me, and taking stock of my apparent rank of corporal, ordered me to join a chain of men rolling depth charges from a store too near the fire to a spot of safety farther along the jetty. This was no time to argue about rank, I was glad of a useful job to do, and for some time I rolled warm depth charges away from the scene of the fire.

The very heat and fury of the fire made it short-lived. Within an hour or so the worst was over. But a flotilla of MTBs had been destroyed and over seventy men had been lost.

Ostend Cathedral is close to the harbour and to the dock where the disaster took place. The force of the explosions was so great that its huge spires were suspected to have been so badly shaken as to be unsafe, and for some time the surrounding area was closed to traffic in case masonry should fall.

The Coastal Force craft which had escaped the flames returned to their berths and I rejoined ML 490. Even on these ships there had been casualties. One CO was killed by a flying piece of metal as he took his craft to safety down the estuary and away from the fire.

A sad day and a bad day for Coastal Forces; by an accident or an act of carelessness, we had done ourselves more damage than we had suffered in months of engagements with the enemy.

During that winter and early spring, the advance of the Allied armies seemed to be slow. There was the failure at Arnhem; the German Ardennes offensive threatened to cut off Belgium once more, and we wondered about the evacuation of Ostend. Meanwhile behind us the German garrison held out in Dunkirk.

On patrol outside Ostend one night, we were surprised to see a light further out to sea. In those war-time days lights either at sea or on the land were so rare as to cause questions and alarm.

We had become accustomed for some six years to pitch blackness during the night, and to show a light invited a bomb on it or a shot at it.

We set off northward to investigate and came upon a small fishing vessel showing a bright light, as many of them used to do for peace time fishing. As we came near the four men on board showed signs of panic and ran to and fro so much and so fast that I could not help wondering whether they were over-acting a part. It was rough out there and boarding was dangerous so we made them understand that they must follow us. It would have been unwise to take them into Ostend without investigating further, so we waited until daylight and as the sea was moderating, we were able to put a boarding party on to the craft. Sub. Lieut. Dickie Bales and two men made the jump successfully as we ran alongside.

Now Dickie Bales was convinced that they were harmless fishermen and had protested to me that we were just harrassing poor starving Dutchmen who were trying at great risk to themselves to find food for their families. So he jumped aboard in a friendly fashion with his revolver out of sight and quite ready to shake hands and wish them luck.

He was wrong and could have been in danger. As soon as he was aboard, they took off their oilskins and revealed German uniforms underneath. They surrendered peacefully and the surprised Sub. Lieut Bales took command as they followed ML 490 into Ostend. They were, in fact, a small unit taking food to the garrison in Dunkirk and, among other things, had a very large amount of butter on board which seemed a strange priority when there must have been so many other things badly needed.

18

Denmark and the Baltic

By the beginning of April 1945 the Armies of the Allies were making steady progress and there was some relaxation of the heavy duties which the Coastal Force units had been carrying out from Ostend. The Admiralty envisaged other work for us and perhaps we should now be involved in the duties for which we had had some training in the previous Autumn: namely, the occupation of enemy waters and harbours following an armistice or peace treaty.

Since last autumn, the ships had been worked hard. They had stood it well but hulls and engines and all other equipment badly needed a thorough overhaul before reporting to a base where little or no maintenance facilities could be expected.

In the second week of April ML 490 left Ostend for the Thames and after an interesting voyage up river, under Tower Bridge, London Bridge and all the others up to Twickenham, we berthed at the yard of J. Mears at Twickenham to undergo a re-fit. Subject to an officer and some of the crew standing by, we all had leave in turn. It was, I think, well-earned and was reasonably generous because the re-fit was not completed until 22nd May 1945 when the last of the crew returned from leave.

It was during this time and while I was on leave that Germany surrendered. This was 'VE Day' and was joyously celebrated by a population which had seen war so close for so long. Pictures and descriptions of that day have been produced in detail elsewhere. While my wife and I knew that there was more to be done before I could return home (affairs in Europe could not be considered as peaceful for some time yet and war, to which I might be sent, was still raging in the Pacific), nevertheless I could see in my wife's face that some of the tension had been lifted.

On the ebb tide on 22nd May, we left Mears' yard with a pilot on board and made our way downstream to Hay's Wharf near London Bridge. Although we still had electricians working on board and the radar refused to operate properly, we sailed on for Sheerness. At Sheerness we landed all old ammunition and took on new supplies. We took on stores, had a new Asdic dome fitted and went to a buoy to 'swing compasses' — that is, to have them adjusted and corrected.

On 27th May, we received orders to proceed north to Rosyth on the Firth of Forth and we entered Immingham that evening. Our radar was still giving trouble and we had an electrical fault in one engine. The base staff at Immingham worked on these and we left on the afternoon of 29th May without all these defects having been rectified. At least we had the satisfaction of good gunnery trials during the passage.

Entering the firth of Forth on 30th May we went first to Grangemouth for refuelling and in the evening we entered the docks at Methil. There was an interesting entry in the ship's log at this date, 31st May, which read 'In view of peace time conditions, the ship's company is organised into three watches for leave and at sea.' Throughout our wartime service in Coastal Forces we had been in two watches which meant that in harbour half the crew could go ashore and the other half stayed on duty. At sea it meant a routine of '4 hours on' and '4 hours off.' Now we only retained a third of the crew on board in harbour, and at sea they had 4 hours on and 8 hours off.

All this time, electrical experts came and went and still left us with a defective engine. We moved from Methil to Leith and then back to Methil. More experts came and went. We even had a few days leave while the engine was taken to pieces but we also had typhus injections to prepare us for the health problems expected in Europe. Eventually the engine was passed as fit and the only defect left was in the radar equipment. The authorities were now losing patience and, defects or not, we were ordered to sail for Kristiansand in Norway on 7th June 1945 in company with ML 119 (Lieut. Paul Johnstone RNVR).

It was a most uncomfortable voyage. There was a force 4-5 wind which first caused a heavy swell from the south, taking us on the beam and causing prodigious rolling for a long period. Then the wind veered to the west and increased so that we were chased by a steep sea making the steering difficult as the waves lifted our stern and threw us forward into the trough where our bows dug themselves into the wave ahead. Worse still, the engine fumes from our short funnel blew continuously forward over the bridge giving us all a headache and a queasy stomach.

Our own engines behaved well but those of ML 119 gave trouble all the way, and we had to reduce speed to 1200 revolutions, which means about 12 knots, and at this speed we suffered much more from the pitching and rolling of the heavy waves. However, we made a good landfall and, feeling tired and rather ill, made fast to a pier in Kristiansand in the evening of 8th June.

Kristiansand looked heavenly in its peacefulness. The crew were kept hard at work cleaning ship, stripping and greasing the guns after our spray-soaking voyage across the North Sea. We were aware that we were going to represent the Royal Navy in Copenhagen and we wanted to look our best in a city only just being relieved of German occupation. Ashore we found that food was short in Kristiansand except for fish which seemed plentiful in the market.

As a precaution against fuel shortage we had carried a deck cargo of 87-octane petrol in ex-German jerricans which were so much superior to the leaky, shiny tin containers we had to carry around the the Mediterranean, and no longer did we have to worry about the fire hazard of petrol dripping from inferior British containers onto our wooden decks. Having extinguished all lights on board, we poured 400 gallons from the cans into our tanks. We retained about 20 cans (100 gallons) as deck cargo to provide against a lack of supplies later on.

There was an oil and petrol tanker in the harbour. ML 119 went alongside her to fill up and we intended to follow, but cancelled this intention when we found that the petrol there was contaminated with water. We had to tow ML 119 away and she spent the rest of the day and most of the next day getting rid of the water in her tanks.

We should have sailed at once but owing to the fuel troubles of ML 119 and the appalling weather outside, we did not leave until the evening of 10th June 1945.

In the night we passed close to a small coaster who warned us of floating mines ahead. The Baltic had been heavily mined and now many were breaking free of their moorings and floating on the surface. The war in Europe might be officially ended but nobody had told these mines, and all over the land and the seas of Europe deaths continued as the weapons of war remained active and uncontrolled.

At five o'clock in the morning of 11th June, we took on board a Swedish pilot off Marstrand and during that day we went south keeping inshore of the chain of islands off the Swedish coast to lessen the chance of hitting a mine. We changed pilots frequently at Vinga, Vorberg, Tylo and Viken. All the pilots were keen to have a cup of tea and were delighted when we gave them a small packet of tea to take home.

In the evening we reached Copenhagen and for about a week we stayed in the harbour. We had to supply hands for shore patrols in the town, some engine defects were attended to and the ship had never been cleaned so much and so well. We were organised in three watches and at least one watch had leave from 1315 to 2200 — two watches had this leave when our engines were under repair.

Ashore, the welcome and the hospitality were unbelievably lavish and warm-hearted. The Danes were showing all the emotions one would expect of a people relieved from an enemy occupation which had been harsh and brutal. In Copenhagen there was the infamous Gestapo headquarters where prisoners had been interrogated with torture and which had been bombed by the RAF to relieve the sufferings of the captives and stop the barbarity of the captors. A Danish school had been hit by bombs dropped in this raid and many Danish children had been killed.

Apart from the natural joy at the ending of the war with Germany, there was relief that we had arrived in Denmark before the Russians and our own friendly and temporary stay in Copenhagen was seen to have prevented a possibly less friendly and more lengthy occupation by Russian forces.

There were still more Germans in Denmark than Allied Forces and many of them still seemed to be well-armed. It was, I think, the general chaos in North Germany and the disorganisation of the transport system which prevented a rapid repatriation of the German forces. Meanwhile they remained and were for the most part well-behaved. The job of the Allied Forces in Denmark at that time was to see that peace was maintained while the organisation of the country recovered and the foreign armies withdrew.

For the first week or so, I found it extraordinary that the Germans still drove around the town in their black Mercedes and on their powerful motorcycles while I had to walk the mile or so from the docks to the Naval Headquarters. Slowly the Germans left and some of their cars became available — but not to me. A more ruthless conqueror would not have treated the defeated troops so leniently and the Danish population were probably much less kind to the Germans than the troops of the Allied Forces.

I saw little of the Danish forces but one Danish Naval Officer was assigned to us as a liaison officer. He was a cheerful young man who seemed to have hardly any experience of the Navy or the sea. He had been through the Naval training establishment and, as he freely admitted his lack of experience, we asked him how he had managed to pass his examinations. 'Well,' he said, 'I came bottom in navigation, gunnery and seamanship but I came out top at dancing.'

This happy young officer invited me to the Danish Naval Headquarters for lunch where we sat in an imposing room overlooking the harbour and the ancient forts. He introduced me to several senior officers who were present but there was one who sat alone at a table and who made it clear that he did not wish to meet me. My host explained this behaviour. 'You see,' he said, 'Captain X (I have forogtten the name) was in command of some of our Naval forces when the Germans invaded us. We soon surrendered and he was ordered not to fight the invaders but he said his duty was to defend Denmark and he was ashamed not to have done so — so ashamed that he refuses to meet officers of the Allied Forces.'

Although all seemed peaceful and a holiday atmosphere existed ashore (despite some food and drink shortages), the MLs maintained a guardship outside the harbour and in the narrows to the south of the harbour and close to the island of Saltholm. We each did a 24-hour spell in turn and that was no hardship because we anchored for most of the time. As it was mid-summer we dived over the side for a swim — and also for a badly needed bath because the shore facilities did not supply much in the way of these luxuries, and we did not yet know our Danish hosts sufficiently to ask for a bath when we were invited out to dinner. And the Danes were much too polite to suggest that a bath was necessary.

We had a neighbour and good friend in Horley during the war. His name was Roland Barkby and he, as a man too advanced in years to do war service, tried his best to look after servicemen who were lonely and far from home. When they were invited to his house for a meal or a cup of tea, he always horrified his wife Leila and perhaps offended his guest by saying as he opened the door, 'Would you like a bath?' Most of us would have welcomed his thought-fulness.

We soon made some very good friends in Denmark and none better than the Dalmarks, Py and Bamse. He was a doctor, an ear-nose-and-throat specialist. She was a delightful hostess. To the 11th ML Flotilla, their home at 171 Bernstorffvej was always open and we spent many happy evenings in their company.

There were other evenings not so happy. With two or three others, I went to a drinks and dinner party at another house. They were hospitable and the food was good. But the drink was wood alcohol which is no more than poison which was distilled in Denmark during the war. It drove motor cars and, taken in very small quantities, it could give human beings the uplift of alcohol, but it could be very harmful too. To have a little too much could be fatal and that nearly happened to us. I felt bad, another felt worse and our third man, by the time we got him back aboard, was paralysed. Luckily the dose he had was not sufficient to harm him permanently and after a very sick 24 hours, he recovered.

And what of this form of Scandinavian hospitality? One of the crew told me that he and his 'oppo' (the sailor's term for his friend among the crew) met and were invited for several evenings to the home of two very friendly and grateful Danes. On their third or fourth visit, the two Danish men pointedly got up and left the party to 'go for a walk' so that their two wives could be left alone to entertain the two sailors. I do not know what entertainment was offered and my sailor friend did not tell me what was accepted, but he did say to me 'That was a wonderful gesture, sir, but it would not do at home, would it?'

After a while, the situation became so quiet and organized that home leave was arranged for the crews. Although some went, many did not wish to take their entitlement to leave. I asked one of my crew why he did not wish to go home for ten days and he said:

'My shoes need repairing and I can't go home in my sea boots.' The condition of his shoes did not prevent him going ashore in Copenhagen whenever he had the chance. He just knew that he might have many days in the future in Hull or Hartlepool or Hendon but never would he have such days (and nights) as he was now enjoying in Copenhagen.

Lieut. Bibby in ML 163 was clever enough to 'acquire' one of the big Mercedes that the Germans had left behind. It was an open touring model and he drove it proudly, and sometimes wildly round the city. In those days the traffic was light, so he could drive fast and with panache and also with the most beautiful girls in town. Someone asked me, 'Who is the Naval Officer who always drives around with a car full of girls?' We all knew the answer to that — Lieut. Bibby of ML 163. One late evening after a party, he drove off the road at Langelinie and round the Gefion fountain and the famous statue of the woman driving her plough drawn by her six sons whom she had changed into oxen. That statue is a much-cherished monument of Danish mythology and to drive around it where there is no road to do so would normally put one into jail — but those were mad and enjoyable days and so long as one laughed, one could do anything.

Drinks were supplied by us (otherwise it might be wood alcohol) and some of the food, too. Our cigarettes would buy anything. Petrol was very short and the taxis and cars mostly ran on gas derived from a kind of small furnace in the boot of the car which burned wood chips and produced gas into a kind of balloon on the car roof which fed the engine. But what did we care: no one was shooting at us and no one was dropping bombs on us. The city was lit up at night and the ships sailed with navigation lights. After years of blackness ashore and of straining one's eyes through binoculars at sea, hoping to see the black loom of a ship, whether friend or enemy, before one collided with it, what a joy it was to feel that night was no longer filled with invisible dangers and visibility by day was no longer to be feared.

Patrol and guardship duties being very light, the crew were able to devote more time than they ever had before to cleaning, painting and polishing the ship. I think they were proud of their ship and pleased she looked so good and so fresh inspite of the hard work of the past years. Both the officers and the crew were permitted guests on board and they showed off their ship with pride. It was hard to impress on our visitors, however, the dangers we always faced from the 2000 gallons of petrol we carried as fuel. We knew the rules about smoking but guests always scared me by their tendency to wander onto the deck with a cigarette and once, to my horror, I found cigarette ash in the engine room.

Hospitality on the ships was coupled with a modest amount of showing the flag on shore, and a certain amount of drill was required to keep our un-military sailors fit for carrying out patrol duties ashore in a smart and orderly manner.

On July 1st and 2nd occurred the mysterious affair of the Icelandic ship *Esja*. We were ordered very suddenly by a message delivered by a despatch rider to go at once and stand by to guard, and at the same time to control, the movements of this *Esja* which was a small passenger and cargo-carrying ship lying in the inner harbour of Copenhagen. When we arrived, the ship was embarking passengers and making every sign of departing. We scraped together some information and it seemed that this was to be the first ship to make the voyage from Denmark to Iceland for many years. There was probably some competition to become a passenger, or perhaps spies or criminals were trying to board illegally? Were we there to prevent a riot? Nobody told us and I could not make contact with Naval HQ — our orders were just to stand by. So we did so: prepared for anything and with an armed boarding party at the ready, looking proper idiots in a narrow inlet of the harbour, with Danish civilians lining the quay in holiday mood waving and shouting to friends about to depart for Iceland. One of the passengers was said to be the tallest man in Denmark, and that was probably right as he towered above the others as if on stilts.

In the afternoon, *Esja* left harbour and anchored outside. We continued our watch and the motorboat from Naval headquarters made several visits, putting more people aboard and even taking some people and their baggage off. Nobody struggled and no shots were fired, so we stood by still mystified. At first light next morning, a Danish naval craft came alongside and the Commander asked my permission to speak to his wife and child who were on board *Esja*. I saw no reason to say no and so I graciously gave my permission — why not? By mid-day, we were relieved by ML 114 and for us that strange episode was ended. Why we were needed to provide an armed presence for the departure of this ship I never knew.

It was our turn about once a week to carry out a 24-hour patrol outside Copenhagen. This was an easy duty and it provided some relief from the social round ashore. We anchored most of the time in the channel leading from the Kattegat to the Baltic, and we all enjoyed a swim over the side in the rather cold water but in the warm sunshine of a good summer. There were plenty of craft moving about: mostly small ones such as fishing boats, the larger ones were usually German minesweepers helping to clear up the mines which their own forces had laid rather liberally in the narrow waters. Some of these mines had in course of time broken from their moorings and had become a real menace in that part of the Baltic: channels which had been swept clear of mines one day could have mines drifting on the surface next day.

Occasionally we visited other ports in the island of Zealand and when we did so, it was customary to take on board a local pilot because the approaches to many harbours were shallow and the channel markings after war-time neglect, or even deliberate misplacement, could not be trusted. While in one such port we received a signal to go urgently to another small town further along the coast where there was said to be trouble with German prisoners of war who, as was normal, heavily outnumbered the Allied troops guarding them. The harbour we were in had a long serpentine entrance through shallow waters rather casually marked here and there with stakes and very ancient and rusty buoys. A pilot seemed essential.

I looked up at the harbour wall above us and there looking over it was a man in a blue jersey and a peaked cap. What luck to have a pilot on hand! 'Can you take us to Nykobing?' I said.

'Ja,' he replied.

'Come aboard,' I said, which he did and we showed him to the bridge where he leaned comfortably in a corner. We cast off from the harbour wall and started to take the channel out to sea. Our gentleman in the blue jersey and peaked cap stood quietly in his corner doing nothing and saying nothing. Soon, following a narrow channel through the mud-flats, we came to a buoy where the channel seemed to divide. Still our man in the corner said nothing and did nothing. 'Which way,' I said, 'Which way do we go?'

'I don't know,' said peaked cap.

'But you must know,' I said, 'you are a pilot, aren't you?'

'No,' he replied, 'I'm a taxi driver.'

We turned back and put him ashore. After all, he had his job to do and I was certainly not going through those channels without some expert advice. All we got out of that evening's work was a good laugh and our taxi driver had a large gin to pay for the amusement he gave us.

We had in our flotilla as First Lieutenant of ML 118 a Sub. Lieut. Alan Palgrave Brown. Now he had an identical twin brother whose Christian name was Alastair and he also was a Sub. Lieutenant RNVR.

I always understood that the Navy tried to keep twins together if they so wished. They did their best in this case by appointing both to MLs in home waters. They could not, of course, put them in the same ML because we normally only carried two officers and neither had yet enough seniority to be made a CO and even if they were senior enough, which of them would be the CO and which the First Lieutenant? And to have identical twins as the two officers in an ML would be most confusing for all concerned. It was impossible for any of us to tell which was Alan and which was

Alastair. So they were each a No. 1 — or First Lieutenant — in an ML and at that time one of the MLs was in Copenhagen and the other was in Cuxhaven in North Germany at the mouth of the River Elbe.

In our present days of light duties, we began to introduce a privilege which many of us had not known since 1939. That was the opportunity to have leave while one's ship was still operational: since 1939 the only chance of getting leave was to have one's ship in dock for repairs — or, a poor choice this, to be a survivor when one's ship was sunk. It caused no surprise when Alan Palgrave-Brown asked for a long week-end leave so that he could travel to Cuxhaven to see his twin brother who had also arranged to have leave that week-end.

We saw him off on a Friday morning and wished him a good journey and a happy reunion with his brother.

He had been gone only a few hours and we were settling down to lunch when a smart young Sub. Lieutenant came aboard whom we at first thought to be Alan returning because, perhaps, his transport had broken down or his transit papers were not in order. But the young man announced that he was Alastair Palgrave-Brown who had come from Cuxhaven to spend this week-end with his twin brother Alan in Copenhagen — and, by the way, where was his brother Alan?

We were all shattered. Poor fellows: Alan travelling to Cuxhaven and, without knowing it, passing on the way his twin Alastair who was making the long and difficult journey to Copenhagen to see him. What to do?

Should he set off back as fast as possible? No, he might once again pass Alan also making the return journey. The difficulty and uncertainty of communications and travel in those days meant that we could see no sense in trying to correct such a sad mistake which no doubt was the greatest of disappointments for both of them.

By a unanimous vote, we asked Alastair to stay for the week-end as our guest and during that week-end we treated him royally: free food, free drinks, special parties arranged on board and ashore — every form of hospitality we could think of. Alastair left us on the Monday having had a wonderful week-end with heartfelt thanks for our hospitality — what else could we do to make up for his disappointment?

On Monday evening Alan returned to us from Cuxhaven and told us that he too had been royally treated by everyone in

Cuxhaven to make up for the disappointment which he too had suffered. And there the incident might have ended had not suspicions grown in our minds. We never knew the truth and the two Palgrave-Browns kept to their story but did Alan ever leave Copenhagen and did Alastair ever leave Cuxhaven? Our own unproved conclusion was that Alan had gone ashore on the Friday morning, walked round Copenhagen for an hour or two and then had come back aboard announcing that he was Alastair. His reward was a week-end of free drinks and parties. Perhaps Alastair did the same in Cuxhaven.

The war in Europe was over: what remained to be done was to help towards the stabilisation of peace, the return of displaced persons, the demobilisation of armies, the release of prisoners, the prevention of starvation and the establishment of some form of law from which order might flow. We in our little world of Coastal Forces found the duties very light and Denmark had suffered less devastation than many other European countries. We expected that before long the Allied Forces in Denmark would be reduced and some of us would be ordered elsewhere.

In the Pacific, the war with Japan was still raging and it was largely a sea-borne war for which more Naval forces would be welcome. There was consequently a distinct possibility, or perhaps a probability, that we would soon be sent to the Pacific. Not, of course, with our MLs because that would have taken too long, but we would more likely be flown out to man any kind of ship which might need additions or replacements.

I would like to pretend that we were heroic enough to be bursting to get out to the Pacific as soon as possible. What did we think? We were tired. Seagoing for nearly six years in war-time conditions had taken some of our enthusiasm away. If we were ordered to the Pacific, we would go with no complaints but we hoped very, very much that the war was over for us.

Nevertheless, we saw little attraction in this constabulary duty around the coasts of northern Europe. There was no real action; there was only a presence to be maintained and crews to be kept on duties such as polishing brass and cleaning paintwork. In the back (or nearer the front) of our minds was 'going home.'

19

Going Home

On 31st July I received orders to go back to the UK, to Sheerness, with MLs 490, 118, 448 and 119. This reduced by nearly half the number of MLs in Denmark, but what was in store for us? Paying off, other duties, going to Japan?

We went north, round the island of Zealand. It was a short trip northward from Copenhagen to Helsingor which we made in the early hours of 31st July, leaving Copenhagen at 0530 in the morning and tying up under the shadow of Hamlet's castle in Helsingor at 0800. This gave us the day to spend in that ancient city and we walked on the battlements and looked across the strait to Sweden.

We left Helsingor at 0630, rounded the north of Zealand, along the northwest coast and into the Great Belt, the strip of water which divides Zealand from Funen. We passed MLs 206 and 190 (Lieut. Bound) on the way and several German minesweepers who were clearing the channels around the Danish islands. At 1830, after a rather long twelve-hour journey, we secured alongside the jetty in Nakskov creating much interest amongst the inhabitants of the small port. The weather had been poor all the way from Copenhagen with a force 6 to 7 northwest blow, but for most of the way we were in the lee of land and were not too roughly treated.

In the afternoon of 2nd August we left Nakskov on the western end of Lofland and made for Kiel in Germany where we berthed alongside the Zeppelin jetty. All seemed quiet and well-ordered there and next morning our four MLs entered the Kiel Canal. We took on board a Kiel Canal pilot. He was a German and it may not seem strange now but it seemed very odd to us then to have a German on the bridge and to be under his pilotage orders. He was a pleasant enough man and we got on well with him.

We made about 10 knots through the very quiet canal and left our pilot at Brunsbuttel at its western end in the early evening. By nine o'clock we were off Cuxhaven at the mouth of the Elbe.

I was very keen to spend the night at Cuxhaven: there was still a strong northwesterly and there were enough floating mines around to disturb one's peace of mind. We had about a 400-mile journey ahead of us, say 36 to 40 hours at an economical speed and I wanted to negotiate in daylight the first 150 miles along the shallow waters of the North German coast. It was my judgement, too, that the weather was getting worse (we had no weather forecast broadcast to us in those days) and we would have to steer right into it. I had yet another reason for a night in Cuxhaven: Palgrave-Brown was making a special request to me to be allowed to see his twin brother and whatever we might have thought about the trick which he did or did not play on us in Copenhagen, I was soft-hearted enough to wish to grant his request.

I had an argument over the radio with the Naval Officer in Charge (NOIC) in Cuxhaven. He ordered us on; I was determined to go in. Palgrave-Brown's need to see his twin cut no ice as an argument, nor did my wish to make most of the passage in daylight, nor my concern about the weather but, of course, we could always find some trouble with the engines and there was no answer to that.

I met one of NOIC's staff later — I knew him in the Mediterranean — and he said that when he knew it was that man Geoffrey Searle in command of four MLs, he advised NOIC to stop arguing and to let me into Cuxhaven because, as he put it, I was always an obstinate so-and-so. In the end, I was justified. The storm outside increased and Saturday, 4th August, 1945 was no day for a small ML to be heading into the teeth of it. So we stayed in harbour that day and NOIC nearly had his revenge: he sent for me and said he was going to request the Admiralty to cancel our sailing to the UK and add our four ships to the Coastal Forces under his command at the mouth of the Elbe.

So far in this long war I had done what I was told, I had sailed or not sailed as the Senior Officers ashore decided. Now I thought it time to play a little politics and try to steer the decision the way I wanted it.

But what did I want? The Japanese war was still going on — the atom bomb had not yet been dropped — so the sooner we got back to the UK, the more likely it was that we should be sent out to the Far East. On the other hand, if we remained longer in North Germany we might be kept on rather boring police duties well into the approaching winter. I voted for the UK as soon as possible. The possibility of Japan looked better than the certainty of a boring and uncomfortable winter — and besides, we ought to get at least a few weeks leave in the UK before we went anywhere else. The Pacific war could perhaps come to an end soon. The door to a peaceful world was slowly opening, we were beginning to look through the opening and making plans for passing into a new life.

I therefore argued strongly with NOIC Cuxhaven that we had been ordered back to the UK and we were urgently needed there — how was I to know why? — and he would be most unpopular with his Lordshps in the Admiralty if he interfered with their well-thought-out and important plans. He knew he was on weak ground and he did not press his case for keeping us in Cuxhaven — so we sailed in the early morning of 5th August. The weather was still bad; it was the end of a westerly gale. We had to spend nearly two days bashing into short seas where the waters were shallow with cold wet water coming over the bridge, and then riding up and down the steeper waves when we reached the open waters of the North Sea.

There was a German-buoyed and hopefully swept channel for the first part of our voyage. The Elbe light vessel was on station. The tanker *British Chancellor* assisted by two tugs was seen presumably with a cargo of oil or petrol. Why the two tugs? Had she been damaged? We never knew. There were some small German ships, some fishing boats and one or two cargo ships to be seen. One of these warned us of a floating mine ahead and in due course we, too, saw it and sank it with gunfire.

By mid-morning we were seeing buoys off the coast of England and by the evening we were appraoching our destination, passing Sheerness and on to Queenborough on the Isle of Sheppey at the mouth of the Thames. It was a holiday atmosphere for us and we chatted and exchanged silly jokes over the inter-communication radio with MLs 118, 448 and 119 who had kept astern of us in excellent close line ahead station all the way from Copenhagen.

The Naval H.Q. at Queenborough was known as *HMS Wildfire III*. The greatest of our enjoyments was to have a good hot bath and we were reprimanded next day for not cleaning off properly the clinkery ridge of dirt which we left at the top of our water level on the sides of the bath.

It was 6th August when we arrived and for the next three days we stood by awaiting further orders. As we arrived at Queenborough, the atom bomb had been dropped on Japan: the significance of this was not at the time fully appreciated because we were not informed as to the meaning or effect of such a bomb, but we knew it was out of the ordinary and could hasten the end of Japan's resistance to the steady advances of the Allied Forces.

Our uncertainties were brought to an end when on 10th August, 1945 the surrender of Japan was announced. It was a Friday. Half the ship's company were given week-end leave and on Sunday the ship was washed down and the crew, properly dressed, fell in on the jetty and marched to the Sunday ceremony of divisions and prayers.

The next week was one of fairly hard work to remove all offensive and defensive gear from the ship. Guns were dismantled and landed; ammunition put into a lighter which came alongside. Depth charges, rockets and smoke cannisters were taken away too. Our radar dome was lifted off by crane and every kind of spare gear, clothing and provisions not required for day to day living were listed, checked and taken away by base staff.

On 21st August, half the ship's company left to return to their home depots leaving a crew of nine ratings and three officers on board. It was nearly the end of the end. Were we sad? Were we pleased? I really do not know. I think I was numbed by the rapid change and I lived from day to day without thinking too much. I was beginning to feel very, very tired.

It was nearly the end of August when we were ordered to leave Queenborough and sail to Poole in Dorset still in company with MLs 118, 448, 119.

At Poole there were rows and rows of abandoned and emasculated MLs which had just been paid off. An unpleasant officer of the base at Poole came aboard and started by making rude and uncomplimentary remarks about the amount of work still to be done to remove certain fittings and equipment. I was in no mood to accept that; we had had a hard month's work since leaving the Baltic and I made my feelings felt about base staff who slept in their beds every night in the comfortable town of Poole and expected the seagoing people like ourselves to do their work as well as our own. We parted bad friends which was a pity, because the crew and I stepped ashore and left ML 490 in his hands and that was the last time I exercised any authority as an executive officer on board one of His Majesty's ships.

As to ML 490: the MLs were for the most part sold for civilian work. They were converted to inshore pleasure cruisers, ferries and so on. Some months later I was sad to see a picture in a newspaper of ML 490 washed ashore on Brighton Beach. She had been under tow without engines from Poole to Dover and her tow had parted in a storm. I suppose she was refloated and I hope she had a better

248

resting place than the pebbles of Brighton Beach.

I went home to my wife and son who were living with my parents in their bombed but now well-repaired house at Horley in Surrey.

Soon after I returned I put on my best uniform, borrowed my father's car and took my wife out to tea in Croydon. Tea may not sound much nowadays, but having tea together was not something we had done much of since our marriage and such an occasion, being together in a tea room and being waited upon, was to us quite as good as a theatre and dinner in London. There was a pleasant tea room in George Street not far from East Croydon railway station and, not knowing the civilian rules about parking in busy streets, I left the car right outside the door. We had a most enjoyable tea together but when we came out there was a policeman, notebook in hand, standing beside our car. I went up to him and he looked at me in a kindly way. He looked at the medal ribbons on my uniform and he said to me, 'I think we owe you something, sir.' He put his pencil and his notebook in his pocket and he turned and walked away.

For the first time in our married lives we believed there might now be some stability. The wars were over and a start had been made in the demobilisation of our Armed Forces. We all had to wait our turn and the administration of the demobilisation must have been formidable. Perhaps, too, there was some sense in not moving too fast for how could commerce and industry absorb so quickly the thousands now coming back to civilian life when commerce and industry was itself struggling to re-adjust to peace time requirements.

After paying off ML 490, I was on indefinite leave and very unlikely to be recalled. That leave lasted for four months.

I did not have four months of relaxation and celebration. Stability in a new way of life is not achieved quickly and easily. The strains of wartime sea-going were over; I was alive and uninjured but like a drug the exhilaration of the challenges, the dangers and the responsibilities of command had uplifted me and now they were gone I suffered the withdrawal effects of a drug. I was tired and depressed despite the achievement of all I hoped for: a safe return to my wife and family.

For a week or two after I came home, everything seemed to be an effort and I had so little energy that I wondered whether I had some serious illness. Perhaps such reactions were the explanation of the suicides, soon after the end of the war, of at least three of my friends from Coastal Forces who were with me in the Eastern Mediterranean.

For me, the depression passed and the realisation of my new responsibilities took the place of those which I missed and which caused the emptiness of the first few weeks. Although not yet demobilised, I saw no reason why I should not try to establish myself in a civilian job and I went back to see my pre-war employers, W. B. Keen & Co., Chartered Accountants previously of 23 Queen Victoria Street in the City of London. Their offices had been bombed and destroyed and they were in temporary accommodation in the upper floors of Dickens and Jones in Regent Street.

They offered me a job on the audit staff and they offered to pay me £500 per annum. There was something depressing about it all. As I was leaving and on my way down the stairs, Eric Channon, the partner to whom I was articled in 1931 and who had just offered me the job, ran after me and said there had been a mistake. His partners had told him that £500 p.a. was too much and the offer of employment was at £450 p.a. — that was all right, wasn't it? I said 'yes', and I left in a black mood, it was a bad start, a new and different world had closed around me and I did not like the look of it.

If W. B. Keen & Co. really wanted me back, they were singularly discouraging. I was seven years older, I had changed: I had forgotten a good deal about accounting but I had learned much more about many other things during those years. They put me back on the same audits as the ones I had done in 1938 and 1939 and I worked for the same men who, being much older, had done those jobs throughout the war. I felt small and useless: I started to look for another job and I took refresher courses in accountancy, finance, law and so on.

In January, 1946 I was officially demobilised and paid off by the Navy with a gratuity of £132, a pair of shoes, a civilian suit and hat.

Meanwhile I wrote letters to possible employers. There was one who saw me in the back room of a bombed-out building. He wore dark glasses and said he had a factory somewhere making aluminium saucepans. He paid his works manager £20,000 p.a. and if I was a good accountant I too would be well paid. There seemed to be something strange about the set-up and the pay was unusually high for those days but he did suggest an interview with his auditors — a well-known firm — and they said, at a very pleasant meeting, that they thought I was too professional for the job. Perhaps that is why I have never become very rich.

An interview with a firm of accountants in Brighton ended up with an offer and the prospect of a partnership, but the lead I followed up with most interest was that with the Anglo-Iranian Oil Company which arose from my contact with Colonel Browne of the Royal Engineers during our balloon flying episode in the English Channel just after D-day in 1944.

Using Col. Browne's name, which he had told me to do, I sought and obtained an interview with a Managing Director by the name of Jamieson. Jamieson was a tough, outspoken, well-liked and often well-feared man who had done most of his service in the oilfields of Persia. I seemed to get on very well with him and he said he would see what they could offer me.

After a few weeks I had a letter from Anglo-Iranian offering me a sea-going appointment. They were about to start exploration in the region of the Bahamas; it was mostly offshore work which would require support ships and I was to have some responsibility in running the offshore side of this oil exploration venture. This, I think, was a very generous offer and quite an attractive one, too, but for me it had a major and decisive defect. It would mean another separation from my wife and son, and how could that be a reasonable proposition when we had been parted for most of the time since our marriage in 1940.

Family considerations came first and I replied, not without some regrets, that I could not accept their offer. I thought that was the end of my opportunities with Anglo-Iranian and I pursued other possibilities of employment. I was very close to taking the offer from the Brighton accountants when in February, 1946 I heard from Anglo-Iranian again. This time they offered me the job of an accountant in their London office at a salary of £550 p.a. (which soon after I arrived was amended to £675 p.a.) I accepted at once and began in March, 1946 a career with Anglo-Iranian (later to become BP) lasting 29 years which could itself be the subject of a personal history though of a very different kind from that of my six and a half years Naval service.

One chapter of my life had ended and another had begun. The broad sweep of events in the years of 1939 to 1946 can be read in better documented histories of that time; but such histories deal with great events and the great men and women of that time.

For me, those years are a treasure chest of memories. I have written my story just to record some of these memories which may not have any significance in the broad history of the war but were part of the life of one who saw the war from sea level.

APPENDIX

FROM . . . COMMANDING OFFICER, M.L. 355.
DATE . . . 24th June, 1942
TO . . . CAPTAIN LOCAL PATROL, ALEXANDRIA.

Submitted.

The following is a report on the evacuation of Tobruk as seen from M.L. 355.

2. M.L. 355 was berthed on the night of 19th/20th June on the west side of No. 3 jetty.

3. Heavy shelling of the town from a position to the south of about the mid point of the South Shore started at about 0700, the shells passing overhead and over Navy House, and bursting mainly in the town.

4. Shells were also bursting intermittently on the South Shore. The Bardia road was was also being shelled.

5. Between 0700 and 0900 there were both high level and Stuka raids mostly directed on the gun positions on the Southern escarpment.

6. At 0900 I reported to N.O.i/c and requested permission to shift berth, moving at 0910 to No.4 jetty inside URANIA.

7. Shelling and air raids continued throughout the forenoon with one air raid on the town, when the hospital was hit. The rate of shelling increased between 1200 and 1300 covering the South Shore, the harbour and the town.

8. During the afternoon I paid four visits to Navy House to see if the Base Engineer Officer could return my Auxiliary Engine which was under repair, as without it I could not work my Asdics. The last visit was at about 1430 when I was promised it by 1600. It did not arrive.

9. At 1740, in accordance with a signal previously received I reported to S.O.O. on S.N.O.I.S. Staff and received sailing orders to take two T.L.C.s to Mersa Matruh leaving at 2130. S.N.O.I.S.

was present at the time, and asking if there were any further orders was told, 'There may be another ship'. I returned on board to await time of sailing.

10. Between 1600 and 1700 a number of M/T came over the South Escarpment and were fired by their crews.

11. At 1800 Lieut. Colonel BASTIN of H.Q. 13th Corps came on board and shortly afterwards the Army Official Mail (13 bags) was brought on board. Lieutenant Stacey R.N.R. also joined for passage as previously arranged by S.N.O.I.S. Lt. Colonel Bastin brought definite news of the break through in the forenoon and the fact that 40 tanks, less a few destroyed, together with lorried infantry and ''Tank-buster'' guns were running loose inside the perimeter.

12. At about 1900 there was a fight between tanks at the head of the harbour.

13 From 1800 M.L.s 1048 and 1069 were alongside, at about 1930 M.L. 1048 moved out and proceeded down harbour. M.L. 1069 with Lt. Commander Brooks, R.N.R. (H.H.M.) left shortly after, and was hit by an explosive shell in the bridge when about 100 yards out, and immediately afterwards by other shells fired from a tank on a road at the head of the harbour. On fire, M.L. 1069 turned back and slowly came alongside me again.

14. Lt. Commander Brooks asked for signal to be sent for a doctor, this was done and he then proceeded ashore towards Navy House. All those still living, (five in number), were taken on board M.L. 355.

15. About this time a signal ''Sail to Alexandria.'' was received from Navy House; while still rescuing the survivors from 1069 a further signal ''Sail to Alexandria now'' was received and complied with as soon as we could get clear of M.L. 1069.

16. In the meantime a T.L.C. believed to be No. 119 got under way from between Nos. 3 and 4 jetties, and was immediately heavily hit by the same tank which was now near No. 3 jetty. H.M.T. ALASIA alongside No. 3 jetty also got under way, but also immediately got hit and set on fire, finally running aground between Nos. 5 and 6 jetties.

17. At 1950 I got under way embarking everyone on No. 4 jetty except a demolition party of a few seamen who continued with their work; and taking advantage of the smoke from ALASIA went down harbour at full speed, zig-zagging and engaging enemy tanks with Oerlikon and Lewis guns. It was reported to me that at

least one tank was alongside Navy House. An M.T.B. was seen stopped and apparently deserted near Kheir el Dine, and Kheir el Dine was seen alongside one of the wrecks in the harbour, damaged. I then entered a smoke cloud, now learnt to have been a screen laid by M.T.B.s

18. At 2000 while swinging through the boom I collided with M.L.C. 146, from which four out of five members of the crew jumped on board, the fifth jumped overboard but was too slow and fell into the water. I was past him before we could rescue him, and owing to intense fire I considered it inadvisable to turn back for one man.

19. I then proceeded seaward up the swept channel and after taking some additional passengers from an overloaded M.T.B. I proceeded independently for Mersa Matruh, continuing on one engine when my Port gear box failed.

20. A list of passengers is given below:-

STACEY, M.D.	Lt. Cdr. R.N.V.R. H.M. Naval Base
GIMSON, D.	El.Lt. R.N.V.R. H.M. Naval Base
HILDER, W. J.	L/Sea. H.M, Naval Base. SSX17274
BIGGS, B. S. W.	Sto. M.L. 1069. KX120146.
ASHLEY, J.	M/M. M.L. 1069 D/MX70134.
GILFROY, T. R.	Tel. M.L. 1069 D/JX170906.
MORRIS, A.	A.B. R.N.R. M.L. 1069 X21205A.
JOHNSTON N. J.	A.B. M.L. 1069 P/M3322.
DOVE, E.	L/Sea. D Lighter 146 P/SSX21651.
BUCKINGHAM J. R.	A.B. D Lighter 146 JX238163
JEAVONS, R.	A.B. D Lighter 146 C/JX212060.
SHIPMAN, W.	A.B. D Lighter 146 C/JX238165.

ARMY

BASTIN, G. E. R.	Lt.Col. A.Q.M.G. 13.Corp. P26948.
BURGESS, G.C.	Serg. 11 Base Sig. Sec. 4th L of C. 7882208.
MIDLANE F. S.	Signalman 4th L of C. 2360928.
LUND, W. E.	L/Cpl. 4th L of C 2357805.
MELSON, W.	Signalman 4th L of C. 2331476.
HEMMINGS, N.	Signalman 4th L of C. 2328592.
KITCHING, J. N.	Signalman 4th L of C. 2591755.
HARMAR E. F.	L/Cpl. 4th L of C. 2330168.
MACDONALD, J.	Signalman. 11th Base Sig. Sec. 2367134.

LIGHTFOOT, J.   Signalman. 11th Base Sig. Sec. 2325394.
MILLARD, W. A.Sapper. 296 Army Field Co. R.E. 7664549.
GOODALL, J.H.   L/Serg. 296 Army Field Co. 1890556.
MAYHEW, A.C.   Clerk. 67th Medium R.A. 907834.
LEWIS, E. S.   Driver. 68th Medium R.A. 66502.
BLUNDELL, H.   Driver R.A.S.C. 150397.
INDIAN ARMY
ABDUL SALAMAT. 36069   AZIZ ULLAH 39223
TAG UDDIN 39434x   ADDUL ROUF 39064
MOTIAR RAHAMAN 39318   SVED ULLAH 39097
SARAJUL HUO 39005   MUSA MEAH 39182
NAJER AHMED 39019   KUSHALAPPA 17/989
NAHANJAN 507606   NIRMAL SINGH 5008712
MILKHA SINGH 508065   AHMED HUSSAIN 639661
SAMMET ALI 39090

21. I should like to bring to your notice the bravery and good work of:-
JOHNSTON, N.J. Able Seaman. P.M. 3322 R.A.N. of M.L. 1069, who, although wounded in five places, brought 1069 back to No. 4 Jetty after she was hit, he collapsed entirely and was brought out by my crew.
BABER, R. E. Able Seaman, S.4190, R.A.N. of M.L. 355., who took the leading part in securing M.L. 1069 and in recovering the wounded when 1069 was burning and at least one enemy tank within 300 yards.
EDWARDS, R. J. Leading Stoker. D/KX96915. of M.L. 355., who with BABER did magnificent work getting the wounded out of 1069. EDWARDS previously distinguished himself ten days earlier during the attack on Convoy "Solar", diving overboard and assisting a seriously wounded man, 3rd Engineer of BRAMBLELEAF, keeping him afloat until a boat could reach him.

Robert Young
Lieutenant R.N.V.R.
Commanding Officer,
HMML 355